Inside a Secret Software Laboratory

Christine Grimm

Inside a Secret Software Laboratory

An Ethnographic Study of a Global Software Package Producer

RESEARCH

Christine Grimm
Zurich, Switzerland

Dissertation University of Edinburgh, 2009

ISBN 978-3-8349-3386-7 ISBN 978-3-8349-7176-0 (eBook)
DOI 10.1007/978-3-8349-7176-0

The Deutsche Nationalbibliothek lists this publication in the Deutsche Nationalbibliografie; detailed bibliographic data are available in the Internet at http://dnb.d-nb.de.

Springer Gabler

Cover design: KünkelLopka GmbH, Heidelberg

Printed on acid-free paper

Springer Gabler is a brand of Springer DE.
Springer DE is part of Springer Science+Business Media.
www.springer-gabler.de

To my parents
and to the developers of the vendor's labs.

Acknowledgements

Conducting this research was a most exciting adventure, which, over time, many people became a part of. A research project of this scale cannot be accomplished alone and does not happen separately from the social surroundings; from the moment the decision is made until completion different people become part of this work. I was fortunate to enjoy the support of many friends, professionals and organisations and I am delighted to be able to contribute this space to my most sincere 'thank yous' and will do so in chronological order.

First of all, my thanks go to my sister Andrea Grimm and Prof. Philippe Kruchten, from the University of British Columbia, for inspiring me to carry out this project, as well as for supporting and guiding me throughout. Most sincere thanks go to Dr. Neil Pollock, Prof. Robin Williams, Dr. Ian Graham from the University of Edinburgh as well as Prof. Steve Saywer from Syracuse University, New York: Thank you for your professional guidance, constructive criticism, encouraging discussions and never ending patience. I thank the ESRC as well as the Small Project Grant from the University of Edinburgh, for partially financing this research.

Special thanks also to my friends in Scotland: Paul, for making me laugh, Annie for being such a lovely and happy person, Lucy, for being such a nice flatmate, Stephen for the many evenings in the Teviot and unexplainable patience in introducing me to the historical roots of Science and Technology Studies. Thanks also to Emma, Leo, Jinging, Gloria, Shariq, Sheetal, Maite and the rest at 16, Buccleuch Place as well as the staff and students at High School Yards, Anne, Eileen, Moyra, James, Becky, Majia, Shulin, Shean, Jeehyun, Diego, Bart and Xiang. Thanks for making it such a 'fun place' to work. I am also most grateful to the Thursday night Reiki group; in particular, I thank Kenny and Marielle for those inspiring evenings and friendship.

Soon I met the developers from the vendor's labs in North American. I am most grateful for the vendor's permission to let me enter the labs as an ethnographic researcher and to the people in the labs for their ongoing trust and friendship, which made this time in North America one of the most enjoyable times of my life. I would like to address these people by name, but for reasons of anonymisation, unfortunately, I am unable to do so.

After four eventful years, my time at the University of Edinburgh has come to an end and I have moved to Switzerland to work in industrial research. I thank my colleagues, for making the labs such a fantastic place to work, giving me the energy and spirit, to complete this book in my spare time. Thanks also to Elaine McKenzie and Moyra Forrest for proof reading and valuable feedback.

I am also grateful to my friends in Germany, for their many years of friendship. Thanks especially to Simone, Birgit, Alex and Ronald, as well as the people living in my street. Last, but not least, I thank my siblings, Andrea, Rita, Roland and Peter as well as my parents. Thanks for letting me grow up in a great family who taught me most of all, to stick together and keep spirits up. Lots of love also goes to my partner Matthias, my daughter Emilie and her yet 'unknown' sibling, for making this beautiful city of Zürich even brighter and sunnier.

Christine Grimm

Abstract

This is an ethnographic study of the creation of a particular type of standard enterprise software package: Enterprise Resource Planning (ERP) systems, which support wide-ranging organisational functions within large and medium sized enterprises. Drawing upon the Social Shaping of Technology perspective and recent related attempts to theorise the Biography of Artefacts, this work addresses the under-researched area of ERP system development and ERP system support. In providing a system vendor's viewpoint, it seeks to overcome current shortcomings in social research, notably from Information Systems and Organisational Studies, which focus almost exclusively on a user organisation perspective. Mostly concentrating on the moment of implementation, existing studies do not help us to better understand the software producer's viewpoint or to find explanations as to how ERP systems are produced and supported in such a way that they can meet the specific requirements of their highly diverse users (the current market leader SAP had over 12 million users (2008)). Overall, we have very limited understanding of what happens within software package laboratories and how such organisations organise their relationship with their wide and diverse user base throughout the different phases of the product life cycle.

Addressing this gap in the social study of software packages, this research offers an ethnographical insider's perspective of the day-to-day working practices within one of the world's leading ERP system providers, encompassing both its development and support functions. Based on rich ethnographic data, the study demonstrates *first*, how a supplier manages its relationship with its diverse user base during the moment when the system re-enters the vendor's circle of responsibility through the software packages support channel. The sophisticated and mature mechanisms and policies are highlighted, which allow the vendor - not without challenges – to accommodate competing exigencies of its user base at this moment of product life cycle. *Second*, this research highlights how the software development phase is organised, by empirically describing and analysing from a social viewpoint, the software development process during a period of organisational change, in which the vendor reorganises itself in search for a new way to respond to the expectations of the market. *Third*, the account reveals unexpected communitarian behaviour amongst software developers at all levels, demonstrating the social character of programming, a feature which has not been adequately recognised by current studies in this area. *Fourth*, overall, this study highlights the need for a change of the current research agenda in social software package research towards a vendor organisation's perspective, if we aim for a more complete understanding of the social aspects such type of technology.

Contents

List of Figures

List of Abbreviations

BP	Business Process
CAPM	Computer-Aided Production Management
Cf.	Lat: Confer; English: Compare
CG	Christine Grimm
COTS	Commercial Off-The-Shelf
CRM	Customer Relationship Management
ERP	Enterprise Resource Planning
ERP Extension	Products extending the core functionality of ERP systems such as CRM or SCM products.
ESRC	Economic & Social Research Council
GUI	Graphical User Interface
HTTP	Secure HyperText Transfer Protocol
ICT	Information and Communication Technology
IS	Information Systems
IT	Information Technology
MIS	Management and Information Systems
M&A	Merger and Acquisition
MRP	Material Requirements Planning
MRP II	Material Requirements Planning II
ORACLE	Company Name
PhD	Doctor of Philosophy
QA	Quality Assurance
RE	Requirements Engineering
SAP	Company Name
SCM	Supply Chain Management
SCOT	Social Construction of Technology
SLA	Service Level Agreement

SOA	Service Oriented Architecture
SMS	Short Messaging Service
SST	Social Shaping of Technology
STS	Science and Technology Studies
UI	User Interface
Xerox	Company Name

1 Introduction

1.1 Towards a Different Understanding of ERP Systems

Things should be made as simple as possible, but no simpler.
(Albert Einstein)

When the first computer program was written by Ada Byron, a friend of Charles Babbage, the inventor of the analytic engine in the 1840s (cf. Tolle 1992), the idea of computers touching upon almost every aspects of our lives was a mere vision. Indeed, since Ada Byron's first program, there have been many developments within computer programming, technology and society, against a backdrop of the industrial revolution and two World Wars, which have contributed to the advancement of computer technology, both hardware and software-related. Today's computer programs are widespread and much more complex than those of the nineteenth century and, only in very rare cases, are produced by only one person. More often, development teams, perhaps involving hundreds or thousands of programmers, work together to build complex applications.

To orchestrate these many developers, can be a challenging task, as Kraft (1977) shows us in his timely account on software development. The early software industry appears to have struggled with finding formal mechanisms to manage the experts and the production process respectively. Large scale projects tended to run over time and budget, producing questionable results with the software developers being empowered by their often unique, and to managers 'mysterious', expertise (Friedman 1989). The first noted suggestion for a solution to these problems was published by Royce (1970). The author approaching the topic from a managerial viewpoint and drawing on his own programming experiences, came to the conclusion that large scale development projects cannot be organised in the two common phases, 'analysis' and 'coding'. Instead, a more complex process was considered necessary, extending and splitting these phases into smaller and thus easier to control, steps. Inspired by the industries urgent needs for a solution, following Royce, many more suggestions for 'best practice' software development management were, and still are coming forward (cf. Chapter 2).

Whilst the software development process appears to have become more complex since the times of Ada Byron, in that more people have to be orchestrated in order to build a functioning program, simultaneously, the number of software users increased. Over the years, software became available to more users, with a particular increase in user numbers with the emergence of terminal computing, facilitated by the Client-Server Architecture in the 1980s (Woods 2003). With more users, the management of user requirements became more complex and important, in particular, since not only the numbers but also the type of user changed. Software was no more only applied by the few experts with limited access to highly valued and protected main frame computers. With terminal computing, people with other professions, such as manager and sales assistant, were now using computers – a situation which provided an ongoing challenge in regards to the design of the software (Grudin 1991; Winograd and Flores 1994).

Although managing the competing exigencies of a user base can be difficult, an increase in user numbers also offers enormous potential. Software production is labour intensive and expensive; however, to reproduce or adapt existing code for different usage in other applications or contexts can be (depending on variables such as the programming style and underlying software architecture) relatively cheap. To capitalise on the high demand, it became part of software producing companies' strategies to apply tools to facilitate re-using code with minimum effort. There are two types of software producers, which can be clearly distinguished in their reaction to these changes: bespoke software providers and standard software package providers. Bespoke software providers produce customer specific programs, which can be used by one or a few organisations. In this context, re-usage of code is limited to the re-usage of standard functionalities. The applications as such are not designed to be translated into different contexts, but to fulfil the requirements of one or few organisations. Standard software providers, in contrast, address a wider user base, aiming to provide a product, which is generic enough to fit into many organisational contexts (but specific enough to, at the time, respond to the user organisation's key requirements)[1]. Thus, not only standard func-

[1] For this research, Quintas' (1994) definition of 'user organisation' is used. Quintas (1994) defines: "A 'user organisation' is one that does not generate income from the sale of software or other IT Products and services, but uses IT systems in order to achieve its objectives" (p: 45). Referring to Quintas' (ibid.) definition of 'user organisation', the following definition for 'vendor organisation' has been derived and is used within this book. "A 'ven-

tionality is re-used but entire applications are 'recycled'. An example of the latter model is Enterprise Resource Planning (ERP) systems, a specific type of standard software, often also related to as 'Enterprise Software', 'Commercial Off the Shelf' (COTS) product or generally as 'Software Package'. ERP system providers offer applications, which can potentially handle all of an organisation's business processes and work flows, with added customising tools, allowing the re-selling of systems to multiple, heterogeneous organisations (Pollock and Cornford 2005).

ERP systems are not a new or unexpected development, but a phenomenon which can be traced back some years. With a general growth in software package production, triggered in the 1960s with IBM unbundling the software from their hardware, an industry focusing on licensing applications evolved (Light and Sawyer 2007). Within this broader trend (which included also Computer Aided Design (CAD) applications), a type of sub-industry emerged which focused on organisations struggling with integrating and running multiple bespoke systems, each fulfilling different functions, in the production area: Facilitated by the emergence of a Common Business Oriented Language (COBOL) and vast improvements in computing memory, the first generation of Manufacturing Requirements Planning (MRP) systems emerged out of existing stock and inventory control systems in the manufacturing industry in the late 1960s (Webster and Williams 1993) and were soon declared as 'state of the art' (Chung and Snyder 2000; Mabert 2007; Orlicky 1975). Further developments, including the inclusion of events on the shop floor into the production schedule in the 1970s, earned MRP systems the title, MRP II (Manufacturing Requirements Planning II). Expanding further, until the 1980s, MRPII remained the leading product for large scale organisations in search of more integrated software products (Yurong and Houcun 2000).

With the emergence of Client-Server Architecture in the late 1980s (MRP and MRP II were based on Monolith Architecture), a new generation of software products evolved, which were based on MRPII, known in the in United Kingdom as 'Computer-Aided Production Management' (CAPM) systems (Webster and Williams 1993). Being one facet of what was widely known as Computer Integrated Manufacturing (CIM)[2], the notion of

---

dor organisation' is one that generates income from the sale of software or other IT Products and services."

2 For a discussion on the different definitions of CIM, see Boaden and Dale (1986).

CAPM soon disappeared. However, the idea of an integrated organisation remained and is mirrored in what is known today as Enterprise Resource Planning (ERP) Systems, a term coined by the Industry Analyst Gartner Group (Wylie 1990)[3].

Today's ERP systems are complex software packages, built with the vision, not only to incorporate 'production' related data and functionality, but to reflect an entire organisation's processes within one software system. With the ongoing automation of business processes, supported by the widespread exploitation of ERP systems, the market in which ERP vendors act is forecast to grow – despite the global financial crisis (Garbani 2009). Already in 2000 more than 60% of organisations relied on this type of software package and it is seen as *de facto* standard for any large multinational company (Hanseth and Monteiro 1998; Meissner 2000; Parr and Shanks 2000; Pollock and Cornford 2005; Woods 2003). Addressing large organisations with their software system, we find two companies, SAP and Oracle, dominating the market[4], partially as a result of many merger and acquisition (M&A) activities, in particular in 2006 (Jacobson et al. 2007). Whilst these activities were aimed at reducing the number of competitors (Jacobson et al. 2007), today, we find a shift in M&A patterns: Complementing growth is now the desire to expand the product portfolio, resulting in organisations such as SAP and Oracle targeting smaller organisations, which provide business solutions in niche markets (Garbani 2009).

ERP systems and their predecessors have been discussed by practitioners and academics for many years, with a notable increase in interest in the late 1990s, leading to a total number of ERP related publications in academic journals between 1997-2000 of 189 (only five of these count for the early years, such as 1997) (Esteves and Pastor 2001). Moon (2007) has identified a further 313 ERP related articles published between 2000 and 2006 (as of 31. May 2006). With such an interest in the topic already, it may appear to be a rather superfluous task to add another study to this collection. However, if we look more closely at the existing literature (see Chapter 2), we can see that, despite the numerous studies, there is a sub-

3 Products named 'MRP systems' can still be bought. Whilst having similarities with their predecessors, these systems are much more advanced. The earlier definition of MRP systems appears not to be suitable for such products.

4 Targeting small and medium sized organisations, we find other players dominating, such as Sage Group, Microsoft, Infor, Lawson and Epicor (Jacobson et al. 2007).

stantial lack of diversity which prevents a more comprehensive understanding of the phenomenon, ERP systems. Whilst we find, for instance, multiple articles highlighting the struggles of the local user organisation to implement the generic software package (implementation studies), there are far fewer articles about how these systems are procured. Even less research can be found on how these systems are produced within the software labs; how the individuals, the team, the project and the organisation are shaped by and shape the software package. Overall, we find that ERP related studies (1) focus upon the moment of implementation, emphasising the struggles between the local user and the global system and that (2) the user organisation's viewpoint dominates, even when other parts of the product life-cycle are investigated (for instance, the software package support phase). This focus on the user organisation's viewpoint and, therein the implementation phase, appears to have two main effects on our understanding of ERP systems:

On the one hand, the multiple existing investigations provide a detailed and needed user perspective on the often tense relationship between the user and vendor organisation during the moment of system implementation. ERP systems are complex and yet highly standardised, built on the basis of particular "best practice" assumptions, which are founded in the belief that each organisation has the same core functionalities and thus can be implemented in multiple contexts (Laforest 1997). Whilst we find today, that indeed standard software is widely used and that there thus must be some kind of common functionality across organisation, this was not always thought to be the case. Indeed in particular in the 1990s, many of the more critical social science academics believed that standard systems would not succeed (Berg 1997; MacLaughlin et al. 1999; Webster and Williams 1993). It appeared at the time that there was such as a 'mismatch' between the local settings and the standard technology that fitting them to the idiosyncratic needs of the many different user organisations would be possible but only with significant and unacceptable tradeoffs. Unsolvable tensions were said to develop – a belief, which was strongly supported by a line of implementation studies, reporting on failed projects and problems. Hanseth and Braas's (2001) account reflects, what has been the tone of many studies:

> The idea of the universal standard is an illusion just like the treasure at the end of the rainbow. Each time one has defined a standard which is believed to be complete and coherent, during implementation one discovers that there are elements lacking or

> incompletely specified while others have to be changed to make the standard work, which makes various implementations different and incompatible – just like arbitrary non-standard solutions. (Hanseth and Braa 2001: 261)

Whilst such a critical viewpoint has been central for many years, if we take a more historical view on implementation studies, we find that over the years, different types of, and more nuanced implementation studies have emerged.

The first accounts published, were, indeed, 'success stories' rather than critical accounts. Written by standard system software vendors or affiliated organisations, the first studies reporting upon ERP systems, did so in a very positive way showing the advantages of ERP standard solutions (such accounts can still be found, in particular on the WebPages of ERP vendors and consulting organisations). Following this early vendor rhetoric was the academic literature, often but not always taking on a more critical viewpoint. Giving voice to the user organisations in describing the implementation phase more critically, were in particular researchers from Science and Technology Studies, Information Systems research and Organisational Studies. Offering detailed and analytical accounts, the studies highlighted the tensions between the generic systems and the local organisation during the implementation phase (cf. Hanseth and Braa 2001; Pollock and Cornford 2004; Tolsby 1998), back then, a missing perspective. In particular, in more recent times, research emerged, coming from academics that appear to have moved on from discussing the pitfalls of global solutions or their possible inability to reflect local settings. Instead, these studies focus on how to best 'survive' the implementation phase (Akkermans and van Helden 2002; Bingi et al. 1999; Esteves and Pastor-Collado 2000; Gosh 2002; Holland and Light 1999; Holland and Light 2003; Hong and Kim 2002; Motwani et al. 2005; Somers and Nelson 2001; Sumner 2000). For these authors, it is no more the question whether systems can be applied widely or not, but how best to manage what appears to have been accepted as the inevitable tensions that arise when ERP systems are implemented.

The current imbalance governing the field of ERP system research becomes most visible in comprehensive literature reviews such as those provided by Esteves and Pastor (1999), Esteves and Bohorquez (2007) and Moon (2007). Only a visual comparison between the authors listed under the point 'implementation studies' with the other areas of the product life cycle, demonstrates with undisputable clarity the current disproportions. Only lightly scattered and slowly emerging, we find, for instance, research occupied with software package design, development, procurement and support. If we aim to understand ERP systems more fully, however, we cannot continue to focus only on the single moment of implementation (even though access to such sites might be easier, the material found more sensational). There is a need to investigate other phases of the product life cycle in more detail.

When approaching ERP systems, equally, we cannot continue to focus solely on the user organisations' viewpoint, as it is the case with the majority of current studies, but need to ask how these systems are shaped by the vendor organisations throughout their life cycle. It is the technology producing organisation, which is reflected in the technology (Kidder 1982) and whose role, across the product life cycle, needs to be understood. This includes phases such as product development, support services and sales. In short, there is a need to investigate all areas of the product life cycle and in doing so, take into account not only the user organisations' but also the vendor organisations' experiences, policies and practices.

1.2 Aim of This Research

The aim of this research is to address some of the gaps in current literature, and more specifically, present a widely neglected vendor organisation's viewpoint on ERP system development and support. The study provides, from a social perspective, first hand and also first time insights, into the practice and policies of one of the biggest ERP system vendors worldwide. Based on ethnographical fieldwork data, this book offers a more comprehensive understanding of how work is organised in such settings, and thus, how the technology producing organisation as well as the user-vendor relationship is shaped by and shapes the technology. In shedding light on the system development and system support phase, the study demonstrates that it is only if we broaden our view and aim to understand the technology producer, that we can more fully comprehend the phenomenon of ERP systems: a complex but yet widely spread standard software system, which success has been declared earlier as likely as finding a treasure at the end of the rainbow (Hanseth and Braa 2001). More specifically, this book highlights:

How does an ERP system provider manage the challenge of serving a highly diverse and geographically dispersed user base?
Maintaining a positive relationship with the user organisation does not stop where sales and implementation efforts do; the management of the user-vendor relationship spans the entire product life cycle, including the moment of ERP system support. It is when problems are reported by the user organisation and thus the system re-enters the vendor organisation in its customised and often modified form, that relationships are constantly re-defined. Whilst current literature provides us with some impressions on how the user organisations experience this critical moment (Light 2001; Nah et al. 2001), the vendor's site and with this the way the vendor is organised internally, to handle the multiple, often highly individualistic and urgent problems, reported from the user site, is, as yet, a mystery.

Research question one addresses this gap in literature and shows, how one of the biggest ERP vendors worldwide, manages this challenge. The findings highlight, for the first time, the complex nature of the user-vendor relationship at this stage of the product life cycle and, in particular, demonstrate (1) how the vendor manages to organise support for the thousands of, often highly complex, requests for help through various mechanisms of dis-embedding and re-embedding problems and (2) the challenges associated with providing online support for such complex technologies and geographically dispersed users.

How does an ERP system provider, from a social perspective, organise its product development phase?
The business model of ERP system providers is based on the assumption that software can be developed in such a way that it can travel from one setting to another, with minor adaptation efforts. The underlying belief is that organisations have similar core functionalities, which can be supported by (a slightly modified version of) the same system (Laforest 1997). It can be speculated that the development of such systems differs from other types of software development, where only one or few organisations are addressed (Keil and Carmel 1995) and thus, that also the social accounts from bespoke system development such as Kraft (1977) and Friedman (1989) cannot be translated into these settings. However, despite the financial success and the still growing market of standard software packages, what we currently find in literature are studies occupied with bespoke system development, and dominating, accounts on the more managerial aspects of software development such as the Waterfall

process (Royce 1970), the Rational Unified Process (Kruchten 1999) or the many methods summarised under the umbrella of Agile Software development methods, such as Scrum (Schwaber and Beedle 2001) or XP (Beck and Anders 2004), all aiming to provide a framework, which shall help to develop software more effectively. Only very few studies (Carmel and Sawyer 1998; Cusumano and Selby 1997; Cusumano and Smith 1995; Sawyer 2000a; Zachary 1994; Zachary 1998) address the social aspects of software package development such as how people actually work in such settings, including an individual, team, organisational and cultural perspective.

Whilst both types of research are insightful, the latter studies occupied with the social aspects in software package labs are still small in number, there are few providing ethnographical detail, and many generalise from their studies about the wide range of standard software packages rather than addressing possible particularities of ERP system development. As yet we do not know what the challenges in such settings are, where a dynamic market with competing exigencies of different stakeholders build a complex environment and where thousands of programmers need to be orchestrated. As Wellman states, it appears that “how people work is one of the best kept secrets in America” (cited in Suchman, 1995: 1) and, as it seems, not only there.

The lack of research in this area is highly surprising. How can we aim for understanding ERP systems, which are generic but yet equipped with customising features, if we do not know how work is organised in such settings, how the technology is developed? How can we theorise upon and impose management methods, if we do not understand who these developers are and how they work? How can we set out to understand the phenomena ERP systems, if we build our understanding on what is happening within ERP vendor labs on few studies and assumptions? Overall, it appears that parts of the field have moved towards an attitude in which the shaping of the technology through the technology producer has become ‘uninteresting’ and possibly ‘unimportant’ – an attitude which needs to be challenged. Addressing the current shortcomings in academic literature and arguing that there is a need for an ERP system specific sociology of software development, this research provides a unique social-organisational perspective on the efforts of an ERP vendor to succeed in the competitive and dynamic ERP system market. In particular, the findings reveal (1) the attempts of a leading organisation to change its development process and product respectively, to regain market share, (2) the struggles at different organisational levels in handling this change, and (3) the unforeseen consequences of such change on the informal work organisation, and therein, on the flow of knowledge.

1.3 Structure of This Book

To address the aforementioned issues, this book is organised into seven chapters.

This first chapter is followed by *Chapter 2*, a discussion on existing knowledge, setting also the theoretical grounds for the later discussion of the collected data (Chapter 4, 5, 6, 7). Particular attention is given to empirical accounts of ERP system development and support and the conceptual literature related to the Social Shaping of Technology perspective.

Chapter 3 is divided into two sections. The first section is dedicated to an ethnographic tale, introducing the North American software labs in which this research took place and with this, sets the context for the ethnographical data presented. The second part of Chapter 3 presents a theoretical introduction and discussion of the research design.

Chapter 4 is concerned with ERP system support. Split into two sections it highlights how an ERP system provider manages the relationship with its diverse user base, during the moment of software package support. The first part is devoted to an ethnographical description of the ERP system support division, presented from the viewpoint of a vendor's support employee. Themes such as the work organisation and policies, which determine the moment at which the ERP system 're-enters' the vendor's organisation through the support channel, are highlighted. In the second part of Chapter 4, the presented ethnographic data is discussed, giving particular attention to the formal and informal work practices.

Chapter 5 focuses on ethnographical data collected within the ERP system development department. Aiming to reflect the events at the site studied, the chapter highlights the vendor's changing strategic direction, the impact of this change on the day-to-day working practices, as well as the software developers' reactions.

Chapter 6 is dedicated, firstly, to an analytical discussion of the data presented in Chapter 5 and secondly, sheds light on the intriguing connections, found between the software support teams (Chapter 4) and developer teams (Chapter 5). The data reveals a, by current literature yet unnoticed, surprising communitarian spirit within the software labs, which at times, expands and even embraces the user.

Chapter 7, the concluding chapter, provides a summary of this research as well as highlights the key contributions. This is followed by a discussion of the limitations of the research as well as a proposal for future investigations, the latter focusing, in particular, on ongoing changes with regard to software architecture and its possible impacts on social research.

1.4 A Note on Style

There are many different styles of writing, each reflecting both the discipline and personal preference. There are three stylistic elements used within this book, reflecting a personal preference and are briefly explained below:

First, the fieldwork data presented has, apart from orthographical errors[5], not been modified, unless indicated otherwise. I decided against grammatical corrections in any form, because I felt it would take away important details, reflecting the spirit and atmosphere of this global organisation with its multinational teams and customers. Second, instead of describing and analysing what has been found at the research site using notions such as 'the researcher' or 'the informant', I include myself as a vendor's employee, who is actively shaping and being shaped by the surroundings. In acknowledging the close connection between myself, in the roles of participant observer and intern, with the field, I present the relationships in the way they were arranged, instead of pretending a distance, which was not aimed for nor existed (cf. Chapter 3). Thus, notions such as 'I' and 'my colleagues' can be found. Third, to facilitate reading, I decided to use only the male word form, where gender specific terms had to be used. Naturally, the male form represents both genders, male and female.

5 When quoting support messages sent between the vendor and user, orthographical errors made by the parties involved were not corrected, since these errors reflect the tone and thus the user-vendor relationship at a particular point in time.

2 Discussion of Existing Knowledge

2.1 Introduction

> *Software presents a challenge because it is, in many ways, an atypical technology; indeed, we may question whether it is a technology at all since it is generally regarded in intellectual property law as being equivalent to literary works. It is easy to see why this is so: software is "written" in a variety of languages. Without the hardware on which to run, software is merely lines of code. However, what distinguishes software from literature is that when installed in a computer it becomes a "virtual machine" – a tool or machine that we experience as a word processor, drawing tool or database. (...) Software is code that creates virtual machines that do things, and it gets just about everywhere. (Quintas 1994b: 29)*

This book is about software, a very particular type of technology or as Quintas (1994) calls it, an "atypical technology" (p: 29). It is technology, which, on its own, is mere text, not an artefact which can be switched on and off or modified in order to achieve a-different goal (cf. De Laet and Mol 2000). As such, software appears to be a passive technology, acting only as a text – unless brought into contact with hardware. Together with hardware, software becomes a "virtual machine" (Quintas 1994b: 29), an actor which influences our day-to-day lives. Thus, software is not only an 'atypical technology' but also an 'atypical text', which does not necessarily shape or is shaped by society through the reader but rather by being read, interpreted and enacted through the machine.

This type of atypical technology has been the subject of much academic research across disciplines. Various conceptual and empirical work, related to the production and use of software, has, for instance, been carried out within Science and Technology Studies (STS). Looking at software from a very broad and interdisciplinary perspective, and aiming at exploring and explaining the phenomenon of how social, political and cultural values shape and are shaped by technology, STS is a very wide field, which, in many cases, also crosses academic boundaries and includes research from other disciplines. Like all interdisciplinary research, a broad and cross-disciplinary view on a particular topic, provides a rich picture, with the same topics being looked at from multiple angles. Combining the different accounts, a bigger picture establishes itself, which allows comprehending the object or situation observed in a much more 'multi-coloured' way than non-interdisciplinary research could do.

Whilst such a situation is fortunate in many ways, for the researcher working in an interdisciplinary field, the vast amount of viewpoints and literature, also from interfacing disciplines, can be overwhelming not only in terms of numbers of articles but also, in trying to understand the different viewpoints. Whilst, for instance, Sociologists can read technical literature from Computer Sciences, the question is, can they also understand what is said. In short, what has to be the basis for selecting relevant literature in interdisciplinary research, is the question of *understanding*. In the case of this book, literature from disciplines such as Management, Computer Science and Sociology (besides STS literature) was chosen, reflecting my own interdisciplinary background, allowing such understanding (see Chapter 3).

Providing an overview on the selected literature from the different disciplines, the following chapter is divided into two sections, one occupied with an empirical viewpoint on ERP system production and one with a conceptual view. The first section, highlighting more empirical literature, presents an introduction to the literature on commodified software and more specifically, ERP systems. Adopting a life cycle perspective (according to Pollock and Williams (2008)), existing accounts are categorised into five phases: design, development, procurement, implementation and support[6]. Whilst all phases are reviewed, the development and support phase is discussed in more detail, being at the heart of this research.

In the second section, conceptual literature is reviewed, highlighting different concepts emerging from within Science and Technology Studies, in particular those related to software production, and therein to commodified software.

---

6 The notion 'life cycle' is used and interpreted in different ways. For instance, when discussing the life cycle of packaged systems, Carmel (1993) does so in the context of software development, including the different software development methods, such as Waterfall or Spiral model and defining these as life cycle. Other authors suggest different and boarder categories. Esteves and Pastor (2001) use a life cycle suggested by Esteves and Pastor (1999) consisting of adaption and decision, acquisition, implantation, use and maintenance, as well as an evolution phase. For this research, Pollock and Williams (2008) notion on life cycle has been found to be most appropriate.

2.2 ERP Systems in Social Research

Embedded in the broader field of standard software package research, Enterprise Resource Planning (ERP) systems have only recently become the subject of increased academic interest. Whilst ERP systems are dominating the market and gradually evolved over the years (see Chapter 1), it is only since the late 1990s and early 2000, that ERP system research has become a more active research field (Botta-Genoulaz et al. 2005). Even though literature is available, as the following review will show, today's research is often unspecific, in that it fails to distinguish between ERP systems and other types of standard software. Whilst in certain areas we find a clear focus (for instance, in cases where authors report upon software implementations), in others authors do not distinguish between different types of software and generalise from their ERP specific account towards standard software and vice versa. In some literature, it even remains unclear which type of standard software package has been investigated. Arguing throughout this book, that there is a need to distinguish not only between custom made and packaged software, but also between different types of standard software packages, within this chapter ERP system specific literature has been prioritised.

2.2.1 *ERP System Design*

> *In order to understand the phenomena surrounding a new technology, we must open the question of design – the interaction between understanding and creation. (Winograd and Flores 1994: 4)*

The design of a system determines the satisfaction of the user organisation and has a significant impact on the software's productivity, quality, and costs, throughout the entire product life cycle (see also Curtis et al. (1988)). Whilst this is the case for all types of software, the additional challenge for software package producers is that not only one, but many, heterogeneous users in different organisations need be satisfied with a particular design. But, how to design a system, which responds to requirements of a specific user organisation and at the same time, is generic enough to be used in different organisational settings?

In Information Systems literature on software package design it is mainly the question of whether user requirements should be included or not, which dominates the discussion. Whilst some authors argue that generic solutions suppliers are actively keeping users at a distance (and thus do not include user requirements), in an attempt to avoid becoming too tied to a specific user organisation, and produce a system, which is unsuitable for the wider user base (Bansler and Havn 1996; Williams et al. 2005) others found that user involvement was of such significance, that also generic solution providers should not act disconnectedly (Carmel and Becker 1995).

Salzman and Rosenthal (1994), following the first school of thought, argue that users should be kept at distance at any point of the product production phase, since user involvement would instead of helping, confront vendors with an unmanageable amount of requirements, which cannot be understood or translated meaningfully into the technology. The authors state that:

> Even if they try, through their own marketing experts, to understand the needs of a major customer, they generally lack the necessary detailed operational knowledge of their customers' industry and way of doing business. (p: 204)

An argument also related to the difficulty of translating user requirements, was made by Wagner and Newell (2004), who outline the problem of having different views, depending on which users are asked. Again, it would be a question of contextual variables, which would make the interpretation of requirements potentially challenging, since each requirement has to be looked at in its own context (such as the role of the user, the political motivation as well as any possible individual agenda).

Grint and Woolgar (1997) (see also section on Social Constructivism 2.4.2) referring to the quality of requirements, ask the question whether the accounts given by the users really reflect the users' needs. The authors argue, that a user might not yet know what is (technically) possible and what might be future requirements for the system, deriving from environmental factors, such as politics or the user organisation's own industry.

Disregarding these discussions on quality and if it would be meaningful at all to include the user, we find Keil and Carmel (1995), building on Grudin (1991), implying that users *should* be included in the design process. Critically discussing the use of direct (developer-user) and indirect (intermediaries - user) links in software development, the authors conclude that the more direct links are used, the more successful the software product. With too many indirect links in place organisations are said to be in danger of not fully comprehending the user's needs, since intermediaries might lack the technical understanding to comprehend user requirements to their full extent. Thus, misunderstandings are said to be common in such settings. An argument also supported by Curtis et al. (1988), who pointed to the same problem in large scale bespoke system development several years before.

In this context, an additional point has to be taken into account: ERP systems exist for many years (both of the market leaders for instance had already started in the 1970s), and are not developed from scratch (Pollock and Williams 2008). Thus, even if managing to collect and translate user requirements correctly, the vendor might be unable to implement the ideas. ERP systems are often historically grown, having unchangeable core functionality which cannot be modified without risking errors in other parts of the system. As such, design does not take place in a "green field" but has to complement existing code.

Whilst the authors differ in their conclusions on whether, and if so, how, users and their requirements should be included in the design process, we find an interesting argument in Salzman and Rosenthal (1994) discussing who can be actually considered as being *responsible* for a misfit between the local organisation and the global system. Whilst the majority of existing studies dealing with the moment of implementation imply that vendors did not make enough efforts to design a system which fits with user requirements, the authors argue that the task and responsibility of matching the generic software and the local organisation is to be left to the implementing party and *not* with the vendor or the implementing organisation. In cases where a fit cannot be achieved through the efforts of the implementing experts, the authors suggest that the user organisation should become more flexible and adapt to the system (rather than the vendors developing more flexible systems).

The literature on the design process is interesting in that it not only discusses how user requirements should be taken into account when designing standard software. It also questions of whether user requirements should be included at all, in the light of the potential lack of knowledge on the users' side, as well as the possible translation problems between the local and the software vendors.

Following the design stage, is the development phase in which the user requirements are (or not) translated into the software on a day to day basis.

2.2.2 ERP System Development

Erran Carmel (1993) notes that if we look at software development, we need to distinguish between bespoke system development and software package development, as both differ in the environmental, organisational and process dimension. Summarising Carmel's process and organisational dimension, existing literature in the field of ERP system development (and packaged software development respectively), has been arranged into two dimensions: an environmental and an organisational dimension (including Carmel's 'Process dimension')[7].

2.2.2.1 The Environmental Perspective

Research summarised under the category 'environmental perspective', is work occupied with factors shaping the surroundings in which software package organisations act and which are thus almost unchangeable from within the organisation: *the nature of the product*, *the stakeholders* and *the industry*.

The Nature of the Product

Software differs from other types of commodities in that parts of it can be reused to a large extent (Pollock and Williams 2008), that it can be reproduced with almost no additional costs (Kruchten 2005) and that it can be sold as a product or as a service (Woods and Mattern 2006).

If we concentrate on the first point, we find that reusing software has been common practice for many years. Already during the time of sequential and unstructured programming, parts of code were stored in code libraries or simply on the programmer's computer waiting to be reused (Pollock and Williams 2008). Followed by procedural programming and eventually Object Oriented programming evolving out of the earlier programming principles (Sammet 1991), the idea of reusing code became

---

7 Even though agreeing with the argument that software development takes place at multiple sites, and thus, not only inside the vendor's labs, such discussion has been left aside. The aim of this section is to look closely at the development of ERP systems within software labs and the different factors influencing this part of the part of the product life cycle. For illustrative literature on developments at the user site, see Fleck (1988), and on technology innovation, see von Hippel (1988).

more and more concrete. Whilst in procedural programming functionality was arranged along loops and conditions and with this could be copied and reused elsewhere (with a different condition or loop), Object Oriented programming goes one step further, and by encapsulating parts of coding, offers complex functionality, available to anyone with access to the often publicly shared code libraries (for instance, Java Code libraries). Whilst all software producing organisations profit from such development, it is the software package industry which went one step further and embraced the principle of re-using code as a business model (Pollock and Williams 2008).

Not only do software package providers re-use parts of coding, they also re-use large parts of their systems by 'translating' them into other sectors (see for instance Cornford and Pollock's (2003) and Pollock and Williams' (2008) description of such a translation in the context of a software package for higher education). As such, investment into the development within one area can also be capitalised upon in other areas. Already taken into account when developing the system, packaged software vendors can spread the risk of an investment into different areas, a risk avoidance strategy which is necessary not only to generate additional value but also, to survive as an organisation even if the new product is not accepted by the market. Unlike bespoke system development, the development of standard applications is not pre-financed from the user organisation. The software vendor has to finance the development of the entire system upfront (Carmel and Sawyer 1998). As such, software package vendors are dependent on the market accepting the product and the possibility of translating code into other areas. An idea which goes along with the attribute of software, that re-production costs of software are insignificant (Kruchten 2005)[8].

Another specific characteristic of software is that it can be sold as a product, which is handed over to the customer or as a service hosted by the vendor organisation. If hosted by the vendor organisation the service can be requested by the user organisation through a data connection, such as the Internet. Depending on the pricing model, the user organisation might pay by traffic, amount of requests or a monthly / yearly fee. If the

---

8 Such a business model can be highly risky in situations like the 2008 global financial crisis. For example, the market leader SAP announced, that due to a fall in sales, revenues for already developed functions are not meeting expectations and thus cost saving measures need to be implemented (Computerwoche 2008).

service is handed over to the user organisation, it is the user organisation's responsibility to handle and maintain the service (or to sign up for a support contract with the vendor). Again, different pricing models can be applied. Many other business models are feasible such as, for example, a combination of bought and 'rented' services (Woods 2003). This particular characteristic of software provides software producing organisations with choices many other technology selling organisations do not have.

The Stakeholders

One of the definitions for stakeholders is that a stakeholder is "a person with an interest or concern in something" (Oxford English Dictionary 2009). Generally, for standard software providers, various parties can be stakeholders: persons with an interest or concern in something, amongst these being the employees, the investors and the media. Whilst all organisations have to keep their different types of stakeholders satisfied, in the context of standard software production, there are stakeholders, which, without having any investment in the company, are crucial for the organisation's success: analysts, market research organisations, reference clients and the media (Carmel and Sawyer 1998).

As highlighted earlier, buying an ERP system is a huge, long-term investment for an organisation and how to come to a decision upon which product to buy is a multi-actor effort (Pollock and Williams 2008). Because of the financial impact and strategic importance, organisations consider carefully which systems to buy. Often not knowing what to purchase, user organisations turn to analyst reports, reference clients, newspaper reports and other organisations running ERP systems, to find help with their decision making process. As such, ERP system vendors are under constant scrutiny by investors, stock-holders, analysts and the media, creating a highly competitive industry in which many different groups, who often follow different interests, shape the public's and with this, the user organisation's opinion and buying decision (Carmel and Sawyer 1998; Sawyer 2000a).

Industry Rivalry

The third environmental factor is the competition in the market and with this the industry rivalry (Porter 1980). In the ERP market we find intense industry rivalry, which is partially expressed and rooted in the fight by ERP software vendors for the best publicity (Carmel 1993; Carmel and Sawyer 1998) and also in the nature of the packaged software production process. Whilst in bespoke system development, competition is high during the initial 'betting phase' (when the user organisation decides on who is offered the contract to develop the system), the software package market competes on the basis of already developed functionality. A commodity is offered to the market, which needs to be unique and different from the competitor's to catch the user organisation's interest and produce a 'wow' effect (Deifel, 1999). With this, software package vendors are reported to be constantly running against time, to keep up with the competitors' innovations, but at the same time, to be offering something new, something which catches the user organisation's eye and with this, allows the organisation to differentiate itself from its competitors (Carmel 1993; Carmel and Sawyer 1998; Dube 1998).

To keep ahead of the competition, we find different strategies amongst different organisations. If we compare, for instance, the biggest rivals in the market (2009), SAP and Oracle, we find heterogeneous approaches to creating a differentiation effect. Whilst SAP is known for following the more traditional route of organic growth, the in-house development of new product features (SAP Annual Report, 2006), and only occasionally acquires other organisations (the acquisition of 'Business Objects' being seen as the exception (Wang and Bartels 2008)), Oracle has become well-known for its shopping activities to gain a competitive advantage through providing new features. Following the "Oracle's Mergers and Acquisitions philosophy" (Oracle 2008) a list of acquisitions made over the years in order to get involved in new markets and to offer new products, can be found on the Oracle homepage (http://www.oracle.com/corporate/acquisition.html). The list presents us with names of previously well-known organisations in the software package market, such as PeopleSoft (acquired in 2005), Siebel (acquired in 2006) and BEA (acquired in 2008). With PeopleSoft having taken over JD Edwards before being bought out by Oracle, Oracle today appears to incorporate what used to be the major competitors in the ERP and market for both SAP and Oracle.

2.2.2.2 The Organisational Perspective

The organisational perspective, in the context of this book, embraces literature occupied with work organisation in software producing labs. Within this area, we find three streams of work: (1) research concentrating on how software developers should work together, including suggestions on different management methods, (2) research focusing on the implementation of such methods and how the managerial practices are shaped by, and shape the local organisation and (3) how software package developers work together in such settings.

How Software Developers Should Work

If we look more closely at the first stream of literature, on how software developers should work together, a substantial body of literature can be found, discussing how various methodological approaches evolved, such as the Waterfall model (Royce 1970), the Spiral model (Boehm 1986), and Agile Software Development methods (Agile Alliance 2008b). These methods suggest guidelines and rules to organise the software development process most effectively.

One of the earliest models for managing software developers, the Waterfall Method (Royce 1970), emerged during a time when projects were constantly running over time and producing questionable results, whilst the tradability factor of expertise in the software industry was on a high[9]. For the management of software companies, this was a most unfortunate situation in which the idea of de-skilling and re-distributing expertise was hoped to reduce the dependency on certain experts. The Waterfall process, responding to the demands of time, was quickly accepted in the hope that with having a more complex and rigid process in place, a more static and controllable environment could be created. Since Royce (1970), various other methods have made their way into literature, such as Boehm (1986) and his 'Spiral model'[10], as well as later developments, mostly based on engineering approaches (Kruchten 2004), all seeking to overcome the earlier method's pitfalls.

In the late 1990s, influenced by object orientation, evolutionary development and internet technologies, a different type of software management method evolved out of what was known as the 'agile movement' (Abrahamson et al. 2003; Strode 2006)[11]. The agile movement aimed at moving

9 See also Saviotti (1998). Saviotti (ibid.) argues, that the tradability value of expertise depends on the cost of acquiring expertise, and the demand for it. Rare expertise is more valuable, can be sold at a higher price and puts employees in a more powerful position.

10 The classical Spiral model (Boehm 1986) emphasises the importance of iterative development. The idea of the Spiral model was to define requirements in as much detail as possible, create a preliminary design and develop a prototype. Following an evaluation of the prototype, these steps are to be repeated until the product is finished. In its original design, the Spiral model suggests iterations with a duration of 6 month to 2 years.

11 The notion of agile software development (which Friedman (1989) would possibly characterise as an approach which emphasises responsible autonomy) serves as an umbrella term, which embraces various methods such as Extreme Programming and Scrum. Whilst

away from the engineering traditions, considering software as a new and special type of product development, which cannot be organized by drawing on engineering methods. Different methods evolved under the umbrella of agile software development, such as SCRUM and Extreme Programming (see also Chapter 5).

Implementation of Software Development Methods

A second stream of literature in this area is occupied with the implementation of such methods. Dube (1998), for instance, presents a picture of a struggling software package provider in an attempt to implement a new, less hierarchical management approach. Describing the problems associated in detail, Dube (ibid.) comes to the conclusion that a change of method can be difficult for an organisation, in that it influences all parts of an organisation. He suggests that, thus, such moves have to be planned carefully (even if the market demands an urgent change) and that in particular the transformation of measures of control has be planned and watched carefully.

Whilst Dube concentrates on problems associated with a change of management practice, other authors, such as Paulisch and Volker (2002) discuss the idea of implementing mixed methodologies. Paulisch and Volker (ibid.), report upon Siemens' practices on combining agile with more traditional methods. Barrett (2004), drawing on work by Storey (1985), Hyman (1987) and Friedman (1989), shows how, in the case of a small Australian Software company, the management moves successfully between different management practices simultaneously, depending on the task the employees are responsible for. The idea of mixing methodologies has also been discussed in more general terms by authors such as Truex et al. (2000), Williams and Cockburn (2003), Barrett (2001), Boehm (2002), Adler and Borys, (1996).

Most interestingly, in this regard, is also Fitzgerald's (1997) work. Besides showing how methods are applied and mixed, Fitzgerald (ibid.) found a strong correlation between applying methodologies and the project manager's experiences. Inexperienced project managers were found to use predefined approaches more frequently whilst more experienced project

---

differing slightly, all methods summarised under the umbrella term follow the same set of values: "Individuals and interactions over processes and tools, working software over comprehensive documentation, customer collaboration over contract negotiation, responding to change over following a plan" (http://www.agilemanifesto.org/).

managers are said to avoid using methodologies. Following these two phases of first following and later reject a method, Fitzgerald (ibid.) found that with the experience growing, project managers move back towards the usage of methodology, however only to evaluate which features of which methodology is most applicable for a specific context and, on the basis of this evaluation, mix and adapt different methodologies.

Equally occupied with the implementation of software methodologies, but from a different perspective in that the authors also discuss the usefulness of such methods in general, we find Sawyer and Guinan's (1998) account. Sawyer and Guinan (ibid.) question the need for methodologies particularly when it comes to relating methods to team performance. Whilst acknowledging the usefulness of project management methods to reduce variability amongst developers and to bring developers together (for example, in form of meetings), the authors conclude that management methods are no suitable indicator for team performance. Instead, the authors suggest, more research should be carried out on the social aspects of software development, which are considered as a far more significant indicator for team performance than methods.

Interestingly, similar findings and suggestions are found in Curtis (1988) ten years earlier. Even though writing from the perspective of large scale bespoke system development, the authors found that software development tools and practices had "disappointingly small effects" (Curtis, 1988: 1284) on software quality and team productivity. Instead, the authors suggest, investigating software production as a behavioural process[12], putting the human and organisational aspects of software development at the centre of attention.

Overall, the historical development of software methods, emerging in particular form Management related literature, and the correlated social studies carried out by authors such as Kraft (1977) and Friedman (1989), highlights the apparent struggles of producing this special type of technology. The still evolving new concepts on managing the experts and the production cycle respectively (such as agile software development), show that industry and academia have still not found appropriate tools to manage this relatively new type of work.

---

[12] The behavioural model the authors suggest, consists of several layers which should be investigated in order to understand the productivity and quality of software production: Individual (programmer), team, project, company and business milieu level.

How Software Developers Work in Packaged Software Labs

The third stream of literature presenting an organisational perspective on software development is occupied with the working practices within software package labs. One of the most interesting studies occupied with how developers work within software package producing labs can be found in Carmel and Sawyer (1998). Focusing on the settings in software package development in general terms (studies exclusively investigating ERP development are non-existent), the authors, referring to Bach (Bach 1995a)[13], found a working culture, which was determined by an individual and entrepreneurial climate, characteristics which are said to be rooted in the history of the industry. Carmel and Sawyer (ibid.) argue that the software package industry is relatively young, representing many of the entrepreneurial characteristics, such as long hours, but with high rewards, and therefore, is more attractive to risk-seeking, career-oriented and aggressive individuals. It is these individuals who then shape the organisational culture within a team or sector, initiating new employees and conditioning them to existing rituals. These characteristics, which are said to differentiate software package teams from their counterparts in bespoke system development, have also been found and supported by Cusumano and Selby (1997), Carmel (1997), Dube (1998) Sawyer (2000a). Such is the consensus that had developed around this view that it is difficult to find literature that refutes or problematise these characteristics.

One account which does so, although not explicitly, is Zachary (1998). Having investigated Microsoft when building the product Microsoft NT, Zachary draws a picture of a different software package developer, who is team oriented, swearing alliance to the team leader (rather than to their CEO). Zachary underlines the role team work plays in such settings, in which the body of knowledge is said to change too fast to be documented and thus, knowledge needs to be nurtured and shared within teams. In regard to the characteristics of the developers, Zachary writes:

> If the success of a software project depends on the vitality of its teams, what is the principle that holds many teams together across distances and corporate objectives? It is not the unrestrained selfishness and individuality, which is often viewed as

13 In his article, Bach (1995) argues, that it is only through the efforts of motivated, heroic developers, that a project can succeed. He argues, that the importance of process is overemphasized and that aspects related to team and people do not get enough attention.

> the American ideal of teamwork. Nor is it the consensus approach for which the Japanese were lionized in the 1980s. (p: 64)

In indirectly questioning earlier accounts on individualistic behaviour (surprisingly, he does not reference any of the above discussed authors), Zachary describes, how Microsoft seemed to have created an environment of "Armed Truce", within which, developers united in teams, are constantly at war with other teams. Consensus was found to be not desired but seen as unhelpful with the team being the most important part of a developers working life. Concluding, Zachary emphasis the rise of the importance of teams and argues, that this will lead to the greatest shift in corporate power in which bosses will be no more authorities but facilitators and politicians.

Discussion

The reviewed literature provides us with an interesting picture on the complexity of software production. What stands out, particularly in the organisational perspective section is, that whilst we find many accounts theorising how to best manage software developers, only few researchers appear to be interested in the way developers work together, their working culture and informal practices, a condition already pointed out more than twenty years ago by Curits (1988) in the context of large scale bespoke system development and ten years later by Sawyer and Guinan (1998) referring to software package development. Before managerial methods can be used sensibly within the specific settings of software package production, we need to first understand how work is done in these labs (Ailon 2006; Bach 1995a; Barley 1996). Whilst authors such as Sawyer (1996), Cusumano and Selby (1997), Carmel and Sawyer (1998), Dube (1998), Sawyer and Guinan (1998), Zachary (1994; 1998), Sawyer (2000a), Sawyer (2000b), make attempts to introduce us to software package labs, future research is needed, carried out in different settings, as well as at different sites, and by other researchers approaching the topic from different angles (for instance through ethnographic workplace studies), providing new perspectives.

In comparing results, we might find that a differentiation between standard software packages produced for a mass market (such as Microsoft Office) and complex enterprise systems (such as Oracle's ERP system) suggests itself as useful. Current social studies of software package development appears to be too generic in that the notion of software packages and the related discussions incorporate, in most cases, all types of standard software packages. Cusumano and Selby (1998) for instance, introduce us to a paper called 'How Microsoft develops software', missing out on distinguishing between the different types of products developed within the organisation studied, ranging from spreadsheet software to ERP systems, which require very different approaches to project management[14]. Hence, it might not only be 'Sync and Stabilise' (cf. Cusumano and Selby 1995) that we find at this organisation, but also other types of methods. Many other authors follow similar broad categorisations (see, for instance, Carmel and Sawyer (1998) introducing us to 'software package teams and what makes them different'). Whilst this generic approach is useful in the light of the limited research available, with the field growing, we need to re-consider the suitability of this categorisation for the future. There is, in short, a need for a specific and comparative sociology of ERP systems.

Having outlined in detail the area of ERP system development, in the following, literature related to ERP system procurement is reviewed.

2.2.3 ERP System Procurement

If we continue our journey through the different stages of the product life cycle, we arrive at the procurement and sales phase. ERP systems are implemented in many organisations –SAP alone had more than 12 million users in 2008 (SAP AG 2009). Deciding to buy and implement large scale standard software package, such as ERP systems, is a big investment for an organisation, giving the procurement process as well as the implementation process high visibility within the organisation. In the light of the number of organisations going through procuring complex standard software products, as well as the significance of such an investment not only in terms of resource but also impact on the existing processes and culture, it is surprising how little attention the procurement process has received.

---

14 A confidential report on project management practices within Microsoft carried out by the vendor studied (and with agreement from Microsoft) reveals, that there is no one answer to Microsoft's project management practices. Depending on the type of software and team, different techniques are applied. The introduction to the report reads: "It is important to note that no two Microsoft divisions do things the same way. The development process the Office group would describe would be different than the process for MSN or for Windows or for Business Solutions. The same is true for user experience or metrics." (vendor confidential report 2005).

If we look for reasons for what looks like disinterest, we find Pollock and Williams (2008), providing us with rather practical motives. The authors argue that the wide neglect of the procurement phase might be rooted in that the procurement of ERP solutions takes place infrequently and the first decisions are taken 'invisibly' to the outside, on a senior management level (see also Harwood 2002; Sawyer 2001). The time needed by Social Scientists to first know about a procurement project and then negotiate access, is often too great. By the time the researcher arrives at the site, the procurement phase is already in its late stages. Tied to limited information on the early stages of the procurement process, researchers can consequently only provide an incomplete picture, which is then often included in other studies occupied with the implementation of the recently procured system (MacLaughlin et al. 1999). From what we learn from the research available is that the procurement of ERP systems appears to be fundamentally limited by the technology being a complex 'Black Box', difficult to open, and the procuring organisations being an equally complex arrangement of political, technical and social arrangements (Kunda 2003). Thus, to assess organisational needs, as well as the technology features and then match both, appears to be a most difficult exercise. Salzman and Rosenthal go as far as stating that:

> The transaction through which software products are bought and sold is based, to some fundamental extent, on mutual misunderstandings. (p: 209)

This situation of mutual misunderstanding is for Salzman and Rosenthal (ibid.) based on the vendor organisation's belief that their software is flexible enough to bc adapted to the user specific context, and the user organisation's belief that the system can be adapted to their needs (even though these needs are often not even clear).

Pollock and Williams (2008) report upon these related struggles within a user organisation when attempting to identify the needs Salzman and Rosenthal (1994) refer to. In their ethnographic study, Pollock and Williams (2008) show how requirements are not agreed upon across the organisation but are particular to different groups, and with this 'local'. The authors highlight how these groups cultivate and defend particular beliefs about competing solutions. Describing the user site's struggles, the authors conclude that what we can learn from this ethnographic study is that the procurement process of such solutions is not merely a political decision but a complex process determined by negotiations and uncertainties deriving from and shared by different groups.

Similarly, although from a different perspective, Alves and Finkelstein (2002) discuss the assessment of the features of such software solutions. Proposing a newly developed approach to deciding between different standard software products, the authors provide us with a new perspective in that they also discuss problems associated with *future* requirements of such solutions. Comparing bespoke system development (using the slightly misleading notion of "traditional system development") with standard software systems, the authors write:

> In traditional system development, requirements evolve as the environment in which these systems operate change. Typical changes to requirements specifications include adding or deleting requirements and fixing errors (Nuseibeh and Easterbrook 2000). Evolution in requirements might lead to a temporary instability but as soon as the changes are managed and requirements agreed, the situation is controlled. However, in COTS [Commercial off the Shelf] -based systems, requirements are extremely volatile mainly because of rapid changes in the COTS marketplace. The vendor requires customers to accept new releases that bring new features that can be either unwanted or conflicting with stated requirements. Thus, this new situation leads to a continuous process of negotiation and trade-offs. (p: 790)

Considering this account, even if today (despite all negotiations and difficulties to identify requirements) a perfect match between requirements could be found, future changes in the system might still lead to an eventual misfit between software and user organisation.

Light et al. (2001) look at the procurement process by discussing more non-functional requirements (operational parameters of a system such as supportability, compatibility) on why organisations would buy a mix of standard software modules from different vendors, instead of one ERP system from a single vendor. Without suggesting what might be the better choice, the authors provide a comparative overview of the advantages and disadvantages of ERP systems versus composing one's own enterprise system by buying single modules from different vendors (best-of-breed), based not on assessing detailed functional requirements but on more general factors such as integration possibilities, reliance on vendors and skills required.

As the discussion shows, even though limited, we find interesting accounts in literature, investigating the procurement phase from different angles. Whilst the user perspective of the procurement process is at least to some degree covered by academic discussion, it is interesting how the vendor's viewpoint of this phase remains unrecognised. The 'sales phase', which would be the counterpart of the user organisations procurement phase for the vendor, remains a white spot on the map of ERP system research, which has not even been identified as such by any of the existing publications.

Following this brief discussion of ERP system procurement, in the next section follows a discussion of the most popular topic in ERP system research: ERP system implementation.

2.2.4 ERP System Implementation

The notion 'ERP implementation' addresses the life phase of a system in which it is introduced at the local site. Whilst often referred to as 'moment of implementation', an ERP system implementation can be an undertaking of several months and even years until the system is ready to represent the complex organisational processes (cf. Worthen 2002). Unlike bespoke systems, ERP systems are designed to fit multiple organisations and hence cannot respond to the unique settings of one organisation without any system adaptation effort on either the site, the user organisation or the system (Moon 2007). 'Customising' and 'modifying' are terminologies which are often associated with this adaptation process. 'Customising' refers to changes in form of parameterisation or additional programming in places which are pre-defined by the vendor. 'Modifications' of the systems are activities outside this predefined space, for which the vendor takes no responsibility and which can cause problems when the system is updated and upgraded (further developments provided by a standard software vendor are based on the assumption of what is compatible with a customised, not modified system)[15].

---

15 Even though constantly referred to in literature, the notions 'customisation' and 'modification' are not clearly defined. For this research, I use the definitions used by employees at the vendor's site, which is the terminology common amongst practitioners.

Counting for the majority of all research activities carried out in the field (Botta-Genoulaz et al. 2005; Klaus et al. 2000; Moon 2007), current implementation studies can be categorised into 3 groups (cf. Pollock and Williams, 2007):

(1) *ERP success stories*. These are mainly case studies written by system vendors or consultants providing a rather uncritical account of ERP implementation (mostly found on vendors' and consultants' homepages; see for instance the SAP or Oracle homepages).

(2) *Failed implementations*. Building a counterweight to the earlier vendor rhetoric reporting upon ERP implementation success, we find later publications focusing on the problems associated with ERP system implementation. Many of the disaster stories on ERP implementation are found in magazines and newspapers. Songini, a journalist at *Computerworld*, for instance, writes in 2005 about the US Navy losing $1 billion on a flawed ERP pilot project. Worthen (2002), writing for *CIO Magazine*, introduces us to a failed implementation in which the organisation Nestle spent millions only to eventually end the project due to a unbridgeable misfit between the local organisation and the global system. In academic circles, whilst we also find many studies on failed implementations, these accounts generally differ from magazine and newspapers articles in that they provide a more profound and analytical account, aiming to advance knowledge by discussing more general topics such as the misfit between generic system and local user organisation (cf. Pollock and Cornford 2004; Regnell et al. 2001; Tolsby 1998) or the impact of an ERP system implementation on globalisation (cf. Hanseth et al. 2001).

(3) Suggestions for Best Practice. More recently, we find literature outlining possible success factors on how to best manage the implementation phase (Akkermans and van Helden 2002; Bingi et al. 1999; Esteves and Pastor-Collado 2000; Holland and Light 1999; Holland and Light 2003; Hong and Kim 2002; Motwani et al. 2005; Somers and Nelson 2001; Sumner 2000)[16]. We find for instance Holland and Light (2003) discussing specific factors which make ERP implementation projects a success. Hogn and Kim (2002) highlight one possible success factor, namely the

---

16 In this context it is interesting to note that, not only have suggestions in the literature about the best practices for ERP implementation dominated in the last few years; more generally an entire consulting branch has developed in which expertise is offered to manage this knowingly difficult phase of implementing standard software packages.

degree to which the ERP system fits initially with the organisation. The researchers found that below a certain level any more adaptations of the system to its local context would only lead to lower implementation success rather than improve the situation. Gosh (2002) argues that the success of large scale ERP implementations and the often related global roll-out of the system to all subsidiaries, is dependent on how quickly organisations can re-engineer their process to the best practice inscribed in the ERP system.

The sequence in which literature on the different perspectives on ERP implementations emerged follows a common pattern. According to Abrahamson (1991), literature on new technologies typically evolves from what are early vendor success stories to more critical accounts as well as suggestions on best practice.

Following the implementation, software systems need to be supported. Literature related to ERP system support, is highlighted below.

2.2.5 ERP System Support

No matter which decision is made within an organisation, to develop or buy a bespoke system or to implement standard software, deciding on a software package is a long-term investment for a user organisation. Not only are the costs for developing these systems or buying the software licence and the subsequent implementation of the system expensive, a major bulk of the total investment on software goes towards maintenance activities. Software is not a static and faultless product; errors can be hidden in the system, which appear only over time and in the context of implementations of the same software in different settings. Furthermore, constant changes in technology, requirements and regulations make regular updates necessary.

Once an organisation has decided on a bespoke system or to buy a software package, an organisation has different options regarding the support. Bespoke systems leave the organisation with a choice of either supporting the system in-house (often in close co-operation with the programmers who developed the system) or out-sourcing the support to another organisation. In the case of package software, there are fewer choices: to receive the updates and upgrades necessary to use the system long-term, it is necessary to negotiate a contract directly with the vendor organisation or indirectly through a third party (in addition to day-today, in-house support activities). Once a decision has been made on the type of software package support, the service can become a significant financial investment[17]. Whilst being for one party an investment, for the company offering the support services, such activity generates a steady and long-term source of income (Gable et al. 2001). Unlike software sales, revenues from support services are less influenced by the economic downturn, since organisations have no choice but to keep service contracts in place, if they intend to continue using the ERP system in their organisations.

Given the potential financial impact of software package support for both the user and the vendor organisation, surprisingly little research has been carried out in this area (with some exceptions: Gable et al. 2001; Light 2001; Nah et al. 2001). Whilst all authors acknowledge the importance of looking at software package support, they do so from a user organisation's viewpoint.

Light (2001) focuses on the user organisation perspective, exploring the tension between customising an ERP system and modifying it[18]. Nah et al. (2001), addresses maintenance activities after an ERP package 'goes live', meaning after the initial implementation phase, and compares the type and frequency of support activities for both bespoke systems and ERP systems. Whilst Nah et al. (ibid.) conclude that the frequency of maintenance activities in certain categories (corrective, adaptive, perfective, preventative, user support and external parties), appears to be similar in both cases, ERP systems differ in some areas, such as the amount of errors reported with increased system usage. The authors identify three reasons for this variance: Firstly, ERP systems are more robust once they are implemented; secondly, in the cases studied, little customisation work was carried out, therefore, little adaptive work had to be carried out and thus errors are less likely; thirdly, as modifications in the system were not allowed under the licensing agreement (see the debate by Light, 2001), major changes, potentially causing problems, were left to the vendor (and with this, were also supported directly by the vendor).

---

17 SAP, the market leader for ERP systems, currently charges a rate of 22% of the licences fees for its standard support service.

18 Customising a system includes the usage of tools provided by the vendor to adapt the system to the local settings. In turn, modifying the system, such as changing the vendor's code, endangers the future compatibility of the system for updates and upgrades as well as challenges the warranty and support agreement with the vendor.

Gable et al. (2001) differ from Light (2001) and Nah et al. (2001) in that, instead of providing an account of how software package support can be organised, they outline a possible research agenda, highlighting the importance of investigating software package support separately from other types of software support services. Gable et al. (2001) write:

> Thus, rather than simply assuming that all past research on software maintenance is generalisable across all situations, this is a call for more work on identifying key factors that impact maintenance costs and benefits, their incidence, problems, and strategy across diverse new software scenarios, with particular emphasis on large, packaged application software. (p. 352)

However, even in this research agenda, we find the current focus of the field on the user organisation viewpoint reflected when the authors (ibid.) write:

> While we advocate research that assumes alternative, less typical perspectives on the maintenance activity (e.g. the vendor view), for the purposes of restricting the discussion herein, it is yet again useful to be somewhat user-organization-centric (thus the 'user-organization' centric context). An assumption herein is that all software of interest is ultimately used by organizations. (p: 356)

To summarise, the research carried out by these academics is interesting and in some ways pioneering work. Whilst authors, such as the above, help us to understand the software package support, it does so, however, only from the perspective of the user organisation. Existing studies end when problems are reported to the vendor. This leaves the world behind the software package vendors' walls unexplored; how software support is organised from within ERP vendors' organisations remains black-boxed.

As there are only few accounts of ERP system support, the search for more insight on technical support in more general terms, leads to the most significant sociological account of support work, which was investigating technical support in the 1980s within Xerox, an organisation providing copy machines (Orr 1986; 1998; 2006; 1996). Orr (ibid.), even though in another time and place, is one of the few authors who highlight technical support, not from a user's point of view, but that of a vendor. With his highly influential work Orr (ibid.) introduces us to the organisation of technical support within Xerox, and more specifically, the section where copy machines are supported. Applying light theoretical scaffolding (Orr 2006), Orr's 'thick description' brings to our attention the importance of understanding the concrete work organisation, in order to understand organisational outcomes, such as support services.

Allowing many readings (see, for instance, Pinch 1998; Wellman 1997; Barley 1996; Bechky 2006 as well as the special issues on Orr's work in 'Organisation Studies', 2006), what appears to be most dominant in Orr's accounts of Xerox, is the emphasis on the 'situated' and 'communitarian' nature of work. Orr introduces us to technicians[19] who consider not only their technical expertise as being necessary to repair the machine, but also the socio-technical context of the object in question. He writes:

> It is not simply a matter of finding out what is wrong with the machine; there may be nothing wrong with the machines as a thing, in and of itself. The problem may rather lie in the interaction off the machine as it is, the uses its designers anticipated for it, and the uses and methods desired, understood and chosen by the customer. (Orr, 1996: 171)

It is the socio-technical context, the interaction between the environment (including the user, but also factors such as the temperature in the room and where the machine is placed), and the machine, which is found to be crucial to analysing the problem and effecting a repair. This emphasis on environmental variables is reflected in the territorial organisation of work in this setting, in which work is not divided according to expertise, but according to territories. A change of territory, to cross territorial boundaries, is thought to result in lower quality work.

Whilst work appeared to be organised according to territories, Orr's technicians show a surprising communitarian behaviour when it comes to sharing expertise. Showing again the importance of the socio-technical relationship between the user site and the machine, 'war stories' (narratives told about prior support incidents) were frequently recited amongst the technicians as a way of sharing knowledge. Whilst documentation was available to solve problems, it was considered as less helpful. The documentation followed a sequential approach to detect errors, assuming that

19 An interesting discussion on the notion of 'technician' and its evolution over time has been carried out by Barley (1996).

all machines are identical, that problems are identical. However, from a technician's point of view this was not the case, as it disregarded the user-machine interaction, creating unique, non sequential problems. In turn, the stories told took into account contextual factors, as well as addressing the socio-technical relationship between the user and the machine, therefore, were considered as being much more useful. Over time, the stories which were recited became common knowledge and were replaced by new stories.

Sharing expertise was also common amongst the technicians in cases where known war stories, as well as the documentation, could not solve the problems. Whilst behaving protectively over their territories, where problems appeared unsolvable, the group of technicians would function as an informally, hierarchically organised group of experts. When advice had to be sought from other technicians, the informal hierarchical order within the group had to be respected and the most knowledgeable person was to be asked only if all other sources were depleted.

Another interesting paper concerned with support in more general terms is written by Pentland (1992), who introduces us to support work within two software support hot-line teams. The author demonstrates how, in various ways, support at the company studied was no longer a territorial activity, but how problems which became detached from their local settings were dealt with over the telephone. Whilst there were many different ways of getting help (documentation, looking at the database and by asking users), two ways of dealing with problems stood out: (1) asking their colleagues a 'quick question', whilst the customer is still on the phone and (2) forwarding the message to someone with the expertise needed to 'have a look'. Pentland (ibid.) found that these kinds of 'organisational moves' of referring to each other's knowledge and of forwarding customers, were crucial for the success of this organisation. He concludes:

> Organisational moves are critical to knowledgeable performances. Without these moves, work would grind to a halt as individuals attempted to deal with problems outside their speciality. (p: 545)

Whilst Orr's, as well as, Pentland's account is situated in another context and time than ERP system support, interesting parallels can be drawn, as we will see in the context of Chapter 4, in which I present the empirical evidence of how an ERP system is supported from within an ERP vendor's organisation.

Discussion

Reviewing the literature on ERP system support demonstrates how little we know about technical support. Again, similar to the area of ERP system development, it can be assumed that the overall focus on the implementation of ERP packages, as well as a user organisation dominated viewpoint, led the field to disregard this phase of the product life-cycle almost entirely. Light (2001), and Nah et al. (2001), being the exception, have become pioneers in this area introducing us to the specificities of ERP system support from a user organisation perspective. In a search for further insight into how support might be organised *within* a technology providing organisation, for this literature review, I turned to more sociological accounts of work organisation from Organisation Studies (Orr 1986, 1996, 1998, 2006; Pentland 1992). The accounts from Orr (ibid.) and Pentland (ibid.), provide different, but interesting insight, shaped by their time and settings. Orr's research is based on fieldwork carried out in the 1980s, in which Internet, email and call centres were not yet a common way of exchanging information. In comparison, Pentland (1992) picked up on support organised through a means of establishing support hot-lines.

Whilst, potentially, both types of support can still be found in different settings, it can be assumed that given the penetration of technology in our day-to-day lives and the global distribution of similar products, it is very likely that a division of expertise as well as geographically detached support, via modern communication technologies as described in Pentland (1992), is more likely than Orr's situated type of support. However, whilst we might find more frequently a division of expertise as described by Pentland (ibid.), the communitarian behaviour amongst technicians and the importance of informal communication of knowledge through 'war stories' as reported by Orr (1986, 1996), can most likely still be found in support teams, as the work of Bechky (2006), Lesser and Storck (2001) as well as Zachary (1998) indicate. These accounts suggest that particularly in today's information economy an informal exchange of information is crucial and to be expected. Whilst we do not yet know how support might be organised within a ERP system vendors support lab, on the basis of these accounts we can speculate that today's support might incorporate elements highlighted in the accounts of both Pentland and Orr.

2.3 Summary: ERP Systems in Social Research

This first section of the literature review aimed at highlighting more empirical work on software package production, and more specifically, ERP system production. The discussion of the literature has shown that some areas within this line of research are investigated in more detail than others. For instance, we find the majority of studies taking place in the area of ERP systems implementation, whilst we know very little about other phases, such as ERP system support. Overall, what has developed appears to be an imbalance of reporting from the user organisation viewpoint and therein of overemphasising 'situations' such as ERP system implementations which, because of the systems wide impact on the user organisation, stir many different emotions. Discussions about the vendor organisation and how organisational structures as well as developers shape the product throughout its life cycle, are rarely mentioned.

Even though no exact line can be drawn between empirical and conceptual literature, there are accounts which are more conceptual in nature than others. It is these more conceptual accounts, which allow us to situate our research in the different research areas, as well as help us to analyse our empirical findings. Following this review of more empirical literature, in the next section, more conceptual literature is outlined, providing an overview of research within Science and Technology Studies, setting the theoretical context in which this research is embedded.

2.4 Science and Technology Studies: Conceptual Perspective

> *The literature analyzing the social character and consequences of computer use is fragmented and often bewildering to nonspecialists. The diligent reader who examines the literatures on such topics as computing and personal privacy or the role of computer-based information systems in organizational decision making will find a cacophony of voices (Kling 1980b). If he or she reads widely and listens carefully, distinct choruses can be discerned. It is difficult to find voices singing precisely the same tune, or even in the same key, but some do sound in relative harmony. To make sense of the singers and to learn from their songs, the reader must identify the tunes and harmonies of the most notable choruses. These tunes and harmonies are patterned perspectives that provide answers to many of our earlier questions. (Kling 1980a: 63)*

Already in 1980, when computers and research into computers were just beginning, Kling (1980a) found that when it comes to analysing the social character and consequences of computers, there are many voices, singing in different tones. Today, it seems that we find ourselves in a similar but even more complex situation, in which the investigation into the social aspects of technology is of concern to many disciplines, resulting in multiple accounts and many more different voices. If we take only Science and Technology Studies, which evolved during the 1960s from drawing together several disciplines such as Science Studies, the History of Technology and Science, Engineering and Public Policy Studies (Sismondo 2004), we find various schools of thinking, which, in different ways, investigate computer technology. One of the streams evolving from within STS, is the Social Shaping of Technology (SST) perspective (Mackenzie and Wajcman 1985), in which this research is situated.

SST is concerned with the ways in which economic, cultural, social and institutional factors shape the direction, form and outcome of technology and technology innovations and with this, aims to explain and further our understanding of the relationship between technology and society (Williams and Edge, 1996) and as such, commit to opening the black box of technology to sociological analysis. Historically, SST emerged out of a critique of earlier technological deterministic approaches (Dierkes and Hoffmann 1992; Edge 1988), which portrayed technology as emerging according to an 'inner logic', untouched by social influences. Therefore, 'impacts' of technology on society were often seen as necessary and responsible for social and organisational change, and for 'the good of humanity' (Downey 1998), a viewpoint which was commonly adopted by policy makers. Surprisingly, also some of the sociological accounts were highly influenced by this technological deterministic school of thinking, resulting in a line of research which relates to the impact of technology on society, rather than the impact of society on technology (Pollock and Williams, 2008). A technology deterministic focus in both areas later let to an accumulation of SST studies in these fields, aimed at restoring the 'balance'.

Not focusing on a single theory, SST is described as a 'broad church' (Russell and Williams 2002; Williams and Edge 1996) incorporating a variety of different concepts which are united by an insistence on investigating the socio-economic patterns embedded in the process of innovations and content of technologies (MacKenzie and Wajcman 1999). Four prominent traditions are encapsulated under the banner of the Social Shaping of Technology: (1) sociology of scientific knowledge; (2) sociology of industrial organisation; (3) technology policy studies and (4) certain approaches within the economics of technological change (Williams and Edge 1996). Whilst these different traditions disagree on some aspects, they are all centred on what might be described as basic principles of SST in that there are always choices and decisions made which lead to a particular technological outcome and impact; that technology's outcome is influenced by social, political, economical and cultural values and, in this respect, can be seen as 'negotiable' (Cronberg 1992; Williams and Edge 1996). As such, SST research is concerned overall with how different variables takc shape: (1) the direction and the rate of innovation; (2) the form of technology; the content and the practices; and (3) the outcome of technology change on different groups in society (Williams and Edge, 1996: 868).

SST inspired many studies of technology, particularly in Britain and continental Europe, for instance, Sociological Research into Information and Communication Technologies (Friedman 1989; MacKenzie 1991; Quintas 1994a; Randall et al. 1993). Numerous studies have been carried out, from which different sub-categories emerged (Williams and Edge 1996): (1) Organisational Sociology of Software; (2) Social Constructivist Analysis of Software; and (3) studies of the Commodification of Software.

2.4.1 *Organisational Sociology of Software*

The organisational sociology of software draws upon industrial sociology and organisation theories, in particular, the labour process theory set out by Braverman (Braverman 1975)[20]. One of the early and seminal works inspired by Braverman was Kraft (1977), who carried out research into work organisation at the same time. Kraft (ibid.) considered Braverman's (1975) research as particularly relevant for the new type of work, namely programming work (p: 19). He introduces us to narratives on managerial attempts at introducing a division of work in software development through de-skilling labour, the motivation for this being that in the 1970s software developers were in short supply and their expertise still relatively unexplored or understood. With projects constantly running over time and budget, managers, driven by reducing costs, saw the division of labour and with this, the de-skilling of labour as a way to limit the degree of dependency on the developers and their expertise, as well as a tool to allow more visibility and control of the programmers' day-to-day work (Kraft 1977). This move was accompanied by some of the first attempts to structure software development into different phases in order to gain more control of the process (Avison and Fitzgerald 2003). Later, Friedman (1989), arguing for a different interpretation of Kraft's conclusion, introduces us to the case of bespoke system production, emphasising the importance of increased interaction between developers and users, and outlines problems associated with the de-skilling and tight supervision of developers discussed by Kraft (1977)[21].

2.4.2 *Social Constructivist Analysis of Software*

Rooted in the sociology of science (cf. Bloor 1976), the social constructivist analysis focuses on how particular socio-technical arrangements occur. Early papers can be found by Pinch and Bijker (1984) on the social con-

---

20 Restoring Marx's critiques of technology and the division of labour, Braverman (1975) argues that the expansion of capital requires the subordination of labour. Referring to Marx, Braverman (ibid.) concludes that this can be achieved by deskilling workers and homogenising the work of the working class (MacKenzie and Wajcman, 1999). Whilst being crucial in any discussion on workplace technology, Braverman (1975) has been widely criticised for not grasping the full extent of Marx argument (Wood 1983), as well as for suggesting a model of deskilling work which is seen as too simplistic and failing in reflecting the complexity of reality (MacKenzie and Wajcman, 1999).

21 It has to be noted that Kraft's (1977) account has often been misunderstood in that he was often criticised for suggesting the de-skilling of programmers. However, Kraft's argument has to be considered in the context of his era (and thus a direct translation of the argument into today's world is misleading).

struction of the bicycle (see also Bijker (1987) and Bijker (1995)). The authors argue in favour of the 'interpretative flexibility' of technology, meaning that whether an artefact works or not is not an intrinsic property of the technology itself, but a social construction. The degree of the interpretative flexibility is said to depend upon the scope of ways with which an artefact can be used. In the course of making choices, the number of variations is reduced resulting in an eventual stage of stabilisation within the relevant social group. If one interpretation of the artefact is accepted by all, closure arises (Bijker 1995). However, even Pinch and Bijker (1994) argue that eventually there can be closure, not all social groups will come to the same type of closure, the same arrangements. Consequently, there are as many artefacts, as there are social groups (similar arguments were made in studies carried out by Star (1989) and Bowker and Star (1999) in the context of "boundary objects", artefacts which are interpreted differently depending on the social group).

Developing as a branch of social constructivism, the social constructivist analysis of software has been concerned with the same basic question, of *how* particular socio-technical arrangements occur. Low and Woolgar (1993), for instance, show how in their settings, certain issues were considered as 'technical' and others as 'social'. Rather than seeing them as opposites, the authors conclude that their categorisation into 'technical' or 'social' in itself is not a natural or easy distinction to make but a complex social accomplishment. Similarly, Grint and Woolgar (1997), acknowledging Orlikowski's (1992) earlier work on the duality of technology, argue that the interpretation of technology is a social achievement rather than a technical consequence. Introducing the notion of 'technology as text', the authors highlight how technology, similar to a text, can have different readings and how it can be interpreted differently, the accepted definition being a result of social interaction rather than a mere technological performance. Differing from earlier accounts such as Pinch and Bijker (1994), for Grint and Woolgar (1997), technology is never stable in that there is only one reading. For the authors, there is no closure in the way technology is interpreted. The authors write:

> Inasmuch as technology embodies social aspects it is not a stable and determinate object (albeit one with political preferences inscribed into it), but an unstable and indeterminate artefact whose precise significance is negotiated and interpreted but never settled. (p: 21)

In that, the authors differ from Orlikowski's (1992) account of the duality of technology. Whilst drawing on Orlikowski (1992) and not denying that there is a social and technical side, a duality in which technology can constrain the interpretations of artefacts through different social groups, Grint and Woolgar (1997) question what these constraints could be and write:

> Such constraints – or enablers- do not acquire their significance without interpretative action on the part of humans, hence there can be no self-evident or transparent account of such 'material constraints'. There are, of course, more persuasive account and less persuasive accounts – but they remain accounts, not reflections. (p: 24)

Mackay et al. (2000) arguing in the same direction and, whilst not disagreeing with Woolgar and Grint (1997), criticise their work for adopting a inside / outside perspective, the users outside versus the designers inside. For Mackay et al. (2000), the software design process is a perfect example of *fluid boundaries* in which both sides, the inside and outside, influence each other, with the role of producer (inside) and user (outside) not always being clear (see also Fleck (1988)).

2.4.3 Studies of the Commodification of Software

Informed by SST, the commodification of software (Brady et al. 1992; Fincham 2002) became the third sub-discipline in this area. Research into the commodification of software focuses on 'black boxed' software, also frequently referred to as 'Commercial-off-the-Shelf' (COTS) products or, more generally, as 'Software Packages'. These systems are no longer used by, or developed for, a single or few organisations, but are a commodity offered as a 'ready-made' product to a large group of potential user organisations; a move which was made possible by the emergence of machine independent software code, allowing the transfer of programs between organisations at the beginning of the 1970s (Kraemer et al. 1980; Light and Sawyer 2007).

The first studies into the social aspects of commodified software were carried out by Fleck, Webster and Williams (Fleck et al. 1990; Webster and Williams 1993) studying Computer-Aided Production Management (CAPM) systems, showing how the relationships between suppliers, user and others act to shape and re-shape technology. Whilst the notion of

CAPM soon disappeared, the idea of standard enterprise software remained and became what we know today as Enterprise Resource Planning (ERP) Systems, a term coined by the Industry Analyst Gartner Group (Wylie 1990). Similar to other software packages such as CAPM, ERP systems are designed to serve not a few but many organisations and are thus to be viewed as an adaptable but not custom built product. As such, it is designed not to fulfil the specific requirements of a single organisation (what would be the idea behind custom built software) but to reach an *approximate* fit with a maximum amount of user organisations. Following such a business model, which is based on the idea of not one organisation buying the product but many, conflicts appear inevitable when the generically designed product meets its unique user organisation. It is these conflicts, emerging in particular during the implementation phase of the system, which have been the topic of most studies into ERP systems (see the first part of this literature review, in which empirical work in this area has been reviewed).

Following these early studies and acknowledging the focus on the implementation phase, more recent investigations introduce us to other stages of the ERP system life cycle such as *software design* (Grint and Woolgar 1997; Keil and Carmel 1995; Pollock et al. 2007; Salzman and Rosenthal 1994; Sawyer 2000a; Sawyer 2001; von Hippel 1994); *software development* (Carmel 1997; Carmel and Becker 1995; Carmel and Bird 1997; Carmel and Sawyer 1998; Cusumano and Selby 1997; Sawyer 2000a; Sawyer and Guinan 1998; Zachary 1994; Zachary 1998); and *software procurement* (Howcroft and Light 2002; Howcroft and Light 2006; Light et al. 2000; Pollock and Williams 2008; Salzman and Rosenthal 1994). Whilst we find more recent investigations into other phases of the product life cycle, overall, supported by the focus on the implementation phase, a general focus on the user organisation's viewpoint rather than the vendor's viewpoint can be noticed in studies carried out in the traditions of Science and Technology studies.

Reasons for this imbalance are multiple (see Chapter 1). However, overall it can be observed that also more current research into ERP systems seems to have a tendency to highlight once more what is happening within user organisations rather than within vendor organisations. For instance, we find recent empirical work led by Light (Light et al. 2000; Light et al. 2001), asking why organisations decide on software packages such as ERP systems instead of bespoke systems. Focusing on how the procurement phase is experienced from the user organisation's viewpoint, experiences from the vendor organisation during this phase (sales phase) are not taken into account. From other authors such as Hong and Kim (2002) and Holland and Light (2003), we learn how user organisations can best manage the implementation phase, again not taking into account the question of how to best manage this phase from a vendor's viewpoint.

Addressing some of the problems within current research in the area of social research into commodified systems and aiming to provide a more comprehensive view on standard software packages by bringing different studies together to provide a multisite and long-term view, we find Pollock and Williams' (2008) 'biography of artefacts'. Embedded in the movement which Edinburgh scholars refer to as SST II, the 'biography of artefacts' framework, outlined in detail in Pollock and Williams (2008), presents a different way of addressing the complexity of current Information and Communication Technologies. The authors argue that existing notions of SST, based on MacKenzie and Wajcman (1985) (who referred to Noble (1975)), were developed to explain the shaping of 'simple', discrete technologies and hence are unsuitable for more complex technologies, such as ERP systems. Pollock and Williams (2008) argue that the social shaping processes occur in multiple places at different times and should therefore be addressed using tools which allow us to take into account this multiplicity. Based on earlier work (Fleck *et al.* 1990; Tierney and Williams, 1991; Brady *et al.*, 1992; Fleck 1993; Webster and Williams 1993; Williams 1997a; Pollock *et al.* 2003), as well as the idea of a biographical concept from other disciplines (such as history), Pollock and Williams (2008) suggest a 'biography of artefacts' framework, which looks at the product life cycle at different sites and times, and is, as such, considered more suitable for addressing complex technologies.

2.5 Summary: Conceptual Perspective

The overview of the conceptual literature shows how many multilayered perspectives on software emerged within STS over the years, some of which can be summarised under the umbrella notion of SST. Most relevant to this work is the line of research on commodification of software. If we compare the conclusions we can draw from the empirical literature in the area (see section one), as well as the conceptual literature, we find, that by being tightly connected, the same types of bias emerged. Whilst the empirical bias is towards implementation studies and a user organisational viewpoint, the conceptual bias is similar, in that it focuses on the explanation of the shaping of the technology at the local sites, leading to an overall user organisation dominated viewpoint on technology.

2.6 Conclusion

In the introductory quote to this chapter, Quintas (1994) states that software presents challenges because it is, in many ways, an 'atypcial technology'. Touching upon many disciplines as well as our day-to-day life, it is a most complex technology to investigate. One way to approach this topic is through the eyes of social studies of technology. Having presented an overview of empirical literature on ERP systems as well as conceptual literature mainly from within STS, the above literature review provides an impression of this, still, multilayered way (akin Kling 1980a) in which we can look at software. What we can learn from the literature and what has been mentioned in detail in each of the summaries within this chapter, is that current studies develop a user organisation as well as technology bias, falling short in presenting and in some cases even acknowledging the vendor organisations' impact on the technology.

In the following chapter, I now discuss methodological issues, specific to this book. What becomes clear is that investigating what is currently under- researched, the vendor's viewpoint, not only requires a different type of thinking but above all, the permission and thus the *opportunity* to enter the often secretive software labs.

3 Settings and Research Methods

3.1 Introduction

When you live something every day, it tends to take over 'cause it becomes second nature. Not only at work but in everything you do. (Tom, Senior Vice President of the vendor studied, Interview: February 2006)

The choices we make in the course of designing our research influence its outcome. For instance, if we investigate the phenomenon in question via questionnaires we receive a different type of data than if we approach a topic with ethnographic methods. Not only is the data we collect different but also the way in which we approach and analyse what we find. Therefore, to comprehend and evaluate the conclusions of research projects, it is necessary to understand the research design behind them.

Before engaging in such discussion, however, a story is to be told; an ethnographical tale about the vendor's labs. In the course of writing this book, it became clear that, in seeking for an 'academic distance', which might be expected by parts of the audience, valuable data, which makes ethnographic research so richly unique and interesting to read, would be lost. Furthermore, I felt that similar to the interpretations of a poem or picture, sometimes interpretations, whilst interesting, can destroy not only the beauty of the work, but also constrain the reader's mind by providing a frame compromising the reader's own creativity. If we, for instance, take Orr's (1996) much quoted account of technical support, we find that surprisingly little analysis has been provided within his original book. If, however, we look at the many authors referencing Orr's work and the variety of ways in which they do so, we can see the strength which lies in such an approach[22]. In order to satisfy the different types of readers, those who are more interested in the analysis and those who like to

---

22 Also in Latour's work we find a strong preference for descriptions (over explanations). In his imaginary prologue between a student and a professor, Latour (2005) writes: "I'd say that if your description needs an explanation, it's not a good description, that's all. Only bad descriptions need an explanation. It's quite simple really. What is meant by an 'explanation', most of the time? Adding another actor to provide those already described with the energy necessary to act, but if you have to add one, then the network was not complete, and if the actors already assembled do not have enough energy to act, then they are not 'actors', but mere intermediaries, dopes, puppets. They do nothing, so they should not

read descriptions and make up their own minds, this book provides throughout ethnographic detail as well as thorough analysis - an approach also reflected in the structure of this chapter.

This chapter is divided into three main sections. Section one, is, as mentioned above, dedicated to an ethnographic tale, describing how I gained access to the field as well as the atmosphere and context of the labs. Since ethnography is about living with the people at the site, I also included a brief section in which I introduced some of the developers. The first section is followed by a discussion of ethical issues I encountered. Being included and 'becoming one of them' is, whilst often desired, not an easy situation and, at times, ethical concerns are difficult to manage. In the third part of this chapter, I outline and discuss in more detail ethnographic theories and the choice of methods. Furthermore, I point to some of the limitations of this study.

3.2 An Ethnographic Tale

> *For me when we are in the same location then we are almost one culture. Even if [you are from] only one culture you can find differences. You can find people who like more daily Scrum, who like to speak open. Different people. When we are in this office we are one culture. (Remy, Project Manager, Interview: January 2006)*

Working in the vendor's labs in North America, as a researcher and intern, was one of the most exciting things I have done to date. It was exceptional. From the moment I arrived in the labs there was not one day when I felt bored or excluded – not even during the Christmas period which for the first time, I could not spend with my family. Very quickly I was included in the labs, gained trust to potential gatekeepers and found new friends. This situation gave me unique access not only to the daily life

be in the description anyhow. I have never seen a good description in need of an explanation, but I have read countless numbers of bad descriptions to which nothing was added by a massive addition of 'explanations'!" (p: 147). Whilst this is a rather extreme statement and does not fulfil the expectations of different types of readers, I chose to provide a mixture.

of the developers[23] in the labs, but also to their lives outside work. In a North American city during winter time where the temperature varied between 0 and -40 accompanied by snow and strong winds, I got the opportunity to become one of them.

My overall goal for this research project was to gain impressions from an insight into the labs, to see and describe the daily practice of the software developers in this lab; to show what happens behind the walls of one of the biggest ERP vendors worldwide. For this reason and because the context of the labs is important to understand the subsequent ethnographic chapters and analysis, I dedicate the first half of this chapter to an 'ethnographic tale'. The account presented is based on my initial impressions during the first two months. Later on, the atmosphere in the labs changed significantly. These changes in the working atmosphere have to be put into the context of a new management approach whose practices started to influence the daily lives in the labs during the third month of my stay in the labs. For the sake of the context and also to keep a historical story line, the surroundings described in the following will not include the later changes. However, these will be discussed in Chapters 5, 6 and 7.

As mentioned in the introduction, to keep the originality of this research, interview and email quotes are not corrected (apart from orthographical errors). Most developers were foreign and had English as their second or third language. Also, I did not edit my fieldwork notes, unless noted otherwise. I felt that both the originality of the way people expressed themselves as non-native English speakers, as well as the way I quickly typed in notes during the day, equally not a native speaker of the English language, somehow reflects the spirit, the particular situation as well as the international settings in which this research took place.

3.2.1 Arriving at the Labs

The vendor runs software labs around the world, some of them focusing on system development, some on software package support and others on consulting, research or back-office activities. The setting I was about to enter in October 2005 was one of the labs which incorporated research, software development as well as third level software support. All areas were related to the Customer Relationship Management (CRM) product offered by the vendor.

---

23 Unless indicated otherwise, the notion of 'developers' represents all people working in the labs (including the support employees).

On the first day, when I tried to find my way through a rather big North American city, the city map in my hands guided me towards a big multi office building in an industrial area, in walking distance of the city centre. Being there too early, I was expected at 8:30, I walked around the office for half an hour before I entered the building. It was a cold and cloudy morning. Closing the big glass door behind me, I found myself in a huge welcome hall with a reception, where I asked how to get to the vendor's offices. Passing by the coffee shop, I took the lift, as told, and went up to the fourth floor. Stepping out of the elevator, I found myself in front of a yellow wall with a glass door, a small grey box and a bell. I pressed the bell and waited. Nobody answered. I tried again. Still no answer. Another person in jeans and a very old jumper stepped out of the lift, holding a tiny grey key-shaped plastic device toward the grey box next to the door handle. With a 'beep', the door opened. As I found out later, the person allowing me to enter the office was Mathieu, a French man working as lab IT (Information Technology) support. He asked me to wait in the little waiting area just next to the door. Looking around, I could see only the wall which separated the office from the waiting area, therefore I had no idea what is behind, "inside" the labs. Soon after the young man left, a woman, also dressed in jeans came and said I should sit and wait for a manager to come. I sat down and waited rather nervously, in a comfortable chair, pretending to read some random promotion magazine lying in the middle of the table. I had not yet met my future boss and knew him and two of my colleagues only from a telephone interview conducted before I got the job. I waited for more than 30 minutes without any news. Though whilst waiting, I had company. Four men in suits, who, as I found out, were also new employees, joined me in the waiting area. After what seemed like an eternity, a man in his 50s in a grey suit arrived. It was Ritzka, the Human Resource Manager, whom I got to know only through email exchange, whilst I was still in Scotland. Never responding to any of my inquiries and delaying my arrival by 4 weeks due to not having my working visa sorted, I was not very impressed on seeing him with. He asked us all to go to the meeting room, where we had to wait once again until he joined us. Ritzka had just started to finally welcome us, when the door opened and a smiling, rather small, thin man asked in English, with a Spanish accent, for Christine Grimm. I was easy to spot as the rest were all men and so he immediately looked at me and asked me to go with him. He explained to me that, as an intern, I was not supposed to attend the two day introduction session with the HR Manager and could start right away. He led me into a big, open-spaced office with a lunch area at the centre. Everything seemed to be very new and one of the first things I realised was that the people sitting there looked all very different. Asian, European, American, African – people from every continent as far as I could tell. Passing by the desks I could hear people speaking in many different languages and with foreign accents. I was fascinated and it seemed as if my manager, who was called Jordi, still walking next to me, could read my thoughts when he commented: "This is like the United Nations" - and indeed, it was.

As I found out later, within the labs, which were spread over two floors, almost 200 employees (2005) from 35 nations, were working together to build parts of the vendor's Customer Relationship Management System, the Service Industry and Mobile Business Solutions, and also carry out research in both areas in a dedicated research department. The company language was English. During the day, people often mixed languages and for me it became normal to hear something said in French or Spanish, being answered in English and I commented to other people in my native tongue, German, just like everyone else.

After commenting upon the "United Nations", my manager and I walked through the entire office to the other end where I was introduced to my new team, and also my new desk, where a couple of books were already waiting for me. My desk was about five metres away from the team I had just been introduced to. Jordi apologised for that, and explained to me that there were no desks free amongst the support team (about 20 people) with which I would work and therefore, I would have to sit at this desk which was close by, but amongst the CRM developer teams (the CRM developers occupied probably more than 65% of this particular side of the office). As I soon realised, this was the perfect desk for my purposes. From here, I could socialise with the developers but still be close to the software support team. At the same time I could oversee the lunch area and the coffee corner, which were not separated in any way from the developers' desk. Additionally, even though there were no proper corridors in this open-plan office, several 'walk ways' were commonly chosen and my desk happened to be along this imaginary corridor. All the people sitting behind me passed by any time they left the office, went to the toilets, or picked up a cup of coffee or a soft drink. This, in turn, allowed me to be in contact with people I would not work with by just sending a friendly smile and which often initiated a quick chat. Below is a picture illustrating the lab.

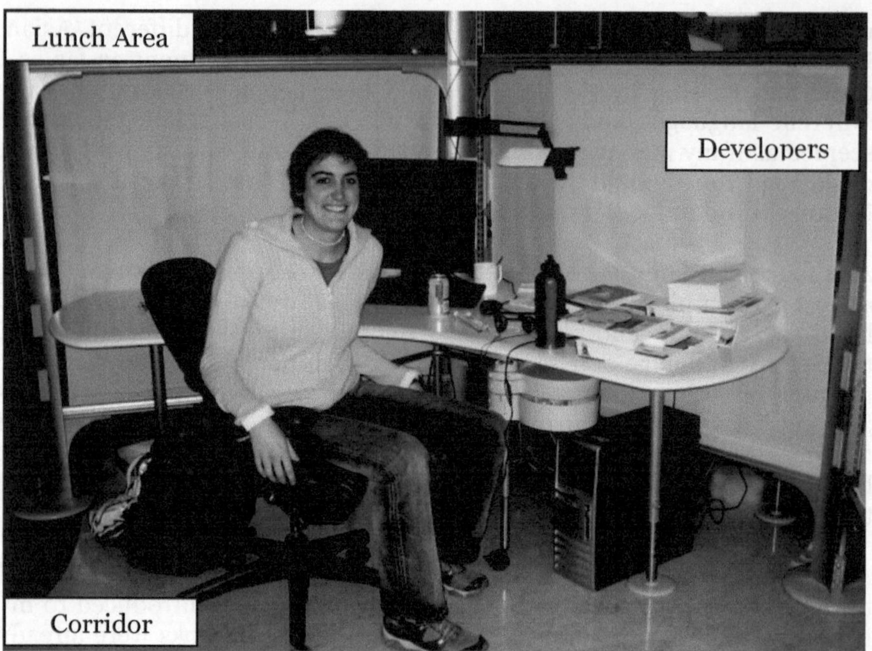

Figure 1: My Desk

Everyone, apart from the Human Resource and Lab Manager, was situated in the open plan office, even the Vice President – an arrangement which reflected the flat hierarchy in place at this ERP system vendor. If the developers needed some space for non-public conversation, meeting rooms were available equipped with a speaker phone, video conference facilities and laptops, if required. Below is a picture of the office I worked in, just the way I recall it from my first impression, when I entered the office.

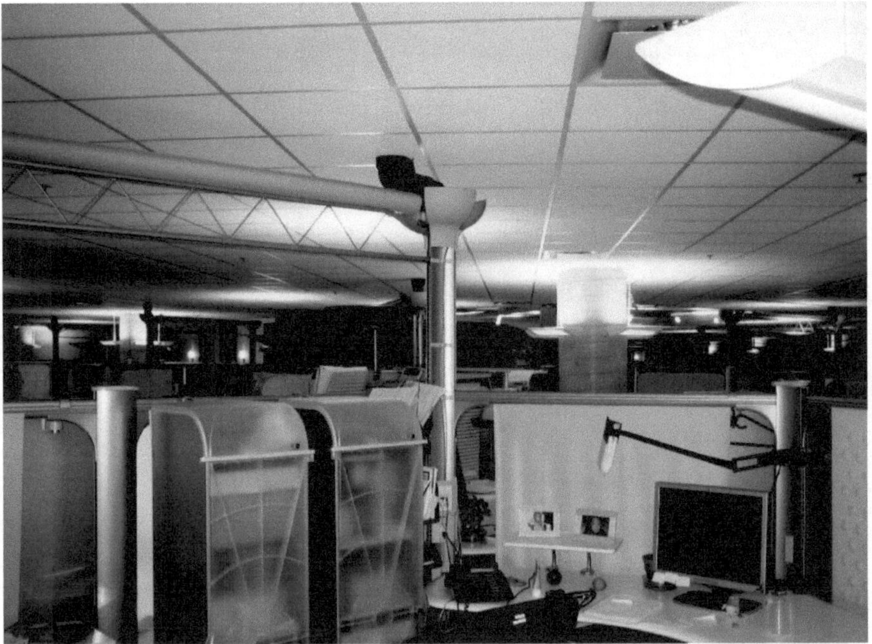

Figure 2: Overview Labs

At the front of the picture is the desk of my colleague Sara, from the support team. From this viewpoint, the lunch area and with this, my desk was just next to the big pillar in the middle. The entrance was at the far end on the left hand side (not visible).

Like the tables of Sara, all tables in the labs were shaped with round corners which was said to increase creativity and co-operation. All furniture was equipped with rollers which made them easy to move. Little partitions, which could be moved like a curtain, separated one desk from another to offer some privacy. In some areas, little corners were formed in which additional tables were made available for spontaneous meetings (see picture below). These tables were also used for leaving the occasional birthday cake or sweets for the team.

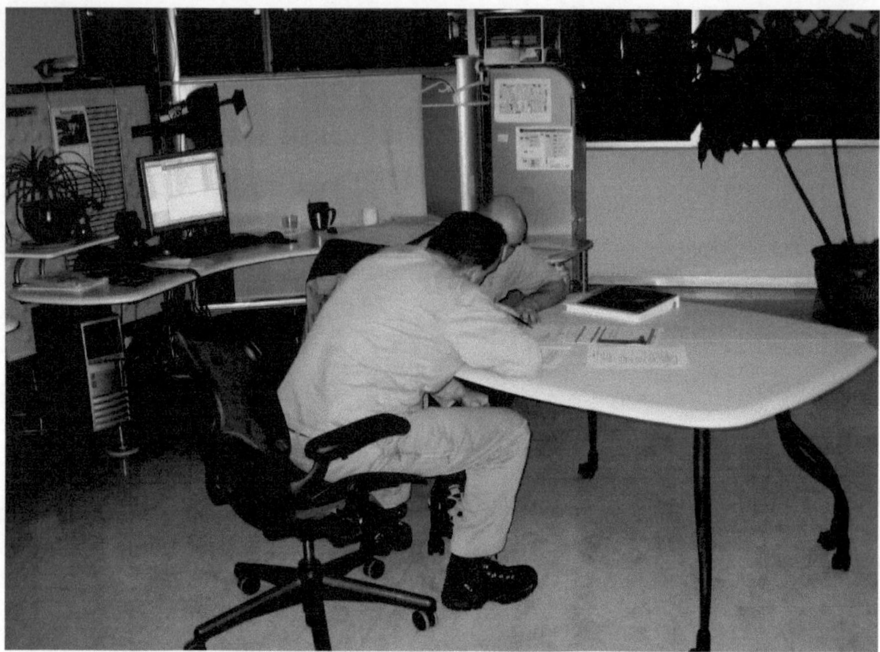

Figure 3: Informal Dress Code

As it becomes obvious from the pictures above, no dress code existed in the labs and I did not have to wear again the suit I was wearing on the first day. Even the Vice President would come in jeans and a casual shirt. As explained by my manager, the idea was that people should work in clothes they feel most comfortable with, so that they could concentrate on their work. One colleague always felt cold and throughout the winter wore a very old Russian military hat to keep his head warm whilst working. This colleague was one of the key architects and highly respected for having outstanding technical expertise[24].

For me the absence of a dress code was surprising. Software labs are known for their informality and I have friends, working in start-ups, who even have a table football. However, from a software vendor with more than eight milliards Euro revenues in 2006 (company report), I somehow expected some kind of formality.

---

24 Orr (1986, 1996, 1998) reports upon similar impressions when studying technical engineers. Also in his case, reputation was almost entirely based on technical skills.

3.2.2 *A Day in the Labs and the Importance of Food*

Working hours in the labs were very flexible and people could start at any time they wanted. It was not very welcome to start at 11am, but nobody would say anything, unless it affected their work or the team's progress. For my colleagues and me in the support team, the entire day was usually organised around the arrival of electronic support messages from around the world, as was lunch time.

Every day at exactly 12pm, lunch was served, usually indicated by the caterer entering the lab at about 11:50am to take away the big trolley on which he would put the food. From the caterer first entering the lab, people appeared to count the minutes and just before he came back the first few would begin queuing up. Almost everyone would use lunch time to socialise. Only a few people had lunch at their desks or talked about business issues during lunch.

Generally, it was up to each employee how long they took for lunch. At the vendor, there was no clock-in and clock-out mechanism, but staff were expected to work eight hours a day. For most however, lunch was a one hour break. After lunch many people went for a walk along the river which was close by and came back to work around 1 pm. Lunch time and the following walk, was for me as observer, always a great chance to talk to different people, socialise and include myself in the developer community. After the walk, people often had a coffee from the coffee machine situated in the lunch area. The coffee machine was surrounded by about 40 different kinds of sachets with any kind of flavour which could be used to prepare a hot drink. For me, after lunch I usually went to one of the, from a European perspective, typically American 'oversized' fridges situated in the corner of the lunch area, which, from the inside, looked like this:

Figure 4: The Fridge

All drinks were free and in the door, which is not shown on the above picture were approximately 14 cartons of different, high quality juices of which I had at least half a carton every day. Often, food was left over from lunch, which was then packed into little containers by the caterer and put in the second oversized fridge. This food was for people to reheat in one of two microwaves, when they worked late (or, if required, started late and consequently worked much later. Nobody distinguished between people working overtime and people who happened to be there whilst working their normal hours and fancied a snack during the evening). Some people who did not work late had the leftover food before they went home, so that they did not have to buy food or cook; a habit which was frowned upon. During my time in the labs there were some other interns in another department who used to do exactly this: eat before leaving to save money and effort. Whilst other people complained sometimes in the evening, that there wasn't any more food, the interns did not seem to notice that they were not supposed to do this (or they did not mind), until the office secretary sent an email round to all people in the office stating the rules as to when one was entitled to eat the leftover food and when to consume the many drinks in the fridge:

> Hello all,
>
> Leftovers from our lunches should remain available to all. No one should ever hide those leftovers in order to selfishly secure themselves a supply of food. If you serve yourself leftovers, you are expected to place the containers back on the shelves where you found them. Moving them to a secret location to create your own personal stash is unacceptable and potentially dangerous (containers that disappear from the fridge sometimes reappear the next day without any indication as to where they were stored and at what temperature while they were away).
>
> Also, the beverages on offer in our kitchens are meant for on-site consumption. At the end of your workday, you should not grab supplies on your way out in order to keep yourself hydrated while on the road. Neither should you drop by on a Saturday, alone or with your entire family, to fill your picnic basket or replenish your cupboards.
> I'm not making this up. It's all "based on a true story," just like those made-for-TV movies.
>
> I would not particularly enjoy having to take more robust security measures and install surveillance webcams, but it's a solution we might have to look into if the situation persists.

> Thanks for your cooperation.
>
> Max.
> (Office assistant) (Max, Office Assistant, Email: December 2005)

When I received this email, I was surprised. The people in the labs were all educated and earned more than the average person in a similar position in another company (company policy). And yet, it was necessary to state when the free drinks and food were supposed to be consumed. However, I also knew that the last point in the email had its merits. Spending many Saturdays in the office, I noticed that there were two people popping in regularly with their families, picking up a drink, walking to their desks and leaving a few minutes later.

Before continuing to describe the atmosphere in more detail, it might be interesting to ask why the vendor provided all this free food and drinks. Why did, and still does, the vendor spend about 15 Dollars a day (this is what it costs at Microsoft to 'feed' an employee in the US) on each employee? Multiplied by over 40.000 people working for the vendor, these are high expenses. Whilst I was still in the field I never asked myself this question. For me it was just a nice 'goody' from the vendor to motivate people and appear as an attractive workplace for high quality developers. I liked that I did not have to cook or shop for food and consequently saved money and time. I also did not have to leave the labs to get food at any point of the day. I could go running along the river after work at about 4pm, take a shower in the labs, eat there and have some juice and then go back to work for another hour until I would eventually join the developers for after work drinks. This motivated me to go to work even on Saturdays (checking the fridge Friday evening to see if there was enough left over from lunch to feed me on Saturday). The labs were well designed, the computers first class and so were the very ergonomic chairs and the height of variable desks. From a work environment point of view, working in the vendor's labs was very comfortable: warm, food and good equipment. Only whilst analysing the data did the question come up. Not having an explanation why food was important other than the obvious, I wrote an email to the Vice President, asking why there is free food in all vendor labs. He commented:

> Is just a perk that doesn't cost much and increases the attractiveness of an employer. There in addition are some more benefits

> like the people don't need to leave office ;-). (Thorsten, Vice President, Email: July 2007)

Looking at what he described as the intention of the free food, the concept worked perfectly on me. For me, the vendor was more attractive and by not having to leave the office to get food and drinks I did not mind spending more hours in the labs. Many times, I felt more comfortable in the labs than in one of the various shared flats I was living in.

At the vendor's Headquarters, which I visited twice before doing my fieldwork in North America, this 'we provide everything and you don't have to worry about your life' mentality was expressed in a built in nursery, gym, several tennis courts, free food and drinks, and supported by the remote location of the Headquarters in a village where, apart from working for the vendor and meeting colleagues, there was little else was to do. On an Internet Blog page, I found an interesting account written by a Google employee, explaining why Google offers these kinds of 'goodies':

> Google provides nearly everything these people need from clothes (new T-shirts are placed in bins for people to grab *twice* a week!) to food – three, free, all-you-can-eat meals a day. Plus onsite health care, dental care, laundry service, gym, etc. (...) College kids tend to like it because it's just like college – all of their basic needs are taken care of. In fact, even most of your personal-life can get tied up in Google benefits. Google provides free or subsidized broadband to every employee. Google runs its own, private, bus lines in the Bay Area for employees. Google provides free or subsidized mobile phones. A college kid can literally join Google and, like they did as freshman at university, let Google take care of everything. Of course, if Google handles everything for you, it's hard to think about leaving because of all the "stuff" you'll need to transition and then manage for yourself. (trixter98052 2008)

Having read this account as well as other software labs stories such as Kidder, (1982) and heard of things like 'family barbecues' taking place in the vendor's Headquarters to include the families[25], I assumed that this is also the way the vendor's labs in North America worked, even though the

---

[25] First astonished and excited, this later reminded me of the John Grisham novel 'The Firm'.

incentive structure was not as sophisticated as at the Headquarters or at Google. There was no built in gym or nursery and families were not included in the company. However, by offering many things on site, the vendor created a comfortable environment in which people did not have to leave the office to satisfy their needs for drinks and food. With this, working overtime, one might assume, was less of an issue.

Interestingly, whilst this appears a logical conclusion, this was not the case in the labs. Except for me, nobody seemed to be motivated to come in to work at the weekend or to stay late, because the office was warm and there was food. Like the informal dress code, this eight hours working regime also surprised me. Seeing people in informal clothes, having food and drinks provided, I expected to encounter some kind of 'hacking culture', in which many developers are so excited about programming, that they forget the world outside the labs (cf. Cusumano and Selby 1997). Instead, I found programmers who were motivated, but saw their profession as a job which brings in money and is fun, but should not exceed normal working hours.

3.2.3 The Atmosphere

Despite the every now and then, disapproving emails about when to eat leftover food and when not to make too many personal calls[26], the atmosphere amongst the developers was generally friendly and people seemed open to helping each other out on a casual basis with business and private matters. Even the caterer would help when needed, taking developers at the last minute, to the airport or, as in my case, help me with finding a new flat and moving. Explaining my surprise about this exceptional 'helping each other mentality' to Jordi, my manager, he commented that firstly, most people in the labs are immigrants and so, everybody knows how it feels to arrive in a new country with your two suitcases and start a new job. Secondly, building a software system this size is an artefact built by

---

26 The office assistant as well as the lab manager were not the most popular people in the labs. Both known for being avaricious – Christmas parties were, therefore, organised in January, when renting restaurants would be cheaper – during my time in the labs, twice, an email was sent round demanding phone calls to be terminated. There was only a restricted amount of phone lines into the labs and if too many people spoke at the same time, no other calls could be made or received. This was, according to the developers stories, to discourage people from making phone calls. At one occasion, the lab manager, who wanted to make a call but not being able to, sent a high priority email stating: "If you are on a personal call right now, please HANG UP immediately. We need the lines to execute our work" (Lab Manager, Email, November 2006).

many. If people do not work together, do not follow the same goals, do not comply with the company's mission, the system cannot evolve.

From what I experienced, besides the multi cultural settings and the nature of the job of having to work together, it also seemed to be the company's spirit and politics which supported a collegial environment. For example, after just four weeks, I had serious problems with the new flatmate I had just moved in with (my first flatmate having been on drugs, this was already my second flat within two months). One evening, when I told her that I would move out she started to hit me and my visiting boyfriend, preventing us from getting into the taxi. After an hour of shouting and fighting, with us unable to leave, I called the police after which we could eventually leave. However, when I returned to work next day, she had left a message on the answering machine and also sent me an email threatening that if I did not pay her $500 by 12am, she would accuse my boyfriend of rape and racism (as she had dark skin). The situation made me feel very uncomfortable. My colleague, realising that I felt terrible, asked me what happened. I explained it to her and she went immediately to our manager Jordi. Jordi called his Line Manager in the Headquarters asking for legal assistance. As I was only employed as an intern I did not qualify for the Legal Support Employment Scheme which the vendor offered to his employees. Though, as I was told, the manager in the Headquarters offered that if the company's insurance would not pay, then the department would. Within an hour I had a lawyer on the phone, with my boss sitting next to me, who cancelled three meetings just to be able to organise the legal support, alerted security in the building, backing up my answering machine and my emails. At lunch time, when things settled down a bit, he told me to go to the police to report the emails and phone calls and then go home. Feeling embarrassed about not having done any work that day and also preventing him from getting his work done, I refused. I recall very well how he looked at me in disbelief and said "You are human. You are not a machine. Go home and rest".

The actions of my managers, the immediate support from the Headquarters and many of my colleagues reflected the way I got to know 'the labs'. Capturing the atmosphere other than through re-telling stories related to particular incidents and explaining them to someone who has not experienced them, is difficult. Interestingly, in explaining them it seemed it was not only me who was surprised by the atmosphere. I do not remember what triggered the conversation, but in the second month of my fieldwork, I was 'talking' to the developer sitting next to me, and in the messenger who wrote:

> [developer] says:
> yesterday I tried to describe to my wife the very ambiance that is in the lab
> [developer] says:
> it is more easy to live than to explain
> [developer] says:
> I tried to describe here our new colleague Gloria
> [developer] says:
> the girl that put 12 sugars in here coffee
> [developer] says:
> or that drink 3 litres orange juice per day
> [developer] says:
> the girl that tells you don't expect anything from me today it is my period !!!
> [developer] says:
> that is funny ...
> [Christine Grimm]says:
> haha.. yes I know she does that. I heard, that in Latin America that's normal. I was shocked the other day with Jordi, who is Mexican as you know, when he commented on my aggressive flatmate with "well, maybe she is in her days"!.
> (Thierry, Developer, Office Communicator: November 2006)

Even my French colleague, who has worked in the labs for more than three years, found it difficult to explain what was so special about the atmosphere in the labs, where so many different nations worked together. For me, the most impressive thing was the amount of tolerance that people showed in the labs towards everything: habits, clothing, working hours, religion. Of course there were tensions between people who did not like each other, but these were rare and from what I saw, not rooted in cultural differences. It was like Remy said in the opening quote to the setting section of this chapter:

> In the labs, we are one culture. We might differ on an individual level, but at work, we are one. (Remy, Project Manager, Interview: January 2006)

Initially, when I entered the labs, I thought of emphasising the cultural problems of having so many different nationalities working together within one lab. However, I soon dropped this idea, because in this particular case, it seemed that the variety of people and also the multicultural environment of the city in which the labs were based, kind of neutralised all multicultural issues and, in turn, an environment in which, potentially, many conflicts could grow into an environment of tolerance. People were so different from each other that, within conversations, nothing appeared to be complicated as everything was different anyway. If everything is different, most things are accepted the way they are. This tolerance was not only visible in the labs, but might also be caused by the general, multicultural environment of the North American city in which these labs were based. Discussing my research with a Belgium developer working in one of the labs in Europe, he commented:

> Well, I do not think that [North American City] or [North American City], or even [North American City] are in any sort of way representative for your typical city. (...) See, I was working about 1,5 years at the University of Waterloo (Ontario). In that place too, hardly anyone had English as their native tongue and if you did hear it, it was mostly because it was like a "common speech" (a la Tolkien). Nobody was ever really bothered with where you came from, what your beliefs were, etc.
>
> My experience compared to, say, life at the university of [European city], or even here in [Headquarters European City] (which has a comparatively large amount of non-[European country]) is very very different. Some of my colleagues sometimes make statements that would be considered racist in [North America]. (...) But this kind of behaviour is integrated in a society which never learnt to deal with multi-culturalism. In fact, multi-culti is nowadays a negative word in [European country] politics. (Developer, Email: March 2006)

Whilst not necessarily agreeing with all the points that this developer raised, it underlined my assumptions that the tolerance and multicultural approach in which everyone could schedule their working day around religious traditions was exceptional not only to this lab, but also because of the city it was embedded in. Belief seemed to be respected in a natural, self-evident way. Muslims were allowed to go to the Friday prayer and seeing them praying five times a day in the staircase without anyone being bothered or concerned equally surprised me. My manager explained to me, for example, that one of the colleagues from the Far East had problems with being managed by a woman. According to what he told me, this was not a big issue and the colleague is now working in a team with a male manager. Apart from this culturally related example of gender issues, I did not observe any other general issue relating to gender. Whilst there were more men working in the labs, the number of women was also quite high.

Besides working together and socialising during lunch times, the developers frequently socialised also outside working hours. Most people in the labs went out together, especially on Thursdays for happy hour drinks in any of the pubs close by. Also the quick pint in the pub after work, as well as private parties to which mostly friends from the labs were invited, were frequent. The people coming from all over the world acted as if they were a big family and even went together on holidays. In my fieldwork notes I wrote

> Saturday, Sunday some of the guys here go skiing. I won't I guess, it's just too expensive. But once again it shows that in this environment borders between work and private are blurred.. however if people meet privately they never talk about work! (Fieldwork Notes, Week 8)

3.2.4 My Work

Employed as intern in the software support team, I was assigned to a team consisting of three people supporting one particular tool of the vendors: CRM application. The four of us came from three different countries: French-Canada, Algeria, Haiti and me, from Germany (Scotland respectively). The colleagues I worked closest with and who assigned me work was Sara, a lady in her 30s from Haiti. She usually started working at 6am to be able to leave at 3pm, to pick up her son. On a normal day, I would start around 7:30. Every morning and also continuously during the day it is the support employees' responsibility to check the system for any new messages from 'external customers' (3rd parties) or 'internal customers' (vendor consultants in the field) which our team would have to take care of. Each day, we had around seven open messages in the inbox from external clients and three or four from internal clients. As I learnt, the rule was to prioritise the messages from external clients. During the day, we would re-select the messages, to see if some new message had arrived which we had to take care of. Depending on the priority of the messages we would work on them, usually by connecting to the client's system via remote login. In particular at the beginning, it was interesting for me to see the different daytimes displayed on the computers we logged on to as we worked across time zones. Once logged in, we would look for solutions and then explain them to the customer. We would never change anything in the customer's system, but explain the issue in a customer message and let the customer do it. It was the vendor's policy which I was repeatedly told: never change anything in the customers system without authorisation. Usually, we worked on several messages at the same time, waiting for the client to respond. To keep track of what we did for whom, I used to have a Word Document in which I would note the different steps to remember for the next day or the next week, depending on how long the user would take to write back. Sara in turn, having done this job for many years, would just write a few words on a post-it – from which I would not have been able to remember anything.

3.2.5 Developer Training

The support people were trained in the same way as the developers and therefore, had the same title as most people working in the labs: Developer. Everyone starting at the vendor as a permanent member of staff (this does not include interns and research staff) goes through an extensive five to six week -long training. As I was told, the training consists of general things, such as programming languages, as well as more specific topics like the CRM customising features. I met some of the new employees from my first day in the labs (and later shared a flat with one of them) and got to know which courses they were attending in the nearby meeting room, whilst I was already working. At some point, some of the new employees participated in a one week Java course. Hearing about this, and that the course was not fully booked, I asked my manager if I could attend. He welcomed the idea. However his manager, who was asked to approve this decision, rejected it. It was explained to me that interns were not allowed to attend the vendor's training courses. Internal courses, taking place in the labs, were reserved for permanent employees only. One of the new employees explained to me later on, that his contract includes the condition that, in case he were to leave earlier then 12 months, after his starting date, he would have to pay penalty fees towards covering the costs of the initial training – a protection mechanism for the vendor to not have people applying to go through the training and then go back to their old job, using the knowledge acquired[27].

In addition to this formal training, once an employee enters the company, he has the choice of participating in ongoing training sessions provided by other employees who are considered as experts in a particular area. During my time in the labs, much of this internal training took place, in which new technologies, in particular topics related to Service Oriented Architecture (SOA), were explained. In my fieldwork notes I wrote:

> It seems that internal education is very important here and there are always sessions giving people updates about technological developments and summaries of conferences. Additionally, there is [vendor] TV online which people really use to learn things they need for their tasks. Learning is part of the daily task and part of a regular 8h working day. Astonishing. (Fieldwork Notes, Week 5)

The expert sessions were mostly held for one to two hours in the afternoon, or, if people from other time zones dialled in, very early in the morning. Usually, meetings were attended by an average of 30 people. I went to the meetings as often as my daily schedule and my manager allowed me to.

As previously mentioned, for my jobs as intern, I did not receive any formal training, but got trained 'on the job'. Developers sitting next to me, as well as my own team from the support, helped me during the first few weeks to find my way through the labs, introducing me to other people, and to install and understand the necessary software. Even though I was part of the software support team, the developers spent many hours explaining work-related things in which I was interested – some of them not even being related to my daily work as intern in the support. As much as developers and support people were looking after me, they were helping each other. I quickly learnt that if there was a customer problem to which I could not find a solution, I could, if no-one else in my team knew the answer, go to the developers and ask. This should not happen all the time, otherwise the developers could do the support task themselves, but

27 The vendor provides trainings to external parties in its own training centres, which are distributed around the world. In Europe, a one week training course costs around 2,500 Euro and excludes expenses (personal experience).

if there are urgent or particularly difficult problems it was fairly common to ask the developer who wrote the program directly, or make a phone call to colleagues in one of the other labs. Most of the developers I came in touch with through asking for help were friendly and open.

On a more formal basis, the developers 'trained' the support in so-called 'hand over sessions'. In these sessions, the developers explained on a functional and technical level new software functionality that their team had developed and which was delivered to the market. The sessions I participate were two to four hours long and were attended by one developer presenting, with Power Point, the new features and the support team responsible for this part of the application. Using this knowledge, the support team should then be able to help the customer with any problems related to this part of the software. After the handover sessions, documentation was signed, confirming that the software and any necessary documentation was handed over and with this, the responsibility for the software, including any software bugs, was with the support team. In practice, these initial briefings were often not enough to cover the complexity of the new program and the day-to-day communication and helping-each-other culture between the people in the labs, was often crucial to allowing a prompt response to a user with an urgent problem.

After the first few weeks which I spent on my own desk, reading and investigating the 'technical surroundings', I started to sit most of the time at Sara's desk. This was less of a shadowing technique as described by Czarniawska (2004) as I actively worked with Sara. Even though she would explain many things to me, my prior experience as consultant allowed me to contribute, to participate and take over work independently. Often, I could also help her by explaining the user's point of view, how it looks on the side of the user, if a customer message is sent back. With this, I could 'pay her back' for her efforts and the time she invested in me (cf. Knox 2005). In turn, she trained me extensively in how to resolve messages. I learnt how to select the ones we were supposed to look after, the practice of investigating an error and how to treat users from around the world. I also learnt about the customer's history, former contacts and impressions. Most of the training I received from Sara was contextual, rather than programming language or application specific. I already knew the main coding language and for the support task, it was important to understand the context, to know where to look for error logs, to memorise common problems and to ask the user the right questions. Support employees need to understand and be able to read coding, but from what I experienced, the problems themselves were often not technical (in a sense of it being a bug in the coding causing a problem) but rooted in a complex accumulation of user actions and interference from other systems. I also learnt, while sitting next to Sara, how to deal with customers, how to address issues in a message and how to explain to the customer which steps to take to help us solving a problem. Surprisingly, even though the vendor sold CRM systems, including the usual pre-defined texts for emails sent to a user (such as 'thank you for contacting [company name].'), the vendor himself did not use these features. Every single message sent to the user was written from scratch and no standard phrases were included.

3.3 Introducing People

Ethnography is about people. All the people I met in the field became important in one way or another to my study, providing me with insights and shaping my point of view. Within this book, I will not attempt to treat the people in the field as 'my informants', but as individuals and colleagues, who allowed me to become part of their lives. As such, I include myself as an actor and also aim to give some of the most important people for this study, a 'face', before letting them act in the following chapters.

The Management
From the management, Tom and Thorsten were most important to me. Tom was the newly hired Senior Vice President (SVP) for CRM worldwide and played a key role in introducing change to the CRM department. On my first day in the labs, he gave a talk to all employees in the labs explaining his new ideas and how he was planning to turn around the CRM division. Tom, around 50 years old, was born in Germany, but emigrated to the US when he was young. For me, his dominant, very self confident behaviour and southern accent were, even though being guilty of stereotyping, what I would have described as 'typical' for people from Texas. Tom was about 1.95 metres tall and with a clear and loud voice.

Thorsten, having German nationality, was the Vice President for CRM, and sat amongst the developers in the labs. Thorsten was a newly appointed Vice President (VP), but had been with the vendor's company for many years. Before joining the vendor, Thorsten worked as an Army Officer. Thorsten was tall, open and joined us for the occasional beer. For me, Thorsten was a main source of information.

The Project Managers
Remy, Matthew, Antoine, Anne-Sophie and Michael were the five project managers on my side of the labs (there were two open-plan offices for the developers), in which CRM was developed. All of them agreed to let me participate and observe their daily 15 minute meetings, which were newly introduced and crucial to the people in the labs in various ways, as I will show in chapter 5 and 6. I also conducted formal interviews with each of them in January / February, 2006.

Remy, coming from Armenia, was a very calm and friendly man in his 40s. Very popular amongst his team he was known for his solidarity. His main worry, which he repeatedly told me about was that he was afraid that with the managerial changes implemented, the work-life balance would change and that he would have to spend more time in the labs. Remy is father of two girls. He has a PhD (Doctor of Philosophy), but never used his title.

Matthew, with whom I have not spoken much, was an English-speaking Canadian. He has two kids and is a hockey fan in his late 30s. Matthew was the only one amongst the project managers with a history in agile project management.

Antoine, sitting next to me, was one of the people I spoke with most and came from Africa. Antoine was in his late 30's: very tall, sporty and fluent in five languages including Russian, French and English. Antoine was, like Remy, well known for standing up for his team and also for being very structured and efficient. Antoine was entirely convinced about agile software development methods such as 'Scrum'.

Anne-Sophie was born in Canada. Her first language was French though she spoke English quite well. Anne-Sophie was average size with blond hair. Her team had the most problems with sticking to the project schedule. Her team rarely spoke about her.

Michael, also in his late 30s was from the Czech Republic and a very calm and structured man. He did not show too much excitement about anything. He always walked around with a light smile and was generally not very talkative. I did not hear anyone talking about Michael, however, I was not very close to the developers from his team (who were sitting quite far from my desk).

The Software Support Team
My colleagues from the support department, most important for my study, were Jordi and Sara. Jordi was the manager of the support team I was part of. He came from Mexico. Known for being very friendly, he was popular amongst his team, very structured and had exceptional diplomatic skills. Jordi was in his 30s and a former consultant.

Sara was the person I spent most of my working time with. Reporting to her, she assigned me tasks and very often I would work with her at her desk looking at customer messages. Sara held a masters degree in software engineering and left academia in search of the 'real world'. Sara was in her early 30s, very focused on her family, very friendly and came from Haiti. She was almost fluent in four languages.

The Developers
Many of the developers were important to this study, but I cannot introduce all of them here. However, there was one person, Thierry, the developer sitting just behind the partition next to my desk, who became particularly important to this study. Thierry spent many hours explaining things to me, chatting on the messenger and sending me emails. Thierry was 30, a father of four (now five), trained as a software engineer and came from France. Thierry studied software engineering. Preferring to work with children, he accepted this job however, was very motivated and had a generally very positive character. Thierry was very popular in the labs and known for his patience, friendliness, openness and programming expertise.

The Researcher
When working in the labs in 2005 / 2006 I was in my late 20s and very much used to moving around. I had already lived in Germany, France, Ireland, Spain and Scotland. Before joining academia, I worked for 2.5 years as consultant implementing the vendor's software. For me, working and researching in the labs was on one of the most exciting things I have done to date.

3.4 Participating in Other Peoples' Lives

All the impressions I gathered and refer to are a result of close interaction with people in their business and private lives. I spent about 50 hours per week in the labs and most of the nights out socialising with various groups from the labs. Being included to such a degree (the last three months I also shared a flat with a developer) allowed me to see many things I would not have seen otherwise; being included allowed me to become 'one of them', which gave this study its depth and strength. I could look into their lives in much detail, be there 'where the action is' (Grills 1998) and experience the dilemmas, frustrations, routines and happiness of the everyday life of the developers. Even though this provides rich data, the fortunate situation I found myself in did not come without challenges: For a short period of time, right at the beginning of my time in the labs, I was absorbed by everything and in danger of missing out on details and specific events in the labs, while being focused on my daily work. Then, particularly in the later stages of my fieldwork, I encountered the problem of losing my status as researcher. The people in the labs created a new role for me and I became involuntarily the 'expert and messenger'. To 'correct' my role was difficult, as defining it was not only up to me but to the network of people I was part of and who saw me in a particular light. The third difficulty I encountered as a result of being included to such a degree was very much an ethical question: What to do if the 'suspects' become friends? How I approached the three problems, is discussed below.

3.4.1 The Necessity of the 'Stranger's Eye'

As a former consultant implementing the vendor's system, I understood the 'language' used by the developers as well as the technical terms and was familiar with some of the problems a developer encounters in his day-to-day life. This allowed me, from a professional point of view, to quickly integrate myself and join discussions about various technical and organisational problems (cf. Merriam et al. 2001). At the same time, however, I became to a degree very engaged in my daily work where, if not reminded by people from academia, I would have lost myself in my role of being a support employee. With this, I would have missed out on details, things which are said to be only visible to the 'stranger's eyes' (Stenhouse 1984). Realising the problem, I developed mechanisms to remind myself of my role and the purpose for which I entered the labs. I took as detailed notes as possible, including things such as feelings and the weather, remembering the suggestions of Burgess (1994), that these would help with reconstructing events once I left the field. In particular, at the beginning I reviewed my observations almost weekly and wrote little summaries at the weekend or summarised some of my findings in emails to my lead researchers. Additionally, I added little evaluation tables which looked like this:

Date	Monday, Nov 07, 2005 07:30-16:30
Keywords	New employee training, [vendor specific software] installation
Main actors	Thierry
Importance	No

Figure 5: Excerpt Fieldwork Notes (Table)

In the Appendices, I copied two of my fieldwork files (week 2 and 14) as an example[28]. Whilst I kept a very detailed diary throughout the five months I spent in the labs, with time, I stopped using these tables. I felt that it would not add any more value and at this stage, I was already aware that I needed to take a detailed fieldwork diary.

Looking at my fieldwork notes today, this was a good decision. The tables, whilst important to remind me in the field, I did not find very useful for analysing the data. What really helped to recreate events though, was that, over time my fieldwork diary also became my trusted friend. Never having written a diary, the fieldwork diary started to become a record, not only of work related, but also personal matters, which in turn, helped me during the writing up process to re-create work related events.

While wanting to keep a certain distance to be able to note the small things in the labs important to my research, I never aimed to become a 'stranger' as Stenhouse (1984) suggests. Before entering the field, I considered this approach, but the arguments in favour of detaching myself were not convincing. I was looking for insider data and I was also not the kind of person who could just pretend to be a part of a group, whilst still remaining a stranger at heart. In the field, there was little time to reconsider and evaluate this approach and I quickly forgot about it. At the research site, so many things happened that I just did what felt to be the right at the time. Having followed the road of not completely detaching myself, and not pretending to be a total stranger (which I was not), and looking back at this decision, I am convinced that this was the right thing to do for the following reasons:

First, Information System studies, mostly, take place in organisational settings. Unlike studying a remote tribe in the rainforest which has never

[28] Because I felt that some comments were too personal, I deleted parts of the notes taken in week 14. I have marked the space where I deleted these personal comments with '(...)'.

been visited by outsiders before, organisational settings are never totally new to a researcher. There are always things which are familiar, which reminds one of another situation and tools (Czarniawska 2004). Knowing the vendor's system and having been trained as a programmer, the developers and their daily work were very familiar to me and hence to take on the role of a stranger would have been an impossible act.

Second, even if I had tried to look at things in such detail as I assume the eyes of strangers might do and would be able to provide a detailed description as, for instance, Latour and Woolgar (1986), it is not every ethnographer's goal to do so. I did not want to describe why and what the developers were doing on such a micro level. My aim with this ethnography is to provide an account about how software is developed, designed and maintained, how the developers work together on a day-to-day basis.

Third, in the settings in which I worked, the fact that my profession for two and a half years had been as a technical consultant implementing ERP systems, allowed me to access the field in the first place. Without being a developer, the vendor would probably not have hired me and getting a working visa for North America would have been even more difficult, but most of all, I would never have understood what the developers were doing or how things, particularly in the software support department, are done on a daily basis. Knowing the system and the company to a certain degree and *not* being a total stranger allowed me to become one of them, live their working lives, engage with the system and participate as an accepted member of the group.

Fourth, studying developers is different from studying any other kind of 'tribe'. Developers are known to communicate mostly through machines in written forms and also constantly 'leave' the labs by working virtually with people in other labs or with clients. This was especially true for the support team I worked with. On many occasions, we had to establish a remote connection to some customers around the world to re-produce errors and look out for solutions. Just sitting in the labs as an observer rather than as a developer able to actively participate and help, would not have allowed me to visit the places the developers did and experience this type of day-to-day work.

Czarniawska (2004) describes a situation, in which a researcher is familiar with the settings and able to not only observe, but participate as 'lucky' and the results as 'superior'. Referring in particular to Melville Dalton's (1959) and Michael Burawoy's (1979) work, she writes:

> It is possible to carry out such studies - which are undoubtedly superior to all other types – either through exceptional luck in obtaining access or because a given workplaces does not require specific qualifications. (p: 785)

She also points to the uncommonness of such a situation happening. Only rarely does a researcher happen to be familiar with the tasks of the people he studies to a degree that he can actually participate in and carry out the same work. In cases where the observer had a different background, the best solution Czarniawska (ibid.) saw from her study was to 'shadow' someone, follow them around to see what they were doing. Even though providing rich data, the problem she encountered was, that people do not want to be watched at all times and answer questions. Consequently, this type of observation works only for a short period of time. Czarniawska describes:

> I followed selected people in their everyday work for a period of about 10 working days (I am not sure if they could tolerate more). (p: 786)

Similarly Latour and Woolgar (1986) point out that, at some point in their research, they felt that they could not ask any more questions without seriously upsetting people. Even though I would not describe this research as 'superior', not being a stranger in the field allows me to today describe and understand the setting in much more detail and depth than someone who does not share or pretends not to share the same background as those people in the field. Gill and Johnson's (1991) quote describes my intention and idea of a good ethnographer best:

> The researcher attempts to participate fully in the lives and activities of subjects and thus becomes a member of their group, organisation or community. This enables the researcher to share their experiences by not merely observing what is happening but also feeling it. (Gill and Johnson 1991: 109)

Apart from all these reasons, to include myself as much as possible was also a 'natural' reaction for me. Being in a different continent, away from my friends and any kind of familiar system and culture, I wanted to become part of my new world, rather than living a life of being physically in a North America city and working in the vendor's labs, but mentally, still be in Scotland. For five months, I wanted this to be my home and the life of a developer to be my life. It was more than playing a role; to the extent that the vendor offered me a permanent position in the labs (which I rejected in favour of completing this research). However, whilst fortunate in many ways, becoming 'one of them', later on, created another challenge: My role within the labs started to change, which was not always an advantage.

3.4.2 Changing Roles

Looking back, it appears as if my role in the labs changed slowly and unnoticed, from being 'the intern with an inexplicable interest in what is going on in the developer teams' (October-December), to 'the researcher' (December-January) and finally, involuntarily, to 'the expert and messenger' (January-February). At the beginning, I tried to stay in the background and maintain my status as intern, the job I was hired for. Over time, I got to know my colleagues better and like myself asking them questions, they also asked me about my past. In my immediate surrounding it was soon well known, that I was not only an intern but also a researcher. Whilst this change of role towards being 'the researcher' was not a problem as such, it was the following change in roles, which became a challenge. Over time, people started to see me as an expert in the newly implemented managerial changes which I actively observed. They saw me as the person knowing what was happening on both sides: the management and the developer. In consequence, for the developers, I became the one who could bridge hierarchies and communicate issues which they were afraid of communicating themselves and who could advise on the managerial change. For the management I became the 'external consultant', who observes and knows what is going on in the working lives of the developers and their level of acceptance of the changes. This situation developed slowly and I did not realise what was happening until very late. In my fieldwork notes I wrote in January:

> Now people are getting curious, they come around like Tracy [developer] asking if it [attending the daily scrums] is related to my research and what I am doing. Also, just today the VP invited me to go with him for dinner to discuss my research, Scrum and [vendor]. After their daily scrum now also Ian [developer] came along asking if I liked it. (Fieldwork Notes, Week 12)

A few days later, I wrote in my diary:

> I regret that Sara [my colleague from the support] saw in my inbox that mail from Tom [Senior Vice President] and then she saw me talking to Thorsten, the Vice President. She looked at me and commented: "You have good contacts". (Fieldwork Notes, Week 13)

I did not feel very comfortable in suddenly getting so much attention. What I wanted to be was the researcher who stays in the background and who has time to do research, my daily tasks as intern, and integrate myself in the developer community. I did *not* want to engage in 'action research' or any kind of consulting or political work. Two weeks later, I wrote:

> People look at me and talk about me and make comments like "the spy" or "I love Tom's ideas, tell him"..etc. It's joking but I don't like it cause behind the jokes there is some truth... I am in the centre of attention. At the same time, I have to do my daily work and feel very distracted by the people trying to chat all the time with me. Now, since I am sitting usually at Sara's desk to work together on customer messages, there are no 5 min a day where I can just sit down, take my headphones and listen to some music while working. Either somebody writes on the messenger, sends an email or passes by. Have no idea how many people I met the last months.. For sure it comes close to 100. (Fieldwork Notes, Week 13)

The developers kept asking more and more questions, and so did the management. At the same time, I wanted to fulfil all my tasks as intern in the support team and also attend the daily meetings of the different teams. With all the people talking to me, balancing my workload sensibly, suddenly seemed to become impossible. To get all things done I had to prioritise my work, and because I could not send people away without offending them and had to do my work as intern, I had no choice but to cut down on going to the daily meetings. The same week, I wrote in my diary:

> I feel guilty and I am afraid that I make the impression of putting my research first by attending all those meetings or that people think I only talk to them cause I am studying them. I am quite

> stressed and wouldn't mind to have 24h on my own. (Fieldwork Notes, Week 13)

The situation became even more difficult for me, when the project managers announced a meeting in the middle of February, in which they asked me to give feedback about how each team performed with the newly introduced daily meetings, which I observed. Without my knowledge, Matthew sent around an invitation to a meeting to all project managers:

> Hi,
>
> I thought it would be useful to meet for 15 - 20 minutes to discuss the daily Scrum meetings.
>
> Christine has been watching our meetings and I was curious to get her feedback.
>
> Regards,
> Matthew. (Matthew, Project Manager, Email: February 2006)

Whilst I suggested a 'come together' at the beginning, this was not what I had in mind. Not happy with being in the spotlight again, there was little I could do other than to accept the invitation to the meeting. The nights before I stayed up late, read books and prepared a couple of comments to make a good impression. I thought that if I had to do it, then at least I wanted to do my best. Calming myself, I also thought I would not compromise any of my promises regarding confidentiality, because, after all, only the project managers were invited and if they are okay with talking openly about things in front of other project managers, then I would be too.

At the time the meeting was supposed to start, I went to the meeting room and saw everyone sitting and talking to the Vice President. As I found out they were running late at a previous meeting, and so I waited outside. After a couple of minutes the door opened and I walked in. Thorsten, on seeing me, came over and asked what we were doing here. Knowing Thorsten, it was clear that if I told him he would stay – what I expected, nobody wanted. At the same time I could not think of any possible excuse except obvious lies. So I told him and he said "That's interesting". And he sat down again.

The problem for me was the following. At the beginning of participating in the daily scrums, I promised each team that I would collect the data only for research and not report to the management, underlining my role as 'researcher'. The people in the labs re-defined my role, in which I involuntarily had to switch by, for example, giving feedback to the project managers. However, with the Vice President being there, I would break the promise of not reporting to the management and potentially offend the project managers, who, during this time of change appeared to be insecure in what they did anyway. The only possible way out I saw at this moment without offending anyone, was to comment only very briefly and generally on the daily scrums. This was a pity because the meeting lost its purpose and I felt like making an impression of being entirely unprepared and explaining only obvious things. Even though hoping that I did not offend anyone and did not compromise my 'neutral status' as researcher (as far as this was possible), I went to each project managers desk / wrote an email and apologised. I re-assured them that I still did not report to the management. Below is the email I sent Remy right after the meeting in February:

> Regarding the meeting last week, Friday, I just wanted to mention that I didn't know that Thorsten will be present as well and it wasn't planned this way. I was sort of trapped since I told you initially that I will not report to any management body but that it is only for academics and for you if you want to have feedback. By reporting without mentioning any specific team, I tried to keep my promise but also not offending Thorsten by saying nothing. I hope this was ok for you. My approach hasn't changed. (Email: February, 2006)

Apologising also gave me the chance to emphasise that I am a researcher and not a consultant, spy or expert. I thought that afterwards, the situation became a bit better and I felt more secure in my position. I also explained myself to Thorsten, the VP, whom I knew by then well enough to do so. He accepted my little speech and smiled. Unfortunately, however, just a few days later, he came back to me, asking me questions such as which team performs best. Again I had to resist giving an answer and argued my case.

Knowing that I would only stay a few more weeks in the field, I decided to maintain my integrity as a researcher as much as I could by avoiding any possible risky situation and tried to disappear by being very quiet. This strategy did not really work and it was my fieldwork coming to an end, which eventually saved me from having to take further actions.

The way the people kept remembering me once I left the field was as the 'Scrum Expert' and 'Messenger'. I still get emails asking me "How is Tom?" or "I would like to know what Thorsten thinks about that. Do you know?" or calling me "Scrum Director" like Antoine did when he wrote:

> Hi Scrum Director ;-)
> We are doing well, still scrumming [daily meetings] but not as regularly as it used to be (no Director = no Scrum :-)) Working hard to meet the deadlines. (Antoine, Project Manager, Email: April 2006)

As a researcher carrying out participant observation, I certainly influenced the way things happened in the labs and contributed to how the people exercised and also perceived the managerial changes, in particular, by being seen as an expert.

From my experience with this research, I agree with Turner (2000) that detaching oneself from the analysis of such ethnographic data by using ideas such as 'informants' and more interestingly, '*my* informants' are only 'cover ups', *pretending* some distance. Turner (ibid.) concludes:

> The anthropologist cannot be present in a social field without participating and becoming a significant author of events, practices and political configurations, thereby effecting what happens and the significance it has for the constructions that emerge for participants. (p: 53)

My influence on social relationships and events in the labs is indisputable and has been unavoidable. Hence, I do not want to pretend I was the invisible observer not interfering with the day-to-day lives of the people in the field. One cannot participate without influencing the course of events, even in an observation setting. One cannot not communicate (Watzlawick et al. 1974).

The combination of my observing the teams and at the same time, having friends in the management, also appears to have influenced the rigidness with which my colleagues followed the plan of carrying out the daily meetings. I remember certain situations in which I went to the corner where the meeting should take place before everyone else and, the project manager looking at me, commented: "Ah, yeah. We should do the daily scrum". I would have just left again, but my appearance reminded him and so he walked around, collected the members of his team and started with the daily scrum. It seemed that, as 'Scrum expert' and 'messenger', I received a certain authority, again, involuntarily.

To recap, this research shows clearly the impact the choice of research methods has on the outcome of a research project. The detail in which I describe the settings in the labs would have not been possible if I had launched a questionnaire or carried out interviews and observation without participating and including myself in a way the case study approach would suggest (Yin 1994). At the same time, being included caused challenges such as not losing out on details or losing one's status as a researcher, as I have outlined above. The third and most challenging problem for me, however, was to handle the trust I received as a colleague and researcher, but most of all as a friend.

3.4.3 When the 'Subjects' Become Friends

Having friends and being included helped me in many ways and it made these five months in North America one of the most enjoyable times. In terms of the research, the extended social network allowed me to understand what was happening in the labs, in the company and in the lives of the developers. Also, by having friends, I got contacts for interviews with people outside the labs through the principle of snowballing (Easterby-Smith et al. 1991). People trusted me and did not mind helping out. Below is an example in which Antoine, a project manager in the North American lab is asking Markus, a project manager in an European Lab, if he can give me some information on their labs and their experiments with Scrum:

> Hi Markus [Project Manager in European Labs],
> I was wondering if you guys are applying Scrum or any other agile dev process in your team. If so, would you mind giving 1/2 hour of your precious time to Christine to share with her your views on this dev methodology? Can she contact you?
>
> Christine is a german-english-now_canadian... intern, who is doing research on Scrum. So, if you could help her or refer her to

> someone who is applying this in [European Lab], it would really be appreciated.
>
> Thanks in advance.
>
> Antoine. (Antoine, Project Manager, Email: January 2006)

Even though being included has been an advantage in many ways, it also caused an inner conflict whenever I socialised with the developers or look at my data during this writing up stage. How to use the information given to me as friend? How to distinguish between 'Christine the researcher' and 'Christine the friend'? How to not betray the friendship by writing down the secrets told? Already worried about this whilst I was still in the field, after approximately two months I started to make an effort to be 'only Christine' and leave 'the researcher' at home, when we were going out. However, this was only possible to a certain degree, as the person who was sitting in the pub, working in the labs and now writing this book, was one and the same, me, a collection of experiences. Also, at the same time, by trying to exclude these experiences, I found that I lose out on the rich picture which the combination of private and working life provided me. After the first nights out, at which I tried to detach myself from my combined role, I stopped as it was just not possible. Instead I started to mark parts of fieldwork as 'private' or 'confidential'. But even this, I only did for a short time as I felt that I just did not have time to do it. Now, when analysing my data and being confronted with the same problems again, I found advice in Hammersley and Atkinson's remarkable work 'Ethnography: principles in practice' (1995). The authors suggest that the key is to constantly be aware of the ambiguity of the situation and carefully evaluate all interactions against the researcher's own ethical principles. Throughout this writing up phase, I have been troubled by what to include in this research and what not. To help me to write freely, I decided to firstly anonymise the data in the best possible way by changing places, names and even the gender of the people in the field. Furthermore, access to the extended version of this research as presented in this book, has been restricted until 2010. With time passing by, the organisation changed and people in the labs I reported upon moved on and, with this, tracing back any of the already anonymised quotes will be almost impossible.

Parts of this research have influenced already published work (Pollock et al. 2008; Pollock et al. 2009). For this article and book chapter, I did my best to only choose data which, whilst representing the work organisation and policies, did not compromise my ethical commitments.[29]

So far, I have introduced the setting in the labs as well as shared some of my experiences as ethnographer in the field. In the subsequent part of this chapter, I discuss in more detail the theories surrounding the chosen method for data collection and data analysis.

3.5 Ethnography

The goal of my research is to find out more about the everyday working practices in software labs and to see how a software package vendor works internally. Knowing the software and programming language of one major vendor already, I chose to try to enter one of the labs of this vendor, unconsciously following Merriam's advice:

> The more one is like the participants in terms of culture, gender, race, socio-economic class and so on, the more it is assumed that access will be granted, meanings shared, and validity of findings assured. (Merriam et al. 2001: 406)

When deciding upon the vendor, I was not sure which type of research approach to choose. It was clear, that in order to experience the everyday life, I needed to carry out a form of research, which resembles the way people make sense of their everyday life, a method to learn about the social and cultural life of developers in a software labs. My aim left me with a choice of either to carry out a case study or ethnography.

The case study approach would have allowed me to get some impressions through carrying out interviews and analysing the many pages of documentation and annual reports on the web. This would have had the advantage that I would not have to spend much time in the field, in particular, since the vendor's lab I potentially would get access to, was in North America. On the flip site however, such a research approach would only allow me to collect data which was given to me. Participant observation would in this case not be possible.

---

29 In this context, it has to be noted that, even though the book implies that it investigates a particular software vendor, for the chapter influenced by my work (Pollock et al. 2008), it cannot be concluded that this is the case.

Even though, it would involve moving to North America, I wanted to be involved to see what is happening, I wanted to participate in a way Hammersley and Atkinson (1995) described it:

> In people's daily lives for an extended period of time, watching what happens, listening to what is said, asking questions - in fact, collecting whatever data are available to throw light on the issues that are the focus of the research. (p: 1)

Fully sympathetic with Bate's (1997) critique of some 'ethnographic' studies, which consist of a few one day visits in some organisation[30], I decided to try to get into the labs for at least three months and carry out participant observation. No matter what data would be available in the labs, it would always allow me to answer my, at the beginning, very broad research question of 'What happens inside a ERP software vendor's labs?'.

3.5.1 Getting Access

One major challenge associated with ethnography is getting access to a field which would accommodate the researcher for several months (Blaikie 2000; Hammersley and Atkinson 1995). In my case and with a history in programming, it was Dr. Pollock who put the great idea into my head, to apply as an intern to one of the worldwide labs. With my background, I was over-qualified as an intern, but the plan was that, with the status of an intern, I would be able to do both, fulfil the tasks I would have to do and still have time to 'wonder around'.

The problem was, however, that organisations such as the vendor were well known for being very protective of its practices and technological developments in its software labs (Meissner 2000) and therefore reluctant to let any 'externals' access the labs. This situation left me with a choice: either I was to gain access through getting a job there and do covert observation, which I found highly controversial from an ethical point of view, or to try overt observation and risk to not being accepted. I decided on the latter, my backup strategy being to write an implementation study and combine it with action research. As a former consultant, access to an implementation project would be no problem.

---

30 Bate (1997) writes: "Organisational anthropologists rarely take a toothbrush with them these days. A journey into the organizational bush is often little more than a safe and closely chaperoned form of anthropological tourism" (p: 150).

So how did I finally gain access? I had, as James Cornford summarised at the Biography of Software Packages Conference in Edinburgh (2008), the most important thing in research: luck. Once decided, I wrote an email to all the people I knew who could possibly have contacts with any of the worldwide labs of the vendor and who would be comfortable in recommending me. I was lucky and got a prompt response from two people, Harald Liessmann, a consultant from Germany and Philippe Kruchten, a practitioner and Professor in Canada. Philippe happened to know the Lab Manager of the North American labs. Having explained my intention to him, he offered to call the Manager. A day later, I received an email requesting that I should send my resume directly to the Lab Manager and that I should do so right away. Harald, in turn, got in contact with the Vice President of another North American lab to which I also sent my CV. A couple of weeks later, I found myself on the phone with three developers from the software support team in one lab, and only five days later with the Vice President from the other lab.

The team I spoke with on the phone first, was very nice and friendly offering me an interesting job in the software support department. The Vice President of the other labs, however, was what appeared to be a very career oriented woman who, whilst offering a very attractive job (user requirement collection and reporting directly to the her), also commented, that I would have to be very self-dependent in my job as "there will be nobody holding your hand!". Receiving a job offer from both labs, I could have carried out a multi-sided ethnography as suggested by Pollock and Williams (2008). However, for several reasons, I decided to visit one lab only. First, there was the issue that this research is mostly self-funded and moving around would have been too expensive[31]. Furthermore, from my personal experience of living abroad, I knew that only a longer stay, like five to six months, would allow me to integrate myself. The option of 6 month in each lab I dismissed for the reasons that I did not want to leave Scotland for a year and also, I was reluctant to extend the time this research would take, by another 6 month. I eventually chose the labs where I got the offer for the support internship, based on my interview experience and also my personal preference for the city.

---

[31] In this context, I thank Dr. Pollock and Prof. Williams, who paid for my flight to North America, the vendor, who paid me a salary as an intern which allowed me to cover my expenses during these 5 months, and the Small Project Grant of the University of Edinburgh, which also helped to finance this fieldwork trip.

Slightly insecure as to whether I made the right decision, what I found in the labs exceeded my expectations: A fascinating, changing site, a very interesting job, most helpful and friendly people and exceptional friends. Unlike many ethnographers' reports, I did not feel that I missed out or that I chose the wrong location, team or people. As one of the developers added, I was lucky that so many changes happened during this time. I have been told that usually life in the labs is a lot quieter.

3.5.2 *A Triangular Approach to Data Collection*

Having gained access to the site, I started work in North America at the end of October, 2005 ending my stay in March, 2006. I began by observing the field while I did my daily tasks as intern and, as time went by, gained trust and, with this the opportunity to conduct interviews. Additionally, throughout this time, I had unlimited access to the Intranet, as well as, various Internet portals of the vendor. The combination of different methods - participant observation, interviews and secondary data - allowed me to see things from different perspectives:

- By communicating with the people and interviewing them, I got an insight into how they saw different situations, how they experienced what others did and how they saw themselves and their own actions.
- In my role as an intern working in the labs, I could observe and experience (as a participant) myself, what the people in the labs were doing every day.
- Having unlimited access to the Intranet, I got an insight into how events, happening in the labs, were communicated through the Intranet.
- Having unlimited access to the various portals, I could observe the users' and developers' sides simultaneously.

Besides being able to reveal some important aspects by cross referencing between the different data sources, I could also experience the difference between perceptions which people drew upon in interviews and their actual behaviour. Even though, this observation is documented at length in academic literature (Bechhofer and Paterson 2000; Denscombe 1998; Gray 2004; Saunders et al. 2000), the extent to which the perspectives differed, as I will show in more detail in Chapter 5, was surprising and convinced me once more, that a combination of methods is crucial. If I had carried out interviews only, I would have come to a very different conclusion, presenting what appears from where I stand now, a 'false' picture[32].

3.5.3 *'Finding' Interesting Topics*

As an ethnographer in the field, my data collection and analysis was driven not by answering with a chosen set of methods a specific catalogue of pre-defined research questions, which I set up before entering the field but by creating an insight into how the developers of one of the biggest ERP system providers work together on an everyday basis, and how they designed, developed and supported the system. Whilst having this very open question in mind, I was also hoping to find certain things I was interested in. Whilst some literature suggests entering the field with an open mind without any pre-assumptions (cf. Actor Network Theory, i.e. Latour (1988)), I think this is an impossible attempt. People anticipate what the field might look like and always have some kind of research agendas which they will try to focus on (and on the basis of which research grants were given in the first place). Also, our theoretical background determines the ways we look at the world. Whilst I tried to stay open minded as much as possible, having the 'advantage' of being a young researcher, rather inexperienced and not too familiar with theories and theoretical frameworks, I nevertheless was not free of expectations of what I might find in the labs. In fact, as mentioned earlier, I was sure I would find intercultural problems, knowing that many different nations were working together in this place. As such, I find myself 'guilty' of not having been open in the field in the first place and, at the beginning, trying to prove my assumption; I picked up anything which was even remotely related to culture, trying hard to give it some meaning even though the incident in which it was mentioned was rather insignificant. For the first few weeks in the field I ran into the trap of searching for something which was just not there (for an impression of my fieldwork notes, see Appendix).

The advantage of an ethnography, an in depth study, is that these things correct themselves if one stays long enough in the field. It is a learning process that an ethnographer goes through in which prior presumptions are reformed and disappear (Hammersley and Atkinson 1995). Eventual-

32 There is no 'correct' picture as such, but reflecting on the conclusions which could be drawn by looking at the interviews only, and comparing these with the conclusions made having followed a triangular approach, it appears that the latter presents a much more complete and accurate picture of the events having taken place in the labs.

ly, the fact that I could not find what I expected to find became an advantage: with my initial idea gone, I was entirely open to whatever happened around me. I was not searching for some idea to be verified or some particular incident. I was able to 'look around' and see what is actually happening in the labs and reflect what occupied the developers, (but not me as researcher). My notes show day-to-day activities and talks in the labs, and so did the unstructured interviews I conducted which interestingly enough, resulted in being all concerned with the same issue: the managerial change. It was then, after listening to the people, that I realised that it was this, that matters to the developers (support as well as development teams) and that has a tremendous impact on the day-to-day work in the labs and the product. Realising the importance of the topic, I then started to ask the developers about how things used to be and their opinions about the change. Once people realised that I was interested, the developers feeling very passionate about the changes, came to me and expressed their opinions - even when I had not asked for it.

3.5.4 Interviews

Working in the field, I carried out 14 formal, unstructured interviews (and many more informal interviews) lasting between 45 minutes and two hours. Each person was formally interviewed only once, hence if I refer to an interview in relation to a person within this book, it will always be the same interview.

At the beginning, I chose only interviewees I knew best and felt comfortable with, asking whether they would mind being interviewed. I was curious as to what they would talk about, what mattered to them, and to gain a different type of insight from the data I collected through participant observation and secondary data research. Finding myself in the fortunate situation of being accepted and not rejected by a single interview partner, after the initial period, I began to choose my interviewees more carefully, making sure that I talked to people from different teams and different hierarchies. I focused on the developers as I was very involved in the support team and therefore already knew a lot about support work (most of the time I was sitting at the same desk as my colleague). I considered interviews with my support colleagues, but did not know what, in addition, we could talk about, as it seemed that everything had already been covered by day-to-day interactions and discussions[33]. Hence, the only

33 There is a difference between what people say and what can be observed. I could have investigated these differences in more detail, but asking questions about the day to day

interview with the support team was with my manager Jordi. I was hoping that by interviewing him, I would have a better understanding of the strategies and policies within the support organisation. Below is a list of all formal interviews:

Name	Role	Form	Date
Remy	Project Manager (same office)	Face-to-Face	January, 2006
Thierry	Project Manager (same office)	Face-to-Face	January, 2006
Anne-Sophie	Project Manager (same office)	Face-to-Face	February, 2006
Antoine	Project Manager (same office)	Face-to-Face	January, 2006
Michael	Project Manager (same office)	Face-to-Face	December, 2005
Lu	Project Manager (next door office)	Face-to-Face	February, 2006
Gabriel	Project Manager (same office but left 2 weeks later)	Face-to-Face	November, 2005
Thomas	Solution Manager	Face-to-Face	December, 2005
Jordi	Support Team Manager	Face-to-Face	November, 2005
Thorsten	Vice President CRM	Face-to-Face and Phone	November, 2005 (Face to Face) August, 2007 (Phone)
Tom	Senior Vice President CRM	Phone	February, 2006
Fritz	Scrum trainer Palo Alto Office	Phone	February, 2006
Markus	Vice President CRM German Office	Phone	February, 2006

work which, I carried out myself too, would have made a strange impression, and most likely would have annoyed my colleagues.

Sharik	Project Manager Palo Alto Office	Phone	January, 2006

Figure 6: Overview of Interviews

I usually booked the meeting room to talk to the people as it was only there that we would not be overheard. Furthermore, I could put the phone on speaker and with this, record interviews which were done over the phone. All interviews, except the one with Fritz, were carried out in one of the meeting rooms in the vendor's labs. This was so as not to interfere with my work or the interviewees' work and also not to draw too much attention to me carrying out the interviews. The interviews usually took place in the late afternoon or over lunch. For people from other time zones, I generally stayed late in the office. The interview with the Senior Vice President took place on a Sunday night. All interviews were carried out in confidential, one-to-one settings.

3.5.5 Participant Observation

Being an intern and carrying out participant observation allowed me to become one of them, to fully participate in the lives and activities of the people working in the labs (Easterby-Smith et al. 1991; Gray 2004). For the particular settings this had three main advantages:

First, in order to observe support work, participant observation is a necessity. As I show in Chapter 4, different members of the support team express themselves mostly through the machine, rather than verbally. For instance only rarely would a support employee call the user. The interaction with the user is managed through the support portal and therefore takes place in written form. It was only through my status as intern and my technical background that I could get a detailed insight into the support work, by not monitoring, but participating in these 'silent communications'. As an employee, I was given the daily tasks of assisting with the problem investigations. During Christmas and New Year, I was, together with my Manager Jordi, the only one representing our support team to the outside world. It was this role which allowed me to 'feel' how the support employee felt and to get an insight into the vendor's formal and informal practices and policies.

Second, it was only by the means of participant observation that I made contact with other teams, the people not supporting, but developing the system. Only by becoming 'one of them' and working in the labs like everyone else, could I gain the trust of the developers and the management and obtain access to their teams and by doing so, observe the managerial changes.

Third, my status as a participating researcher, allowed me to gain an overall impression of the vendor's practices. As an intern, I was allowed to move around in the labs without looking too nosy or intrusive (most of the time at least. Occasionally I felt left out on purpose, by not being invited to meetings, but this was very infrequent, and maybe only my perception). As an intern, I was *supposed to be* curious and ask questions about everything going on in the labs and in the corporation. People became used to me being around, trusted me and actively and passively, allowed me to find out about their work. I could not have collected this information through any other method.

In addition to participant observation and interviews, I also had access to secondary data such as the Intranet.

3.5.6 Secondary Data

Mostly in the evenings and at weekends, I read and collected secondary data by reviewing documentation on the Intranet, and various brochures published for internal / external use. I also had access to all the restricted user and support portals. I could see the interface that the support uses, and also the interface the user encounters when reporting a problem through the web interface. This allowed me to reveal differences between information displayed to the user and information displayed to the support employees. In addition to that, I participated in many educational training sessions which were provided to the developers by other developers during one to two hour presentations. The training sessions were held frequently and were often related to changes rooted in the re-design of the system from Client-Server Architecture to Service Architecture (SOA).

The texts I could access online through the various interfaces, not only provided a permanent documentation about what is happening, but also gave me an insight into what happened before I entered the labs. For example, I had access to all communication happening between the user and the vendor via the support portal during the last few years. This gave me a more complete picture about the working practices in the labs.

The triangular method allowed me to look at events from different angles, to cross reference data. Without wanting to imply that an approach based on only one method only is not 'correct', from what I experienced in the labs, the way people reflect upon what they were doing differs significantly from what they are actually doing. In the case of this research, conducting a case study based on interviews and secondary data, disregarding the option of participant observation as the method of investigation, would, in my opinion, have led to different conclusions. Hammersley and Atkinson (1995) use the metaphor of locating a position on a map when discussing the advantages of mixing methods. The authors explain:

> For someone wanting to locate their position on a map, a single landmark can only provide the information that they are situated somewhere along a line in a particular direction from the landmark. With two landmarks, however, their exact position can be pin-pointed by taking bearings on both landmarks; they are at the point where the two lines cross. In social research, if one relies on a single piece of data there is a danger that undetected error in the data-production process may render the analysis incorrect. If, on the other hand, diverse kinds of data lead to the same conclusion, one can be a little more confident in that conclusion. (p: 231)

It is clear that one can never be sure about the results, but as the authors state, by combing complementary methods we can be more confident in our conclusions.

3.6 Evolving Research Questions

Defining the research question is a process. As mentioned earlier, when I set out on this project, my main objective was to investigate what was happening within this software vendor's labs. I had hoped to find certain information on intercultural teamwork, but this was only a vision. With this I most probably failed in Berg's (1995) eyes who states:

> The purpose of research is to discover answers to questions through the application of systematic procedures. (Berg (1995) in Blaikie (2003): 59)

Like an organisational anthropologist, I entered the labs to study a 'tribe' rather than to get answers to a set of pre-defined questions. This does not, however, mean that I entered the labs unprepared; research courses, articles and in particular, the most useful book from Hammersley and Atkinson (1995), helped me to develop the necessary skills and to find guidance in times of uncertainty.

Interestingly, not even one of my nebulous and unspecific previous assumptions of what I might find, were verified. In a sense I confirmed Hammersley and Atkinson's (1995) claim that the course of ethnography cannot be predetermined. Not having a pre-defined strategy and definite questions in mind allowed me, rather than to emphasise and write about what was not an issue, as was the case, for instance, with intercultural problems, to redefine my interests during the course of observation and 'look around' to reflect what matters to the people in the field. In this case, it was a new management approach, which I did not even know about before entering the labs. Whilst this became clear when working in the labs, for the case of support work, I was not sure what would be the "story". This, not knowing, throughout the fieldwork period, allowed me to look at support work with open eyes, from different viewpoints and just report upon what appeared to be important to the support employees on an everyday basis. It was only when I returned from the field and started to analyse my fieldwork notes that research questions developed, reflecting very clearly the nature of research. In relation to the support work for instance, my data showed most interesting insight into the mere day-to-day working practices within such labs. This broad and organisational viewpoint is reflected in the accounts presented throughout this book and, with this also what over time, became the two research questions:

1. *How does an ERP system provider manage the challenge of serving a highly diverse and geographically dispersed user base?*

2. *How does an ERP system provider, from a social perspective, organise its product development phase?*

3.7 Limitations

A well known quote from Einstein is, that "It is the theory that decides what we can observe". This appears particularly true if we look at academic research and the multiple, almost uncountable, ways we can investigate a particular phenomenon. It is things like the theory, the literature, our personal background as well as the academic environment, which influence our point of view. Events and settings can always be seen in different ways and it is these different ways which are reflected in our research and conclusions. The world within the labs did not arrange itself into chapters, sub headings and stories, but it was me, as the ethnographer and creator of the text, who arranged it this way. I wrote this narrative in the light of what I saw, what specific people told me and what I read in the company's internal documents. My personal background as well as the academic literature surrounding the topic and methodology I read before, during and after the time in the field, is reflected in my writing and analysis (Hammersley and Atkinson 1995; Suchman 1995).

Furthermore, after returning from the field, I started to work for one year on the ESRC (Economic & Social Research Council) funded research project "The biography and evolution of software packages", in which both my lead researchers were involved. With regards to the involvement of my lead researchers, some might argue that such closeness leads to repetition. Whilst the argument has its merits and certainly no research is free from influences (which is also not something one should try to achieve), I believe that this closeness helped me to question things even more than I would have done otherwise. Whilst I, for instance, first tried to align myself with the claims made in the context of the project, which are also represented in written form in the most interesting book of Pollock and Williams (2008), in the third year of conducting this research, I started to re-write most of the chapters, no more aiming to align myself but to further, and question these thoughts in a way that I would question not even any other type of academic account. In search for uniqueness, I aimed to go beyond the results of the project, believing that it is only if we try to push further than existing knowledge that we can grow and contribute.

In light of the various influences, I do not claim to have found 'how things really are in the labs' and how development and support 'works' in a sense of describing a single reality (Bowker and Star 1999). What I want to contribute to academic research is an account of what happened in the labs from my perspective, which is influenced by many factors, including the people I talked to and worked with, as well as their, and my, political, historical, technological and academic background (Barnard and Spencer 1996). Critical voices from other disciplines might undermine this study for being biased and question its credibility and research approach. Whilst this is a long lasting discussion between disciplines in which both sides have valuable arguments, as a qualitative researcher, I believe that questions related to the credibility and plausibility can actually be addressed with more (and not as often thought of with less) confidence in relation to participant observation and interviews, than it can be in the case of, for instance, a survey research. Qualitative methods give the researcher a chance to better understand what is expressed and allow immediate discovery and clarification of misunderstandings. In the case of sending out a postal questionnaire, misunderstandings can seldom be detected, if at all (O'Reilly 2005). Qualitative research such as ethnography also allows one to highlight limitations such as the various influences, rather than pretending that the results are objective and impervious.

Whilst confident in the validity and credibility of ethnographic research, having spent most of my academic life in Management School, I know that being certain and making the above argument is not enough to convince more quantitative minded researchers. I therefore set out to obtain more advice to ensure the validity of this research also in the light of a more critical audience. Once more, I found advice in Hammersley (1991). The author insists that every account is socially constructed (similar to what has just been discussed above) and feels that the validity of ethnographic studies is ensured as long as a researcher is committed to his work, thoughtful, fully aware of possible prejudice and that he should give the audience enough information to be able to judge the validity of the story by themselves. In following Hammersley's (ibid.) advice, besides being committed to and aware of the possible effects of prejudice, I described within this chapter, the settings, some of the people I met, the research methods and my approach to various problems I encountered as researcher. Even more details about the case can be found in the subsequent chapters. By giving a detailed description of both the case, as well as the experiences I had as an ethnographer, I leave it to the reader to decide about the credibility of the study. All forms of descriptions, reports and studies can be undermined if one is aiming to do so (Latour and Woolgar 1986). Even though agreeing with Latour and Woolgar (ibid.), we should nevertheless try our best to explain our approach, reflect upon what we are doing and emphasise an ethical approach to data collection and analysis; an attempt I make throughout this book.

3.8 Conclusion

Carrying out ethnographic research was most interesting and at the same time, most challenging. Whilst the open approach allows the researcher to wander off in any direction and discover the world of the local settings, it may sometimes seem easier to have the security of pre-defined research questions and hypotheses which one can prove or falsify. Ethnography is probably even more than any other method dependent on luck - luck to gain access to the site in question and luck to find 'interesting' things. It is the field which determines the scope and with this, in a way, also the significance of the findings.

Ethnography was chosen for this case as it suggested itself as the best method to get an in depth account of how a vendor of this size works internally and was also necessary to gain access in the first place. Whilst the approach, as well as the methods used, have their limitations, by following the idea of a triangular approach and providing details on the field, the settings and my personal background, I hope to have minimised the possible pitfalls and countered the most common criticisms of ethnographic research.

In the following two chapters, I present the ethnographic data collected via documentation, interviews and participant observation. Both chapters aim to present the rich detailed pictures only ethnographic research can offer. Whilst the subsequent Chapter 4 also includes an analytical part, Chapter 5 focuses on ethnographic data only. The analysis of Chapter 5, as well as the analysis of the connection between the support department (Chapter 4) and the developer department (Chapter 5) is the subject of investigation in Chapter 6.

4 ERP System Support

4.1 Introduction

God became the ultimate support for all mankind only after he replicated [vendor's] customer support model.
(author unknown)

Today's business world cannot be imagined without computers. From the stock exchange to the day-to-day business in a bakery, computers appear to be everywhere. Within big corporations we find entire departments occupied with the procurement of the latest technology, others with their implementation, and others with supporting their day-to-day operation, making sure that the applications function smoothly without interrupting the business. Interruption of these systems and thus the business can be expensive and in some cases, disastrous. Whilst Hollywood films continuously introduce us to exaggerated disaster scenarios caused by computer failure, reality is less dramatic. Nevertheless, technology dependent industries, in particular, are terrified of encountering a major system failure. If, for instance, a bank encounters a major error in their systems which cannot be fixed immediately (or the functionality can be taken over by another system) credit cards will not work, cash points will go offline, online trading systems are 'temporarily unavailable' and teller transactions are temporarily suspended, with no cash leaving or entering the financial institutions. To avoid these types of scenarios, organisations which are highly dependent on their computer systems have, despite having various and extensive security mechanisms and backup systems in place, service contracts, guaranteeing 24/7 attention from their major software providers.

This short excursion shows the often crucial role both in-house, as well as third party support play. Interestingly, if we turn to academic literature, we find that support work has received relatively little attention, compared, for example to system development and implementation. Whilst we can find some accounts of in-house support teams, almost nothing is known about the in-house support of complex technologies, such as ERP systems. Gable et al. (2001), Nah et al. (2001) and Light (2001) pioneering the field, appear to be the only authors recognising ERP system support as a valid research field[34]. Whilst these accounts are very valuable and provide us with a first impression of the topic, the authors focus exclusively on ERP in-house (at the user organisations site) support activities – a focus which reflects the general obsession in the field with looking at ERP systems from a user organisation's viewpoint. As yet, we know little about how big corporations like SAP or Oracle are organised internally, how they manage to provide support for thousands of users around the world and around the clock and with this manage the user-vendor relationship at this stage of the product life-cycle. For instance, what happens, when an organisation raises a problem with their system provider? What are the processes taking place within the software providing organisations? How do standard software vendors deal with the challenge of offering support to a highly diverse, geographically dispersed user base, running customised and often modified versions of the vendor's system?

To address these questions, this chapter is divided into two parts. In the first part I describe with ethnographic detail the course of events taking place when a problem is reported by a user until the issue is solved. In doing so, I address (1) how a message comes to life[35], (2) how the problem is redistributed in search of expertise, (3) the attempts to solve problems once expertise is found, (4) how the technical support organises its day-to-day work around user problems, and (5) the power of user feedback. Throughout these different stages, formal as well as informal practices are taken into account.

The second part of this chapter is dedicated to a detailed analytic discussion, based on a prior ethnographic account. In particular, I address (1) the mechanisms of dis-embedding and distributing problems, (2) the mechanisms of, at times, re-embedding problems and (3) the power of formal informal problem priorities.

---

34 The work of Pollock, Grimm and Williams (2008) has not been included in this argument, as it is partially based on research carried out for this project. It should be noted however, that it is the first published account on software package support showing practices within the vendor's software labs.

35 The description of the user site in this section is based on my own prior experience (working for two and a half years as a consultant) of raising support messages through the support portal. These experiences have been verified during this writing up period by logging onto the support system to investigate potential changes within the portal. Apart from the fact that the web based portal is now the only way technical support can be addressed (before, one could also raise messages directly within the vendor's ERP system), in terms of the message creation process, nothing noticeable appears to have changed.

4.2 The Birth of a Support Message: The User's Site

> We are unable to SSL-enable the web interaction centre. We need instructions as to how to do this. Parameters are in the profile to enable WAS and we have run the ping command successfully over HTTPS [HyperText Transfer Protocol Secure]. We have modified the error page to redirect to the following standard URL:/[vendor]/public/bsp/[vendor](...) which causes CRM_IC to go in as HTTPS. Whenever we try to execute CRM_IC transaction from the GUI [Grapical User Interface], we get the logon page in HTTPS, however when we log in, we get redirected to HTTP. Cheers. Duncan
> --
> ---
> Business Impact
> 30.10.2005 10:14:06 Duncan
> Endangering go-live of [vendor] driven project

It is the constant receiving of problem reports, such as the above, which frame the day-to-day work of the support staff at the vendor's site. If we just look at the message without any technical or organisational knowledge, there is much insight. For instance, the way the message is written is rather informal which points to the absence of any pre-defined texts in this context. Furthermore, formal greetings or introductions are missing. The message is also very technical, addressed to an audience familiar with this particular area and system functionality. There is also an urgency to it, which is stated in the signature within the message. There is a 'business impact', endangering the 'go-live' of a vendor driven project. Whilst we can read many things into this message, most interesting are the things which cannot be concluded or understood by only reading and analysing a text. How does, for instance, the support team approach such a message? And, first of all, how is such a message created at the user's site?

4.2.1 Creating a Support Message

ERP systems are highly complex to implement and run. To support these complex systems, organisations usually have internal support departments looking after the system on a daily basis, as well as some kind of external support which is consulted should updates, upgrades and documentation be needed or 'unusual problems' occur. The vendor studied, offering such type of external support does so by means of an Internet-based support portal[36] where registered users can find a variety of information, as well as report a problem to the vendor's support team.

The user of the support portal and, with this, also the person reporting a problem are not, what is commonly understood as 'end-users'. A system end-user (for instance an Accountant or Sales Manager), doing his daily job using the ERP system, would not be able to understand the complexity of the system to report a problem to the vendor and be even less capable of implementing a suggested solution. It is only selected people who have access to the support portal, such as the internal ERP system support team or contracted consultants. If such a selected user decides to report a problem, in the particular case of the vendor studied, the portal guides the user through the system, starting by asking which system component the problem is related to. Having selected the corresponding functionality for reporting a problem, the user is re-directed to a webpage showing a search engine. The search engine is accompanied by a message inviting the user to fill in a search term associated with the problem he intends to report upon. For the user, hereby 'configured' by the technology[37], there is no possibility to avoid this step and without searching, create a support message. To be able to proceed to the next screen, at least one key word has to be entered. Once the search term is submitted, the search engine goes through documents describing known problems and their solutions. When the system has completed the search, the user is confronted with links to documents which might, from the vendor's (systems) viewpoint, help the user to solve the problem on his own. At this stage, the user can either ignore the results and proceed to 'message creation' or check the documents and rate them according to their usefulness. If the user decides to screen the documents and provide a rating regarding their usefulness, this information is later used by the support team to narrow down the problem (and helps to prevent them from suggesting solutions the user has already seen). In cases where a useful document is found, the solution can be implemented and, with this, the user would

[36] Until April, 2006, the support functionality was available directly through the vendor's application.

[37] See also Grint and Woolgar (1997) and their concept of 'configuring the user'. The authors state that "by setting parameters for the user's actions, the evolving machine effectively attempts to configure the user" (Grint and Woolgar 1997: 71).

leave the support portal, having found what he was looking for: a solution to a current problem.

If the user cannot find the solution to a problem, he can 'raise a message' and send it to the vendor's system support team. To do so, the user is offered a text field, in which he can describe the problem in his own words, without any kind of restrictions in the form of pre-defined texts. Besides describing the problem in this 'blank field', the user is asked to fill in certain contextual information such as the system component in which the problem occurs, the communication language, a subject heading for the problem and the priority with which the message should be treated. Further optional information can be given such as the description of how to re-produce the error, the contact medium (SMS or email) and attachments.

For the vendor, this kind of contextual information is most important as it allows the messages, arriving every day, to be sorted into different categories and problems to be re-distributed to the experts. Whilst all classifications are central to the vendor, from the researcher's perspective it is the message priority, which is most intriguing. Not only does this parameter provide some classification information, it also plays a major role in defining the user-vendor relationship at this stage of the product life cycle.

4.2.2 Setting Message Priorities

Message priorities are set by the users at the moment of message creation and indicate the urgency of the problem from a user's viewpoint. Within the support portal, the user can select from four different types of priorities provided by a 'drop down menu': low, medium, high and very high. It is these priorities which are linked to the service contract (commonly known as 'Service Level Agreement') and therefore have to be respected by the support staff. To help the user decide upon the priority and also, to limit the power of users who tend to overstate the importance of their problems, documents are published on the support portal explaining, in detail, which priority to choose under which circumstances. The following example (extracted from a document available from the portal) shows the definition of the priority status "very high":

> [The vendor] has defined the following priorities for problem messages:

1. Very high:
A message should be categorized with the priority "very high" if the problem has very serious consequences for normal business transactions and urgent work cannot be performed. This is generally caused by the following circumstances:

- Absolute loss of a system
- Malfunctions of central [vendor] system functions in the production system
- Delays to the planned production start-up or upgrade within the next 3 workdays

The message requires immediate processing because the malfunction can cause serious losses.

What the customer must do to ensure prompt processing of messages with priority "very high":

- The affected system should be open
- A contact person must be nominated for opening the system who must be available to provide the necessary logon data
- A contact person must be available to provide information on the problem
- The problem should be described in as much detail as possible:
- The message should contain instructions on how to simulate the problem
- If possible, the problem should be written in English. (Vendor Notes, Vendor Support Portal: November 2005)

Publishing documents explaining which message priority to choose under which circumstances, the vendor gives clear guidelines which preconditions have to be fulfilled for a message to deserve a particular status and the related attention. Interestingly, whilst outlining the relationship between the type of problem and the priority level, this type of documentation also highlights user's duties. In the case of 'high priority' problems, the user is, for instance, asked to provide a 24/7 contact. It is this reciprocal responsibility to which the vendor refers to in some cases, when the user is found not to show the necessary commitment to solve a problem, as I will demonstrate later on.

Once all the parameters are set and the problem is described, the user can send the message. For the user, a period of waiting starts, whilst for the vendor's support staff, the work is only just beginning.

4.3 Distributing Problems

The vendor runs multiple support centres around the world, which are internally organised in first, second and third level support. New messages are always taken on firstly by the *first level support*, also known as primary support. Being the first point of contact, the first level support is placed in different labs around the world and with this, across time zones, allowing the vendor to offer a 24/7 service: Wherever and whenever a user raises a message, it will be immediately taken on by a support employee who is awake and in work. In an interview, a manager, Jordi, explains the role of the first level support:

> The message is immediately taken, depending on the priority taken, by someone wherever they are in the world, whoever is awake in the primary support centres. A big one is in India, Dublin and Spain. We have one in Asia pacific, I think its in Japan, one in China, in Austria, in America... Anyway. They take the messages. They have some kind of expertise depending on the component the message is assigned to. It might be the case that the customer has not read the documentation properly. And they just give them assistance on that. And then the message is solved. If primary support can't handle the message, then they send it to the next level. (Jordi, Manager, Interview: November 2005)

Addressing the global distribution of the first level support, the manager explains its role. The first level support is said to have generic knowledge about the component and knows where to check the documentation, depending on the nature of the problem. If the primary support team is able to solve the problem, and the message has found its expert, the message will be closed by the user. Other levels of support, unless explicitly searching for the incident on the database, will never know about these problems.

Whilst the majority of messages are solved by the first level, in cases where their knowledge is not sufficient, the problem is passed on to the next level of support, the *second level support*. The second level is staffed by application experts, employees who have special knowledge for the particular part of the system the message has been assigned to. If the problem cannot be solved by the first or second level, once more, the message is forwarded. *The third level support*, also referred to as "development support", has expert knowledge about the particular application, is familiar with programming and knows about other applications which commonly interface with the vendor's system (and can therefore cause an error). Third level support teams are assigned to a more specific part of the application than other levels of support. For instance, the first level support might be responsible for the finance module and within this, for the accounting features. A third level support employee might, in turn, be assigned to the finance module, the accounting features and, within the accounting features, to the tax system. As such, within the application, the third level support has expert knowledge. At the same time, however, the third level support has to have a much broader idea about the entire application and other interfacing non-vendor systems than the first level support, to be able to understand complex problems.

When forwarding a message to another level of support, what one has to do is regulated beforehand. In the vendor's Intranet I found the following documentation on the topic of forwarding messages:

> The first processor in the Product Support chain checks if the content of message is understandable and if data is missing. Then the message is examined or the component is resigned.
> The customer message must contain the following information:
>
> - Name of the person reporting the customer message
> - Technical information on the problem context
> - Description of the problem
> - Priority
> - The reporting source of the customer message
> - Component where customer message occurs
>
> If problem description is incomplete, respective data is requested, for example by a standard checklists if available. (Vendor Intranet, December 2005)

Whilst these formal requirements are stated on the Intranet, in practice messages are forwarded to the next level without respecting the above protocol. Wondering why 'we' as third level support receive messages which do not include the above stated information, my colleague Sara explained:

> I'm not aware of any such rules. My understanding is that if they [primary support] find that it's a bug in the application, then they forward it to us. Otherwise, they process it. Of course, in case of [component], since primary support knowledge is limited, they might forward other kinds of messages to us. (Sara, Third Level Support Employee, Email: August 2006)

Within the labs, I have not heard any support employee referring to these regulations. It appeared to be 'common knowledge' when to forward a message: if one cannot find a solution (re-distribution of message to the next support level) or if the problem is related to expertise provided by another team, specialised in another component (re-distribution of message on the same support level). Whilst there were these informal and formal rules of when to re-distribute messages between the different support levels, there were other 'unofficial' reasons for which messages were redistributed between different expert teams within the same level of support (horizontal distribution): to avoid problems.

4.4 Avoiding Problems: The Game of Ping Pong

Support problems arriving at the third level support are often very complex. Alone, the allocation of the problem to the right system component can take days, because it is often unclear which part of the system the problem was actually caused by. Whilst the user provides some information about which component might have triggered the problem, some problems 'hide' and therefore the component a message is assigned to is not actually the part of the application causing the problem. It is this complexity, which, on the level of horizontal distribution of problems, in some cases, leads to so called "ping pong games". It is then, when problems are forwarded to another team of experts, to *avoid* a particular problem.

Such behaviour of actively avoiding problems can have several causes: The user organisation and the support employee might have a history, which is remembered by the support employee as particularly difficult; the problem might be so complex and 'look' troublesome, that the support employee does not want to take responsibility for it; the support employee is too busy (or too lazy) to look after the message; the message simply does not look interesting, but like a lot of work.

Whilst often discussed, such situations occurred rarely. In the labs I only once experienced such practice. In the case in question, it was actually Sara, my colleague, who was the 'victim'. One day, my colleague and I were working together on a message, when we received a very complex looking user problem. After many hours of investigation, the only solution we could think of was that the problem might be caused by another part of the application, the Java engine, of which we knew little about and also were not responsible. Our guess was that the Java engine running on the system was too old and incompatible with other parts of the application. As every step taken has to be documented within the message, we explained the status and results of our investigations, and suggested that on the basis of our findings the Java team should take over the message. We re-assigned the message in the system to the Java Team and with this, triggered an automatic re-distribution process of the message. Only seconds later, the message would be displayed in the inbox of the Java team (equally, third level support).

Having left the office for the day, the next working day started with a surprise: the message was sent back to us with a note from the other team that, from their point of view, the problem was not related to the Java machine, and therefore should remain with us. Convinced that this was not the case and assuming that the team actually did not spend any time having a closer look at the problem, we sent the message back and asked the team, once more, to please investigate more closely. Another day passed and eventually the message bounced back to us. By that time, the problem, which was prioritised as 'high' was already several days old and needed immediate attention. So as not to lose any more time by sending the message back and forth, we raised the incident with our manager who agreed that the problem was not on our side, but indeed most likely caused by the Java engine. Immediately, he addressed the issue with the manager of the Java Team. Simultaneously, we were asked to re-send the message. This time, the Java Team did not send the message back. If and when it was eventually solved we never knew and did not want to know. With the Java Team eventually accepting responsibility for the message, the problem left our circle of interest.

Whilst the incident described above was 'only' annoying and time consuming, the bouncing of messages can have a serious impact on the user-vendor relationship. The following narrative from an 'escalation manager' sharing her experience in the support newsletter (a monthly newsletter distributed by email to all support employees) highlights such a case:

> The customer message was initially forwarded to the wrong component and subsequently went back and forth between the customer and [vendor] support with no ownership taken for the message. Having received no information for a month, the customer requested to close the message as "it was taking so long that I might as well just live with the bug as [vendor] is obviously not concerned in fixing their own bugs". I picked up the message while monitoring messages for the specific market and contacted the customer directly. I listened to the customers frustrations, understood the situation and promised to take action. While the customer appreciated the efforts he advised - "you are flogging a dead horse". I took immediate action and forwarded the message to the responsible team, informing them about the customers negative experience. The message was subsequently resolved in less than a day. I received the following email statement from the customer: "I am very satisfied, I am even tempted to start using the customer message system again. (Vendor Newsletter, Email: January 2006)

In this case, it was the time loss through such behaviour which seemed to have caused the incident. Usually, if a support employee is assigned to a message he constantly updates the user on the state of the investigation. However, in the case reported within this best practice newsletter, nobody felt responsible and therefore the customer was not updated.

4.5 When Experts and Problems Meet

Whilst incidents such as the above occur, these are exceptions. In most cases, communication between the different levels of support appeared to be more professional in that employees took responsibility for whatever problems arrived, as long as they were related to their area of expertise. In the following, I now highlight the formal and informal working practices from the moment the problem and the expert meets, using the example of the third level support, the support level, in which I, as ethnographic research, was based. In particular, I will show (1) how the expert from third level support and the problems 'find' each other on a day-to-day basis, (2) what it means to solve a problem and, (3) which steps are taken to find solutions.

4.5.1 *Problems Arrive*

Every morning when the support employees come into work, they log into the system and open up a selection screen. The selection screen is in most cases set with default values indicating the system component which the support employee is responsible for. Moving on from this screen, the support employee sees a simple list of messages which the teams of the first, second and third level support, specialised in this component, are responsible for. The messages displayed have different statuses: 'new', 'in progress by user' or 'in progress by vendor'. Together with this information, the message subject, the name of the support employee responsible, the priority and whether it is an 'internal' message (raised by vendor's consultants or sales men) or an 'external message' (raised by the user organisation), the latter to be prioritised, is displayed.

Messages with the status "new" are usually only glanced at or are not considered at all. New messages are the responsibility of the first level support and not (yet) of interest to the third level support. Sometimes, however, in particular in cases where new messages have a high priority status, the third level support employee would quickly open the new message to see what kind of problem it was. High priority messages are often complex and critical for the user organisation's business and, hence, after initial checks, forwarded within hours to the next level of support. In the case of the team I worked in, there was no second level support and if messages were new and high priority, we knew that the chances were that these problems would be with us very soon. By briefly checking the problem description, the third level support employee can make a mental note and prepare for the possibility that there might be a high priority message arriving throughout the day. Interestingly, there was a kind of 'code of conduct' in place between the first level and the third level support in that the third level support would never solve or take responsibility for new messages, even in cases where the solution is known.

In one case, whilst sitting next to my colleague Sara, she commented on a newly arrived message. She said she knew exactly what the problem was and how it could be solved. She explained me, that there is documentation available where the customer can find coding which needs to be added to the system to solve the problem. I presumed that, knowing the solution, she would take over the message and answer the user directly. Instead, however, she moved on to the next message, commenting that new messages are the responsibility of the first level support. If we, as third level support, were to take over new messages and with this, interfere with the formal process, we would undermine the professionalism of the first level support. Only messages which are *forwarded* by the other levels of support are investigated by the third level support team. This was also the case for the message quoted in the introduction to this chapter: The first level support was not able to solve the problem and forwarded it to the third level (in this case, there was no second level support). The following quote documents this step.

> **Info for Customer**, 01.11.2005 08:40:06
> Dear Duncan,
> I forwarded your message to our development of [...] WebClient. One colleague from there will get in touch with you asap. Thanks for your understanding for this procedure. Kind Regards - THomas - Global Support
>
> **Internal Memo**, 01.11.2005 08:41:40
> Hi DS, [development support]
> Please read the issue on top !
> In the meantime the following notes are considered:
> #827958 JavaScript-Fehler in [...] WebClient
> #737824 Probleme beim Zugriff auf Web-Anwendung über HT
> #722908 Systemprüfung für [...] WebClient scheitert
> [...]
> I haven't no further hint for this case.
> Please take over for further help. Thanks and Regards – Thomas (Thomas, First Level Support Employee, Support Message: November 2005)

Whilst this message provides an example of day-to-day communication between the different support levels which appears to be both informal and friendly, the different types of information in this message are interesting: The first half is classified as *"info for customer"*, whilst the second half reads *"internal memo"*.

"Info for customer" is a message type which is visible to the customer and the support teams. Classified as 'info' the purpose of this kind of text is not to provide a solution, but to update the customer on the progress. The support employee from the first level support team also added a second note, classified as "internal memo". Whilst this information can be seen when opening up the message from within the labs, this information remains hidden to the user. Internal memos can be information required to be communicated, but not to be seen by the user such as, for instance, critical information about the component in question, a description of the current user vendor relationship, or as given above, simply the current state of investigation.

Even though internal memos are not sent to the user, at the vendor, the communicated 'Best Practice' is to put only information into internal memos which, if read by the customer, would not cause any harm. In the support newsletter the following article appeared:

> BEST PRACTICES: WHAT IF THE CUSTOMER READS MY INTERNAL MEMO...
> What the colleague wanted to do: Add an internal memo. What he/she did: Send an info to customer. Result: Big trouble BEST PRACTICE: Never put anything in the message - not even in an internal memo - that you don't want the customer to read. (Vendor Newsletter, Email: January 2006)

4.5.2 Solving Problems

Once the message arrives at a particular support level, the message is investigated. I now highlight what it means to 'have solved' a user problem as well as the different steps a third level support employee would take to solve a complex user problems.

When is a Problem Solved?

Interestingly, solving problems does not necessarily mean to 'fix a problem'. A problem is also solved, when (1) the support could prove that the system works 'as designed' and therefore the user request is not, as such, a problem which can be or needs to be solved (2) the support could demonstrate that the problem is not caused by the vendor's application, but by an unauthorised modification of the system or by another application (3) when a workaround could be suggested, which would not solve the problem, but help the user to get what he is looking for. In each of these cases, the problem is considered as 'solved'.

In the following, an example of a case in which the system worked as designed (and thus there was no problem to be solved), but where, out of courtesy, a workaround was suggested. The problem the user addressed the support with was that a URL attachment in its own web-based support portal (run with the vendor's software) was not accepted by the system.

> Hello Thomas,
>
> In [vendor application], attachments in Solutions and Service Requests are handled in a completely different way. While investigating the issue, we saw that the code for attachments in requests only handled files, not URLs. That means that a change to open URL attachments in service requests would not be done so easily.
>
> If you absolutely need that feature, we suggest that you make your own modifications. If you don't want that, then you might want to create a customer development request.
>
> We could also suggest a workaround, meaning that you could put the URL inside a word document. The URL would be displayed as an active link. Furthermore, the word document would work properly as a service request attachment.
>
> Best Regards (First Level Support Employee, Support Message: November 2005)

Within the message, the support employee explains that the demanded functionality is not supported by the standard system and therefore, from the vendor's point of view, not a problem as such. However, he also indicates that investigations have been carried out to nevertheless help the user to find his own, individual solution to the problem. It was suggested, that if the user needed the functionality immediately, that he should either modify the system or open a customer development request. Whilst the first could potentially endanger the systems compatibility with future updates, if the user organisation were to opt for a customer development request, additional coding could be provided by the vendor enabling the requested feature. In my fieldwork notes I acknowledged this incident and made a note of what was explained to me regarding a "customer development request":

> Today I learnt what a customer development request means and also we suggested a work around. A customer development request is something the client has to pay for but it's supported and [vendor] will be responsible for the code. However it [customer development request] will not be updated just maintained in case it interferes with an update / service pack. If contracts are signed it's [the third level support] who has to do the development. (Fieldwork Notes, Week 7)

Whilst the type of solution is a different one, then in cases where there is a problem with the system (a system bug), the problem still has to be investigated. The process of investigating and solving the different types of problems, are highlighted in the following section.

How to Solve a Problem?

Most problems reaching the third level support are very complex and, other than the standard application documentation which has usually already been checked for hints by the first and second level support, there is no type of written account, helping the support at this level to investigate problems. It seemed to be mixture of experience, expertise, luck and good relationships with the developers (who programmed the application in the first place) which facilitated problem solving.

When approaching a problem, different employees appear to have different tactics. For instance, one colleague from another team would always call the user on the phone, not to discuss technical details, but to establish a relationship of trust. In my fieldwork notes I wrote:

> The way messages are handled depends a lot on the support person. [support employee] says he always calls the client first to establish a personal relationship. "its personal style" is what [support employee] says. (Fieldwork Notes, Week 13)

In contrast, our team almost never called the user (except in emergencies), partially because my colleague would consider it as a 'waste of time', partially, because it was difficult to get hold of the users, usually working in different time zones. Also, in some cases the user might have been called before and might not want to repeat what he has already communicated to other representatives of the vendor's organisation. The latter was particularly true for problems which have been 'ping-ponged' around before someone took on the responsibility. In such cases, the message creator might have been called several times already, as it is easier to ask than to read through many pages of comments (a message can be 10 pages long).

First of all, our team would typically read through the message and, if it was very long, summarise it on a piece of paper or by using a text editor. If there were no immediate solutions to suggest, we usually sent the message back to the user, requesting a remote connection to access the localised system. Accessing the user system remotely was essential for the work of the third level support. Whilst the user can attach screen shots and error descriptions to the message, in some cases it is necessary for the support employees to see the error for themselves, and place it in the technical context of the Information System environment at the user's site. Connecting remotely, the support employee investigates the setting of the systems, the error logs produced and the technical surroundings. In particular, the latter was seen as important as the vendor's system is embedded in a unique technical environment, which can strongly influence the systems behaviour.

On one occasion, for instance, I witnessed the finding of a solution to a very difficult problem which was caused by a lack of communication between various applications, related to the vendor's 'single-sign-on' mechanism. The idea behind the 'single-sign-on' mechanism is that the user has only to login once for an entire pool of different applications. The applications in the user defined pool were, in this case, from different system providers. Whilst standard interfaces between the different systems existed and should have allowed 'plug and play', the parameters sent between applications to allow a single-sign-on got constantly lost somewhere in between applications. As a result, the passwords were not transported and the user was asked to sign on for each application separately. Only remote investigation and debugging in the user's local environments could reveal the problem and show at which stage the parameters got lost.

The uniqueness of the user settings was also the reason why the support almost never connected to the standard applications. Naturally, within the labs, the support had access to any part of the vendor's application with any kind of special functionality. However, with each customer system having a uniquely customised system, running in a unique technical environment, interfacing with a variety of user specific applications, reproducing the error in the vendor's own standard system was seen as a rather fruitless exercise.

Whilst establishing a remote connection is crucial for the work of the third level support, it appears to be not always the easiest of steps for the user. The user is often confused and also experiences trouble running the vendor specific application to allow a secure remote connection. In some cases, if the user is in a different time zone and does not provide all the information necessary at once, setting up a remote connection can take several days.

In cases where even the remote connection does not reveal any clues as to how to solve the problem, in our team, the support employees would turn to the documentation – however, with little hope of finding a solution. The documentation was written to explain the application and to find easy problems. It has been already checked by the first and second level support. In desperation, old messages are also glanced at. Whilst there was more hope of finding clues in solved messages, spotting the right information in the vast amount of information was a question of luck. Prior messages are only classified according to their component, responsible support employee and message subject. Whilst it would be the latter which is of interest when searching for solutions, the subject lines are in most cases of no use. The subject is usually entered by the user who might not have English as a mother tongue and at the moment of message creation does not yet understand where the problem is coming from. Furthermore, a problem is often related to another issue or reveals other problems. Even though, in theory, the support employee and users are asked to open up new messages for each problem, in practice related problems are documented in the same message and are, therefore, not represented in the subject description. Following these actions, if there was still no solution found, the last resort was to ask the developers.

Asking the Developers for Help

The third level support teams are co-located with the developers, to facilitate fast information exchange between both groups. This information exchange was a regular practice both when the support staff encountered problems for which a solution was difficult to find, and also in cases where the developers were just curious about 'how the users were doing' and how they liked the programmes created by these developers. Almost every day, the support and developers exchanged news about their work. Whilst these day-to-day exchanges did not address particular user problems, they formed the basis of a relationship and created a level of trust in which the support would feel comfortable enough to ask the developers about cases where difficult problems were encountered.

I was introduced to the idea of consulting the developers after about four weeks in the labs, in the context of a very difficult problem. I was responsible for searching for the solution and despite screening documentation, old messages and establishing a remote connection, I had no idea where the root cause of the problem could be and what to do to solve the problem. I asked my colleague and, like me, she did not know where to look or what to look for. We were simply unable to identify the problem. The message was classified with high importance, and I thought that this would be the end. It was then that Sara suggested asking the developers. I was delighted that there was one more option we could try and wanted to walk straight over to one of the developers who I knew was one of the most knowledgeable people in the labs. Telling my colleague what I was about to do, she took my arm mumbling something about “No No. Not [developer name] yet” and moved towards a friend of hers, working in the developer team.

Over time, I learnt that there was a clear hierarchy of whom to address with which kind of problem. First, there were the friends working in the developer teams. If the friends could not help, the person who once wrote this part of the application was identified and asked. Only if the problem could still not be solved, the ‘gurus’ (developers considered as undisputed experts amongst their peers) would be addressed. In the case described, we could not locate the problem, even after having spoken to one of the developers who might know. It was this developer who sent us to the ‘Guru’. With a feeling of reverence we addressed the expert who looked at our problem right away. After a short discussion, he gave us a few hints. Following up these suggestions, within a few hours we had the problem located and a solution to suggest to the user organisation.

Overall, I was pleased that we finally managed to solve the problem. At the same time, I was very surprised by this ‘helping culture’. In an interview with the support manager, I expressed my astonishment. Jordi, the support manager commented:

> Jordi: You have to be very strategic, have very good relationships all the time with all your developers, colleagues in primary support, solution support and Solution Manager. (...)
>
> CG: It's amazing, the people help each other, like [developer]. You just go there and ask if you have a problem.
>
> Jordi: That's very good here but we have other locations where the developers sit somewhere else. But then you send an email or ... - everyone is helpful here. And I tell you why: Cause you never know when you need the others.
>
> CG: I guess it depends also on the type of management. If it's team rewards...
>
> Jordi: Exactly. I have had already the issue where someone said: It's not my responsibility, why do I have to help this person. Then I say: you know what, that's not the other person's responsibility either. We work at [vendor] and its [vendor]'s responsibility. So, if you can help please help. (Jordi, Third Level Support Manager, Interview: November 2005)

As this quote also shows, in the labs there seemed to be an atmosphere reflecting some kind of pride in belonging to this corporation - a communitarian spirit which I did not expect, given the size of the vendor and also the common portrayals of software programmers as individualistic workers with limited social interaction. Whilst this communal working practice was of great help to the support, at the same time, it was very useful and educational for the developers: For the developers, communicating with the support was the most direct way to see what the problems were at the user site, which kind of functionality they were looking for and how they felt, overall, about the application the developers created.

4.6 Whose Fault Is It Anyway (and Who Pays For It)?

Generally, depending on the type of error, the responsibility to correct the problem lays either with the user or the vendor site. As such, problems can be classified in four categories: (1) The problem reported is caused by the vendor's software and therefore it is the vendor's responsibility (2) the user bought a product which, from his perspective, is faulty, whilst from the vendor's perspective it works as designed. Problems falling into this category are the users' responsibility (3) the error reported is caused by a modification of the system. Modifications of the system are not covered by the Service Level Agreement and hence are the users' responsibility (4) the error is caused by incorrect customising. The latter type of error are the most common types and looked after by the vendor's support team.

Whilst the responsibilities can be clearly identified in theory, in practice there are grey areas. One of these grey areas which revealed itself in the field was the difficulty to distinguish between what the vendor classed as *customisation* errors and *modification* errors. Systems such as the vendor's products are customisable to a high degree to allow the user organisation to adapt the system to its local settings. *Customising* can be carried out within the system by setting different parameters in the complex and powerful customising tool or by adding additional programs which access the system through pre-defined and vendor approved access points (so called "User Exits"). Whilst these types of localisation tools are designed in a way that the integrity of the system is not compromised (and updates can still be run), for the user organisation these customising features are sometimes not enough. Often, the user organisation aims for a closer fit between the standard system and its organisation, which might make modifications necessary. In such situations, the user organisation might edit and change the vendor's code or add programs where pre-approved interfaces (User Exits) are not provided. In these cases, where the system is *modified* and, as such, differ from the standard version, under the Warranty Agreement, the user organisation becomes self-responsible for the application. In my fieldwork diary I noted what my colleague explained to me:

> If the customer problem is caused by modifications to the customer system that were not initiated by [vendor], then this is not a maintenance case. (Fieldwork Notes, Week 14)

One of the support employees educated the user who sent a request for help with a problem caused by modifications made in the system more formally:

> Unfortunately, the error you describe cannot be resolved by our complimentary Customer Support, since the cause of the error lies in a modification of the [vendor] standard system or in a customer development.

> If you like, you may take advantage of our remote consulting services. Should you wish to do so, please amend your message to this effect and send it back to [vendor]. (Sara, Third Level Support Employee, Customer Message: December 2005)

Whilst both sides are aware that the responsibility for problems occurring in modified systems lies with the user organisation, there were cases in which users attempted to shift the responsibility for the problem in the direction of the vendor. In one particular case for instance, for several days, my colleague and I investigated a problem which we could not reproduce in the user organisation's standard system (user organisations who modified their system were asked to run two systems, the modified and the standard version, in the same environment) and therefore not advise upon. The problem we investigated was lengthy in nature: customers logged in on the Internet portal, but would not be automatically logged out after 12 hours. We set up example cases in the evenings, checking them in the morning. In all cases, the users were automatically logged out and with this, the system worked as designed from our perspective. We updated the user regularly, indicating that we could not see the problem. The user insisted that there was a problem and that it occurred irregularly, which would be why we could not re-produce it. 'Irregular problems' were not uncommon and as an intern, it became my task to monitor this case and to see if there would be an irregular case in which the users would not be logged out from the system. However, even after watching the system for a week, the situation remained the same: the log out functionality did not fail once. On several occasions, we asked the user if this is a problem which definitely occurs in the standard system (the system we tested on) and not in its own modified version. The user never answered this explicit question and we assumed that this was the case. Otherwise, the user would not have been entitled to raise a message, a fact which was clear to all users.

With time passing by, the user got more impatient and threatened to raise the message to the highest priority. This was the time when we really started to worry. Further investigation, however, still did not show any problems in the system and we finally decided to produce a final statement in which we explained that we could not re-produce the problem despite extensive testing and therefore assumed that, at that moment, there was nothing wrong with the system. It was only then, that the user changed his tone in the message. With sudden and unexpected friendliness, the user stated that it might be after all, that it is a problem which only occurred in their modified system.

Whilst I felt rather angry, since to me it was obvious, that the user acted on purpose, hoping that we would find a solution to his home made problem, my colleague advised me that even though this is not the best behaviour, they are still our customers and we have to be friendly. In a very polite way, she answered the message herself. Being in a particularly good mood, and also wanting to show the 'unprofessional customer' how things are done professionally, she outlined some ideas of how to solve the problem in their modified system and concludes:

> (...) I gave you a few hints above. However, I would like to point out that I can only give support for the standard version. [Customer] is responsible for it's own customized version. Therefore, if the standard version is working, then I cannot offer support for [Customer]'s version because it shows that the problem is not coming from our side. (Sara, Third Level Support Employee, Customer Message: December 2005)

Whilst my colleague's answer was friendly, from this day on, anytime a problem was raised by this customer, we would immediately ask for a remote connection to re-produce the problem to assess if there really was a problem in the standard system. Trust was betrayed and we remembered.

To summarise, connecting remotely to the user organisation's system is very important for the support work. It not only helps to investigate problems in detail in their 'natural' and specific environment, but also to (re)-establish boundaries of responsibility.

In the above section, I have highlighted what happens when the expert and the problem meet, which steps are taken to find a solution and how responsibilities between users and support can be clarified. In the following section, I address the scheduling of workflow: the order in which the problems are dealt with and, in this way, highlight the importance of message priorities.

4.7 Which Problems Should Be Solved First?

Every morning when entering the system, the support can select, according to their own parameters, the messages their team is responsible for. Every morning, the support employee decides autonomously which message to take care of first and how to organise the day. Whilst the order is decided upon in the morning, this initial planning of the working day is usually adapted during the day, depending on the arrival of new messages or a change of message priority by the user. The main criterion determining which message is to be solved first is the formal message priority, which can vary between low, middle, high, very high and escalation. Whilst the user can select the "low", "middle", "high" or "very high" priorities from a drop-down menu within the portal, to raise an escalation, the highest level of message priority, the user is asked to make a phone call. Escalations are the exception in that they do not happen very often, but are to be looked at first, followed by the other categories from very high to low. Whilst it is these formal criteria which frame the relationship with the user and formally determine the sequence in which messages are dealt with, within this formal space, the support employees follow their own criteria. For instance, a support employee faces several messages having the same priority. In this case, things like whether a user is liked or not can make a difference. The user might have been impolite in the past and hence the support does not feel drawn to the message. Also, the problem might not be 'interesting' or might 'look like a lot of work'. In these cases other problems might be dealt with first. In the following, starting with an escalation incident, I highlight the formal and informal prioritisation of work through which a conscious and unconscious battle for power between the support and the user reveals itself.

4.7.1 Message Priorities: When Problems Escalate

Whilst happening rarely, escalations are usually directly or indirectly 'pre-announced' and emerge out of existing problems which, from the user's point of view, have not been solved or responded to adequately. This was also the case in the message from Duncan, the message with which I introduced this chapter. In a follow up phone call, Duncan announced that he would escalate 'internally' (at the user's site) what would clearly lead, sooner or later, to an escalation with the vendor. Aware of the dangerous situation, a support employee informs his colleagues in an internal memo:

> Internal Memo
> 01.11.2005 12:09:12
> please note that the customers has already upgraded to the latest kernel release and are still experiencing errors. The customer is now escalating this to the highest level internally so therefore a speedy resolution would be highly appreciated. (Support Employee, Customer Message: November 2005)

Even though the customer escalated the issue only internally, at the vendor site, this internal escalation was treated as a customer escalation and triggered a, to my mind surprisingly, organised process. Formally, the following actions are initiated when an escalation is called in: the person who received the escalation information contacts their manager and the support teams affected. A so-called 'judging team' is created: a type of task force, to investigate the issue and, first of all, to determine whether the call for escalation is accepted. The grounds on which an escalation is justified are outlined in a document available to the user on the support portal and reads:

> A [escalation is a] major situation that causes a substantial negative business impact for the customer or [vendor]. A customer project must be escalated if the customer's [vendor] based solution has or will have:
>
> - System standstill
> - Server performance issues
> - Functional gaps
> - Implementation issues
> - Operational issues
> - Public relation issues
> - Legal or compensation issues" (internal documentation)
>
> (Vendor Support Portal, January 2006)

It is these conditions upon which the judging team will decide whether to accept an escalation or not. Whilst none of the support employees I questioned recalled a case in which an escalation was not accepted, the vendor maintains the right to reject an escalation to avoid users overemphasising their problems. As well as identifying whether the customer has a good reason for an escalation or not, the judging team also determines, based on the context, whether it is a *'message escalation'* or a *'customer escalation'*.

A *message escalation* is an escalation relating to a single message, which is critically influencing the customer's business or has been considered for any other reason as unacceptable by the vendor. In comparison, a *customer escalation* means that the customer – vendor relationship is in a critical stage in that the customer is not at all satisfied with the vendor's products and services. Hence, customer escalations are more critical than message escalations as the general satisfaction of the customer and the project's continuation is at stake.

Whilst there are two types of escalations, customer and message escalations, the reasons for escalations can be multiple. Jordi, the support manager explains:

> We have escalations cause of business reasons. Like they can work business wise. So their productivity is in danger. The other escalation is if they are going life very soon and they still have bugs or problems. (...) Sometimes the problems, when they escalate are more related to the fact of not using the software the way it was designed. They want to have a specific scenario that we don't support or we were not aware of. And we still have to support it and we do so really really fast. And there are other types of escalation I am not aware of now, I am not sure of. (Jordi, Third Level Support Manager, Interview: November 2005)

As we can see from this quote, there is a surprising variety of reasons why escalations are raised. Escalations can be related to technical problems, but not necessarily so. Interestingly, the support manager explains that in some cases the user buys the system and expects certain functionality for which the system has not been designed. Expressing his dissatisfaction, the user might raise an escalation. However, even though such a case would not really be the vendor's responsibility, the support would still do its best to satisfy the user and, in this way, plays a major role in maintaining and repairing the general user-vendor relationship, and with this protecting future sales.

The Escalation Is Accepted

Once the vendor accepts the escalation, depending on the type of escalation, different steps are taken. In the case of a message escalation, a process monitoring team is established to ensure the problem is solved as soon as possible. If a customer escalation is called out, the vendor appoints an 'Escalation Manager' who acts as a single point of access for the customer and support team. The Escalation Manager is someone who is familiar with the industry / the user, and works close to the user's company. Jordi, the support manager explains:

> If it is a formal escalation it is taken care of by an Escalation Manager. The Escalation Manager will be close by the location where the customer is. If the customer is in the US east coast, we have an escalation manager for him. The Escalation Manager is then going to check why they are escalating. (...) What that [escalation] means is, that we pay special attention to this specific customer. We don't work on anything else. (...) It doesn't necessarily mean that we have to be there at 3 in the morning. I haven't done it in 4.5 years. But it could happen that they say, sorry you have to work until it's solved. (Jordi, Installation and Maintenance Support Manager, Interview: November 2005)

If we follow the more complex process of customer escalations, the moment the Escalation Manager takes over, he informs everyone involved to gather additional information. Emails are sent round and phone calls are made to ensure the Escalation Manager is up-to-date and familiar with the situation. Once the Escalation Manager knows exactly what has happened, he develops, with the help of the different teams involved, a de-escalation plan.

In the case of the message which follows and which turned out to be a customer escalation, a 'priority one co-ordinator' (also called Escalation Manager) called the user only 20 minutes after the initial internal memo in which the internal escalation at the user's site was announced. Leaving a summary of the call in the message, the priority one co-ordinator states:

> Call to Customer
> 01.11.2005 12:26:28
> Called Duncan [last name] on [phone number]. They are unable to save info on the CRM system which went live yesterday the 31st October. Customer needs to get this solved asap although they are willing to wait for the development team tomorrow morning CET. Please call Duncan on [customer phone number] mobile for an assistance.

Priority 1 Coordinator (Support Employee, Customer Message: November 2005)

With this message, the priority one co-ordinator informs everyone about the current status. Behind the scenes, a de-escalation plan is designed identifying the problem as well as the expertise necessary to solve the issue. Throughout the process, the Escalation Manager is the main point of access for the customer and the support. All information has to be sent to the Escalation Manager.

As can be seen in the following comment, eventually, part of the initial problem was solved; however at the same time, a new, hidden problem emerged. Explaining the situation to the user, the support employee writes one day later:

> Reply
> 02.11.2005 08:12:28
> Hello, what we've done so far is that the customizing for HTTPS usage is properly defined. The table CRM [...] must contain an entry for the current client, the default contact center id [vendor] and a reference to a rfc destination of type 'H' under SESSION_DESTINATION. From customizing of application this seems ok. What fails now is the creation of the second HTTPS session using the [...]59 destination. Here we should redirect to the basis department. If you would be so kind to supply the necessary [...] trace entries we could follow up.
>
> Best Regards,
> Tobias (Support Employee, Customer Message: November 2005)

The quote shows how further steps are initiated. The support employee suggests forwarding the message to the Basis Team, the team supporting the basis functionality of the vendor's system. Following the best practice suggestion, when forwarding a message, the support employee adds an internal memo for his colleagues, describing the problem in more detail:

> Internal Memo
> 03.11.2005 09:52:40 Tobias
> Hello Viv,

> can you remember your baby [..]WC? We're in trouble with HTTPS support. Now the customer has reached the following state: The customization of [...] Webclient is now correct. The RFC destination VISAGE_SSL exists and is functioning correctly. The application comes up with 2 HTTPS sessions. So application startup works from our side...
>
> But now alerting throws errors. Could you please check what is going wrong here? Or forward appropriately? Thanks!
> Logon data is: [...]
>
> Best Regards,
> Tobias (Support Employee, Customer Message: November 2005)

Once again, the message is in search of expertise. The support employee asks his colleague to either solve the problem or forward 'appropriately'. Keeping its high priority status, many more comments in the message show how the complexity of the problem unfolds further, with other errors in different parts of the application revealing themselves. The message was forwarded several times with different expert teams addressing the various issues. Still, all actions were co-ordinated by the Priority One Co-ordinator. Despite joint efforts, however, the vendor did not succeed in solving the problem in time or provide a workaround and the customer, eventually, had to 'back out' of some of the features of the new system, which were causing the error. With the move to prior technology, the problem did not endanger the customer's business anymore. An internal memo states that the support should, however, continue working on the problem:

> Internal Memo
> 04.11.2005 03:30:07
>
> Hi Guys,
> [user organisation] have decided to go back to http for production because the system has become unusable. HTTPS is now enabled in [test] environment. Please continue analysis however use [user system] instead of [user system]. Userid's and passwords are the same.
>
> Regards (Support Employee, Customer Message: November 2005)

This move back to previous technology was seen by the support team as a reason to ask the user to lower the priority. Hence the support employee suggested:

> Reply
> 04.11.2005 08:10:22 Tobias
> Hello, because productive use now seems to be on http, we would like to reduce
> the issue's priority. Please see attached note. (Support Employee, Customer Message: November 2005)

As the implementation at this particular site continues, more problems were identified, which were all logged in the support message, which was already several pages long. Having been lowered from escalation status to 'very high', it soon reached escalation status again. The technical problems affected the user site to such a degree that the entire project was now endangered.

> Internal Memo
> 17.11.2005 09:55:57 Antoinette
> Mail from Tom [customer].
> The issue remains for the customer after applying the recommended notes. Now critical to the success of their CRM project which went live 31.10.05
> Mail to SPM->Request for processor. (Support Employee, Customer Message: November 2005)

For another month, problems continued to emerge and negotiations were taking place. The last comment in the message shows that several months later, the customer still encountered critical problems implementing the vendor's system.

> Call from Customer
> 06.12.2005 09:04:05
> Contact person: Duncan
> Reason for call: Request to speed up processing
> Subject of conversation: The customer requested to speed up the processing. Within the [user organisation] the customer is not able to process inqueries from [user clients]. (...) It is creating a serious backlog and there is no workaround on this issue.

> Could you please provide the customer with some feedback as soon as possible?
>
> ph. [phone number]
>
> Best Regards (Support Employee, Customer Message: November 2005)

It was then, when, after many pages of different error descriptions and suggested solutions, the support staff suggested opening up a new message to deal with the new problem. The support policy states that a new message can be opened if new problems arise. Even though, this would allow to better use solved problems as point of reference, in practice, this was rarely done. Whilst one of the reasons might be that the support and user simply forget to follow this formal guideline, another might be that in many cases problems are still related, even though one might not have thought so beforehand. Separating problems would therefore only disturb and delude the issues and with this, slow down the solution process.

For all involved, escalations – even if solved in the end – are very stressful and also very expensive. For the vendor organisation an escalation means not only potentially losing a customer and being made liable for compensation payments based on the service contract, but also requires high labour costs, as all forces concentrate on the one incident. For the support employee, escalations are something everyone wants to avoid. In the case of an escalation the support employee is in the spotlight and his present and prior performance monitored by the Board of Directors, which is generally involved in escalations.

Whilst introducing us to a most surprisingly organised process, the escalation process also demonstrates the power the user is given through the prioritisation of their problems. Whilst in the case of an escalation, there is little room for the support to redress the, at this stage, 'unbalanced' power relationship, in the day-to-day lives of support employees informal practices are commonly used to 'balance' power. From what I experienced, heard and saw, two forms of 'power balancing' were exercised by the third level support employees: (1) the practice of negotiating space and (2) the application of informal criteria, which also influenced the 'type' of help provided to the user.

4.7.2 *Negotiating Space*

As shown in the previous passages, the support employees' day-to-day work is governed by the message priorities. However, in some cases it is difficult for the support employee to comply with the rules and answer all messages within their formally defined time frame (through the message priorities). For instance, the support employee might face an overload of high priority messages, or a local holiday interferes with usual working hours. Not being allowed to change the priority of the message, the only option remaining for the third level experts is to ask the user for more time[38]. The following message indicates the problem of time zones (as well as presenting us with another example of the importance of priorities and mutual responsibility if high priority messages are raised). Again, this message is related to the introduction quotation of this chapter. The answer below shows the first reply to the initial customer request, coming from the first level support only 13 minutes after the message was sent:

> Business Impact
> 30.10.2005 10:14:06
> Endangering go-live of
>
> --
>
> Reply
> 30.10.2005 10:27:35 Jeffrey
> Hi Duncan,
>
> Thanks for the info...You have logged this msg in Priority "Very High".. Please be aware of the Priority & its restrictions re Note [...] You say in the msg that this is affecting the "go live" of the project.. Can you please tell me when this is..? Also, please provide a 24hr contact number & open all relevant conections re note 67739.... Also, please provide me with the steps needed to recreate the issue.. Please also be aware that im not an expert in the issue & have limited knowledge in this area...in saying this i will try resolve the issue..

---

38 In the case of the first level support, this is less of an issue. First level support teams usually have a 'double' in another time zone, in another country, who can pick up messages requiring particular expertise (thus the vendor can offer 24/7 support). The experts working in the third level support, however, rarely have a double within the organisation. Hence time zone constraints and local holidays play a much bigger role.

However, we may need to eventually pass this msg to development support [= Third Level Support] they are currently out of the office until 6am CET tomorrow. Please be aware that you may have to wait until then for expert help...

Please open all relevant connections.....

Rgds
Jeff (Support Employee, Customer Message: October 2005)

Whilst I have already shown how this message developed further, only two days after raising the message, negotiations related to the priority of the message took place (ironically, this request was sent only six hours before the customer called out the escalation reported upon earlier):

Reply
01.11.2005 06:39:16 Thomas
Hello Duncan,
Thanks for your efforts ! Could you pl. checks following notes for service (...)

However, today is holiday in [country] and I would ask you,
if these problem still [exist] until it can be postponed tomorrow
to set the priority onto "HIGH" !?

Kind Regards.
Thomas (Support Employee, Customer Message: November 2005)

Two weeks later (after the escalation) the customer was called, but could not be reached. It was then, when the support staff found the user guilty of not fulfilling his side of the contract, and therefore lowered the priority.

Call to Customer
15.11.2005 11:09:36 Maren
Duncan is gone for the day. not reachable

Reply
15.11.2005 11:22:52 Maren

> [...] I will lower the priority. As described in note [number] a contact person needs to be available 24h. (Support Employee, Customer Message: November 2005)

These cases of re-negotiating priority levels demonstrate, once more, the dominant role of priority levels in the context of ERP package support at the vendor. In the case presented, there was a total of six times where the priority level became the subject of discussion. Three of these incidents have been extracted and quoted above. The first incident, quoted above, shows us how the support employee attempts to educate the user about the circumstances and responsibilities related to a message sent with the priority 'very high', whilst in the second incident the support employee asks to lower the priority. If the customer insists on a very high priority, the support employee would not be able to take the public holiday. Whilst in the first case, an attempt was made to educate, the second case was rather like a begging. In the third case, it was the vendor who found the user guilty of not fulfilling his side of the contract (offering a 24/7 contact) and lowered the priority. It is only in circumstances, where the message creator clearly does not fulfil its duties that the support employee is allowed to change the priority levels set by the user.

Whilst the previous paragraphs highlighted the drama related to the arrival of very high priority messages and escalations, the majority of messages are assigned to a lower priority. It is in these contexts that the support employees are able to act upon their own discretion. Whilst priorities still determine the formal frame, within the set boundaries, the support can act autonomously - and does so.

4.7.3 Informal Priorities: The Support's Discretion

Most messages arriving at the third level support have a priority status of 'high'. In cases where there are several messages on the same priority level, it is factors such as, the prior relationship with the user, the mood the employee is in and the type of problem which determines which message is dealt with first. In the labs, several incidents of the support's discretion could be witnessed. For instance, in one case, my colleague commented, when opening a message:

> Ah.. that's [client]. They always put their messages on high importance on a Friday afternoon even though it's not. We can leave that till Monday. (Fieldwork Notes, Week 6)

In this example, the particular client was well known by the support employee from prior incidents (such as trying to impose errors on the support, when they occurred in the modified system and are therefore the user's responsibility). She explained that 'they', working in a different time zone, always have their team meetings on Friday afternoons after which they would always raise the high priority messages. From her perspective, this was highly unfriendly as having dealt with the user organisation on several occasions, she expected the user to know that she was working in a different time zone and would be about to leave the moment the high priority messages arrive[39]. To educate the user (in this case it was usually the same representatives raising the messages) and also demonstrate power, these messages would usually be left open until after the weekend.

In a similar manner, a customer who was well known for raising issues always at the last minute was treated indifferently. A request was ignored hoping that this would educate the user not do so again:

> She always comes last minute. Maybe we should teach her not to do so by not helping her this time (Fieldwork Notes, Week 6)

Other messages are replied to slowly as, in the past, the customer has always taken very long to reply, whilst prioritising his message. Hence, the support employee made an immediate judgement, when seeing messages from this particular user side, that the message will not be too urgent, despite the high priority status and comments:

> The Indians will take forever to respond anyway (Fieldwork Notes, Week 10)

In another case, a newly arrived message appeared to be very complicated. The support employee, having had a bad night's sleep the night before, commented that, today, she was not in the mood for such problems and we should move on to the next message and leave the new one until the next day.

---

39 This client was an exception in that messages were always directly sent to the third level support, rather than being dealt with by the first level of support. Remote connections were almost constantly kept open to facilitate the fast resolution of the many problems reported from this user site.

Whilst these types of discretion, for various reasons, were part of the day-to-day work organisation, in some cases, despite discretion being applied and priorities re-negotiated, there might still not be enough time to look after all messages. It is in these cases when 'accidents' are not unwelcome.

In one situation, my colleague and I were completely overwhelmed by the amount of messages on high, or very high priority, with one being on the edge of escalation. Whilst we were often working together on messages, this time I got sent to my desk with the task to carry out further investigations on one of the high priority messages. We did not yet know what the problem was so I decided to establish a remote connection to re-produce the error (a connection, which was opened only days before in relation to another problem on the same user side). Having established the connection successfully, I arrived at the user's site facing a login screen. I typed in the password. It was not accepted. I repeated this three times and with this, locked the account. It was my fault as I found out later, because I had confused the passwords given. The passwords I used were stated within the message which was already several pages long. Within this long message, the login data for the work station, the backend CRM system, the front end CRM system (web interface) and for the administration of the front end CRM system were spread out. Additionally, passwords changed over the course of the message and some of them were stored in a secure space attached to the message. As all other users always stated their login data within the message, I did not know about this secure space and hence did not check. My locking the terminal at the user site, caused a delay of several days. First, the customer was in India and as a result, in a completely opposite time zone. Second, the person to reset the password appeared to be out of the office the next day. Once provided with new passwords, I wanted to login again. This time however, the user had closed the connections. Remote connections are only open during a certain time window, specified by the user. Again, I could not login to test, and again, we needed to ask for the connection to be opened up. In my fieldwork notes I wrote:

> To finally be able to connect seems to take ages. You can see it also in the messages how often we try, how often it doesn't work until the connection is finally set up properly. (Fieldwork Notes, Week 4)

Whilst this was by accident, the incident was, from my perspective, not unwelcome. Even though unwanted, we gained time since statistically, only the time the message was at our site (and not the user's site), counted against us in regards to the Service Level Agreement. By the time the user had sent us all necessary data, we had other messages solved and time for his problems. Remembering my major mistake on another occasion where we, once again, had far too many messages to look after, my colleague asked me – jokingly – to try to login at a customer's site, but to lock the access by typing in a wrong password. That way we could send the message back to the customer and gain some time. Whilst of course this would be very unethical behaviour and most likely has never happened, I can only imagine that in a case of desperation, such action might at least cross my mind[40].

4.7.4 *New Tools to Frame the Relationship*

As I have highlighted above, when having a full Inbox, the support employee would look at the messages and work on them according to their formal and informal priorities. As I heard from my colleague, recently (2006), a new tool was implemented at the vendor site, automatically prioritising messages not only according to the formal priorities, but also according to criteria which are considered by the vendor as important, such as whether a user organisation is a 'reference site' or of any strategic importance. My colleague Sara described the tool in an email:

> For prioritizing messages, we're now using a new monitor that prioritizes the messages for us according to a number of factors (agreement with customers, time spent at [vendor], priority). This way, when you have a ton of messages, it's now much more easier to select which one to work on. (Sara, Third Level Support Employee, Email: August 2007)

Whilst my first thought was that this would take away the little freedom support workers have in organising their working days, this technical configuration seemed not to be perceived as dominating:

> I don't feel it takes freedom away from us. The messages are prioritized but we still pick the ones we want to work on. It's just that [vendor] prioritization method is clearly shown... I just use

40 I cannot speak for my colleague in this case. I can only describe how I felt as a support intern. I would rather risk looking stupid than having to state that I did not have enough time to look after the message.

> the tool. I just don't question their rules. (Sara, Third Level Support Employee, Email: August 2007)

The support employee does not seem to be intimidated by the new system, but considered it as a help, as an advisor to make decisions which are in harmony with the vendor's strategy. Therefore even though the vendor appears to frame the user-vendor relationship during the support phase even more, not being obligatory, the support's discretion is still exercised.

In the last few paragraphs, I outlined the space of the support employees which is defined by the boundaries set by formal prioritisation. Even though, having less impact than the formal prioritisation, which is linked to the service contract, informal prioritisation allows the support to act at their own discretion. In doing so, however, the support is constantly aware that despite being able to exercise power upon the user in some cases, it is the user who has the 'last word'. When messages are closed, the user is asked to give feedback and it is this feedback, which is included in and the basis for the yearly appraisal of each support employee.

4.8 User Discretion: Evaluating the Support

The support evaluation form presented to the user is designed as a short questionnaire, which pops up anytime a message is closed. Six questions are asked relating to the message processing time, the performance of the responsible employee, the satisfaction with the support and the vendor's product in general. The customer can rate every question with a maximum of ten points and also add some lengthy text, as the following customer did:

> I appreciate the great work [vendor] support representative performed. (...) I am completely happy with the answer I got, it is COMPLETE, I don't need to clarify again, I really appreciate this. (Customer Message, January: 2006)

The questionnaires are analysed automatically and added to the statistics. In the above case, the customer was really happy at getting a "COMPLETE" answer, which will certainly reflect back on the responsible support employee in a positive way. In other cases, however, the user was less satisfied and expressed his opinion in the feedback. What was written in the blank field was:

> It was taking so long that I might as well just live with the bug as [the vendor] is obviously not concerned in fixing their own bugs. (Customer Message, January: 2006)

In this case, as I have previously described, the response lead to an immediate action from an Escalation Manager who called the customer to repair the relationship. While the user was eventually calmed down and the problem solved, for the support employee this statement will not disappear, but crop up once more in the annual appraisal.

'Misbehaving' in an unfriendly manner towards the user, similarly led to a negative customer rating and eventually caught the attention of the Managers who published the following incident in the support newsletter as a negative example. The answer the support employee gave the user was the following:

> Hi, Next time it would be nice if you send me only one mail with the important information. I'm not inclined to single it out from the huge amount of mails. ... It is not our fault that you are behind schedule with your project. ... I won't be stressed because you waste your time. ... Be lucky that I help you nonetheless. (Customer Message, December: 2005)

Without the user's feedback, this incident would have most likely remained undetected, unless the user had given feedback on his own initiative.

Whilst in the cases presented, the User Evaluation Scheme appears to function as a quality assurance scheme, the existence of such practises does not always work in favour of all the parties involved and can actually lead to active avoidance of messages with 'dangerous potential'. Earlier, I explained ping-pong games, which was the passing of messages from one support employee to another, as a last chance to 'escape' the responsibility for a particular message. Because 'ping-ponging' a message takes time and the user might not be informed about the fact that at least some activity is taking place, the user can become particularly dissatisfied with the vendor's service, as every support employee knows. This, in turn, can lead to a further avoidance of the already delayed message with the support employee being afraid of receiving and later having to explain a negative user evaluation in his annual appraisal. The example below shows how the support employee fears the customer's feedback:

> When the message came to me, the customer was already very angry. What could I do to avoid a bad [evaluation system] result? The message was created on November 2nd. I took the message on December 16th, more than one month later. At that point, the message had been 42 days at [vendor] and 2 days at the customer's side. I picked up the message, called the customer and discussed about the solution and suggestions regarding this problem. The customer accepted my suggestion, but he raised one question: "As this message was processed by [vendor] for such a long time, I have decided to give a very low [rating]. Will the low [rating] affect your KPI [key performance indicator] rating?" At that time, I suddenly realized that it was very good that I had called the customer. I told customer: "Yes." The customer didn't give any comments and hang up the phone. Later I found that no rating had been given for this message. (Vendor Support Newsletter, Email: January 2006)

The support employee, in this case had the advantage of talking to a user who was aware that a negative rating may influence the support employee's key performance indicators and therefore decided to not give any rating. If the user had given a negative evaluation, the support employee would have had a chance to explain the situation in his yearly evaluation. However, for the employee, it is easier to avoid troublesome messages and keep forwarding them, rather than having to justify a bad rating.

4.9 Summary

The ethnographic account of the support work at this vendor site presented within this chapter provides, for the first time, insights on how an ERP vendor of this size approaches the challenge of managing its relationship with its user at this point of the product life cycle. I have shown the challenges associated with offering support for an often modified and customised product, to a highly diverse, wide and geographically dispersed user base.

In this chapter, I have outlined the different stages a problem can go through throughout its life time, and the impacts of these different stages on the support's day to day working life. It appears whilst the mechanisms to mobilise the problem and re-distribute it to wherever expertise is available facilitates this type of global online support in which both, problem and support expertise is globally dispersed, it is the message priorities, which determine the power relationship between both parties at this stage. The influence of problem priorities is particularly visible, where it is set to its highest priority, escalation. It is then, when the message priority not only influences the support's working schedule but exclusively 'rules' the support staff. No other problem is to be worked at, no other task to be completed, as long as a problem's priority is set to escalation.

Whilst some processes within this setting could have been uncovered through the means of reading the vendor's documentation on support processes, it is the dynamics as well as the formal and informal approaches to problem solving or problem redistribution (to avoid troublesome problems) unfolding in this ethnographical study, which provides a unique picture on the often tense power relationship between a global ERP provider and its local user organisation, on a day to day basis.

Within the first part of this chapter, I provided the first ethnographic narrative on ERP system support, drawing on data collected within one of the biggest ERP providers worldwide. In the following, I re-address and analyse the ethnographic findings, focusing (1) on the mechanisms of disembedding and distributing problems, (2) the mechanisms of, at times, re-embedding problems and, (3) the power or formal and informal problem priorities.

4.10 Analysing the Support

ERP system support is one of the phases which have been largely disregarded in academic literature. In particular, an ethnographic study of ERP system support from *within* an ERP system provider has not yet been carried out. Whilst this research provides the first ethnographic study providing such an account, investigating technical support as such is not a novelty (although a rarity). For instance, we find studies such as Julian Orr (1986, 1996, 1998), who offers a most detailed and interesting sociological account of technical support in the 1980s. Studying the formal and informal work practices within a copy machine vendor's support department (Xerox), Orr introduces us to a world in which it is the tight relationship between the user and the vendor, the understanding of the socio-technical context of the problem reported, which is crucial to problem solving[41]. Whilst there are parallels to the vendor's case, it cannot, however, be translated directly into the context of complex ERP system support or in more general terms, into today's world, in which the Internet and online services are dominating the support world. Today, with more and more technical products being made available, global, rather than local customer support has become the norm. If problems occur, most organisations prefer to be contacted online, whilst others do not even offer any other type of support. This does not mean that local support entirely disappears; technicians still come for on-site visits, if necessary. Only many parts of the support services have been moved to and incorporated in, the virtual world.

Already from Light (2001) and Nah et al (2001) we learn about this shift of support from local to virtual in the context of complex products, such as ERP systems. Rather than receiving an on-site visit from the system vendor organisation to fix a problem, the authors report on how the user is asked to open up a support ticket online and wait until the vendor replies - likewise online, providing a solution in the form of written guidelines. Somehow, providers of online support channels found a way to offer support to their customers without having to take into account the local, socio-technical context which appears to be important for problem solving to Orr's technicians, in the 1980s.

In the ethnographic account in the first half of this chapter, I have shown the day-to-day working practices of a support team, which is almost exclusively connected to the users via an Internet portal. However, to make problems mobile so that they can be transported into the virtual world and therein to the expert team, the problem has to be somehow detached from its local and social environment. In the following, I highlight from an analytical viewpoint, how the vendor attempts to translate problems into the virtual world and the challenges associated with this type of support practice.

---

41 For a full discussion on Orr's work, as well as on other work in the area of technical support, see Chapter 2.

4.10.1 Dis-embedding and Distributing Problems

The biggest challenges for organising global online support appear to be, firstly, the organisation of distributed and fragmented expertise held by hundreds of support employees; secondly, the necessity to make problems mobile in order to find and meet these distributed experts; and thirdly, to ensure that the 'right' problem meets the 'right' expert.

In the context of ERP products, the first challenge, the fragmentation and distribution of knowledge amongst a large group of individuals, appears to be unavoidable. ERP systems are simply too complex to be understood fully by a single person. At the same time, if expertise is distributed around the world and likewise the products, somehow either the expertise or the problem needs to be mobile. For globally sold products, making the expert mobile might result in, for instance, an expert flying from USA to Great Britain, to solve a problem. Whilst this is possible, it cannot be done for all problems (the vendor receives up to 100.000 problem reports each year). Hence, it is the problem, which has to become mobile, to travel around the world in order to find the expert. To do so, the problem would have to be detached from its local context. This, however, can be challenging as, amongst others, von Hippel (1994) points out. Von Hippel argues that it is difficult to detach information from its local context without falsifying it, in particular in the case of complex information. In this respect, he introduces the notion of 'stickiness' of information. In the case of ERP systems, we might say that we have complex information at hand which needs to be detached as ERP systems are very complex products, much more complex than most other types of available technology. The complexity of such systems is most vividly presented in the many studies involved with the moment of ERP system implementation. Whilst there are many issues which make the implementation phase difficult, only by considering the customising tools, can we see the complexity and wide range of possible errors, which can occur only in this context.

ERP systems can be customised at a very detailed level and in this regard, are designed to differ from implementation to implementation. The complexity is reflected in the amount of time it takes to implement and customise an ERP system. The implementation team, usually consultants, is often on site for a year or more and (considering only customising activities), choose from hundreds of parameters to tailor the system in the way that fits in best with the customer's organisation. The picture below shows an example of the two biggest ERP system providers' customising tools, SAP and Oracle. Similar interfaces can be found for other ERP systems.

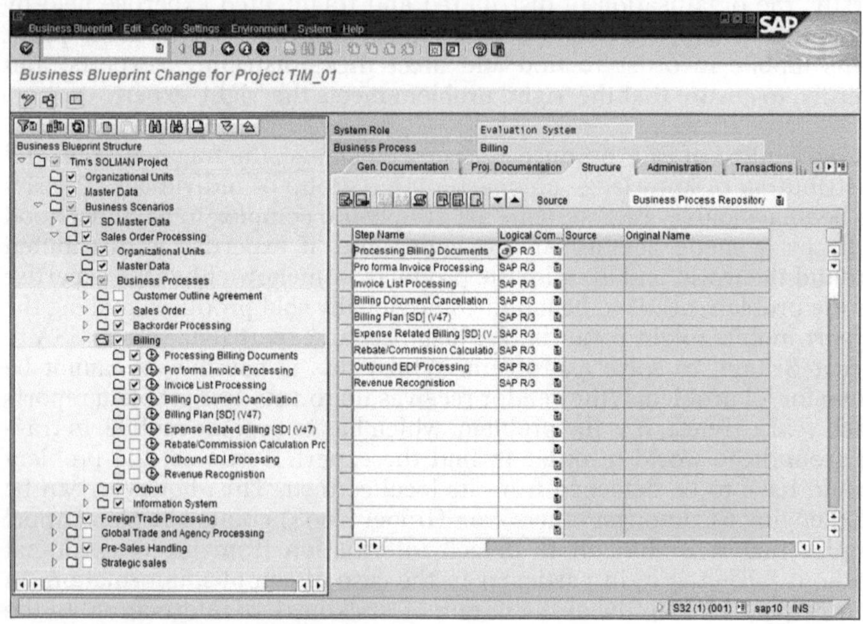

Figure 7: Example Customising SAP

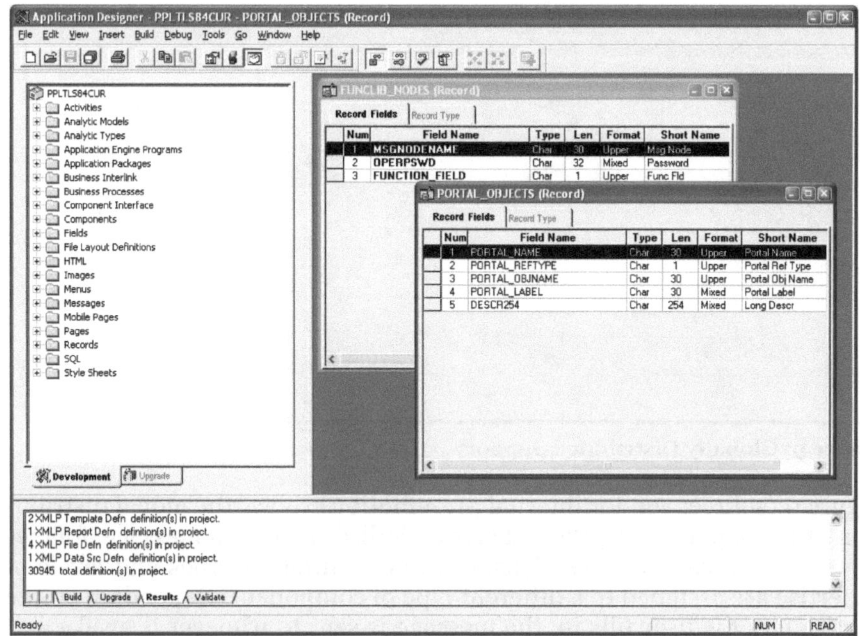

Figure 8: Example Customising Oracle

Taking the example of Figure 7 on the left side, we find the customising menu behind which hundreds of tables and parameters are stored. The right side of Figure 7 shows the details of the functionality selected on the left side. Different parameters are displayed on multiple table tabs (see the upper part of the figure). Given the complexity of information, if we look only at the system customising, it appears that detaching problems from their local context and making them, in von Hippel's (1994) words 'unsticky', is an impossible mission. However, as we learn from the ethnographic data, the vendor seems to have found mechanisms to detach problems despite their complexity and make problems 'mobile'.

The basis of this detaching mechanism to mobilise problems, seems to be the parameters users attach to each problem description, such as the system module, release, and technical environment. It is on the basis of these parameters that the support system detached the problem from the user in a way that it can be distributed automatically to the different support teams. The first level support teams, being the first people getting in touch with the detached user problem, are distributed around the world.

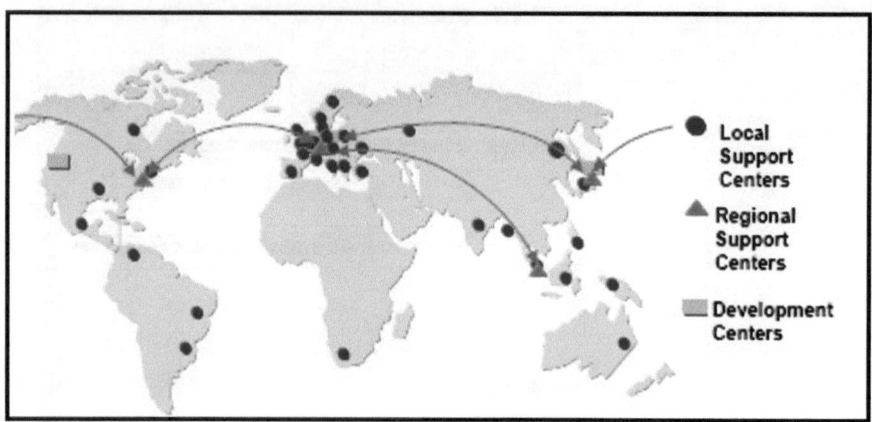

Figure 9: Globally Distributed Support

Figure 9 (source: vendor internal presentation) shows the global distribution of the support labs, the red arrows indicating how a message 'follows the sun'[42]. In each of these labs, experts of different types and levels of expertise are assigned to a different type of component. Depending on the parameters the user fills in, the message is sent to whoever is awake and at work, having the expertise which is needed for a problem with the given parameters.

Once the message reaches its first destination, as demonstrated in the ethnographic account, several things can happen. First, the message has been assigned to the right component and therefore found a first level support expert, who is able to solve the problem. Second, whilst the message might have found the right team, the first level support does not have the expertise to answer the user and, as a result, forwards the message to the second or third level support team. Third, there is the option that the user failed in assigning the problem to the right component which meant that the message has to be re-assigned to another team. Forth, whilst we have found informal practices such as ping-pong in the context of third level support, this is also most likely to be the case for other levels of support. Thus, as a fourth possibility, we might speculate that the first level support forwards the message to another team (on the

42 As mentioned earlier, the 'follow the sun' principle is only applied for messages with first and second level support. Developers working in the third level support are experts in a particular area. This expertise is not duplicated across labs.

same level), because the employee does not, for one reason or another, want to engage with the problem.

Whilst there are many examples in which these mechanisms work perfectly and messages are re-distributed appropriately by the system and solved by the support employee without any further involvement of the user, this is not always the case, in particular when it comes to complex problems which are forwarded to the third level support. It is then, when the mechanisms are in place, which allow the support to re-embed the problem in its local context. This is when the support visits the user site virtually, by establishing a remote connection to access the user's system.

4.10.2 Re-embedding Problems: Visiting the User Virtually

Investigating problems in support settings can be a regulated or unregulated process, depending on factors such as the organisational culture, the product and the environment. In the context of technical support, we know little of how problems are investigated and solved once they have found their expertise. If we draw our attention, once more, to Orr's (1996) intriguing account, we can see how the technicians followed their own judgement on where to start and where to follow up, when investigating problems. Whilst documentation was provided, it was considered as unhelpful. The documents were said to follow a sequential diagnostic path and problem solution, whilst problems were found to be wild and dependent on the individual socio-technical context and as such not following the sequential approach suggested in the documentation.

A similar situation unfolded at the vendor's third level support: Whilst general application documentation (but not specific problem documentation) was available and was said to have been used by the first and second level support, problems arising at the third level support were mostly unique. The unique nature of problems at this stage could not be solved by reading through the documentation. However, even though the problems were individual, a pattern can be detected on how third level support approached such problems. If no solution could be thought of immediately, the support employee would always request a 'remote connection' to access the user site, to re-produce the problem and see it with 'one's own eyes'. With this, the support *re-embeds* the message in its local context and creates a 'virtual local'.

Establishing a connection to the user organisation to investigate the problem is a very interesting step which shows (1) how problems sometimes cannot be solved without taking into account the local context, and (2) how boundaries between user and vendor responsibility at this stage of the product life cycle, are not always set and, in some cases, need clarification and reinforcement.

In regards to the first point, whilst the idea of re-embedding problems shows parallels to Orr's (1986, 1996, 1998) accounts of the importance of understanding the socio-technical context of the user and the machine in question, in order to solve problems, interestingly, in the vendor's case, it appears that the re-localisation efforts focus on a different issue. Whilst, for Orr's technicians the socio-technical context was important, for the support staff this action is taken solely to understand what is described in the labs as 'technical context'. The re-embedding of the problem takes place in a silent dialogue between the support and the machine, potentially even through the night (local time user organisation) when all users are offline. Only in rare cases does the support employee investigate the problem *together* with the user, to understand the different steps which the user took when experiencing the error (akin Orr's technicians)[43].

Whilst establishing a remote connection was important to understand the local (technical) context of the problem, it was also used at the third level support to (re)-establish boundaries between 'vendor's responsibility' and 'user's responsibility'. As we learn from Light (2001), for the user organisation, there is a fine line between customising the system and modifying the system, the latter compromising the support service agreement, limiting the vendor's responsibility for errors. Whilst Light (2001) describes it as a fine line, the specialists taking care of implementing and servicing the system are generally aware (and are expected to be aware) when crossing the line between customising and modifying the system. However, there are cases described within the first part of this chapter, where the user challenges the vendor by claiming an error to be the vendor's responsibility. For the user organisation, the advantage of such action is to not have to deal with the problem on their own, but get professional help. For the vendor, errors which are only occurring in the modified system and not in the standard system, but are claimed to occur in the

43 Only one case has been witnessed in which the user was included in the search for an error via telephone conference. In this incident the 'user' was a vendor's consultant at the user's site and as such, had the status of a 'colleague'.

latter, are an expensive adventure. It appears to be that the vendor's responsibility is to provide proof that it is a problem which is not covered by the service contract. By accessing the system locally, re-embedding the problem in its context and trying to re-produce it allows the vendor to relatively quickly re-establish boundaries and clarify responsibilities. If the problem cannot be re-produced in the standard version of the system running at the user site, the problem is the user's own responsibility.

To summarise, the virtual visit to the user site, as the above discussion has shown, is important to the vendor in two ways. First, it allows the vendor to re-embed complex problems in their local settings to understand them better and, second, to clarify responsibilities for problems.

Whilst the message re-distribution and problem solution process has proved to be very complex and dependant at first, on the formal parameters attached to a problem, such as component and system environment, there is one additional formal parameter, which is set by the user when raising a message that distinguishes itself from the other categories: the message priority. Whilst all other categories help the vendor to detach and distribute problems, the message priority takes on another role. Tightly connected to the Service Level Agreement (SLA), which states, amongst others, how fast messages with different priorities have to be solved, the priorities build the grounds and also determine the power relationship between vendor and user at this stage of the product life cycle.

4.10.3 The Power of Formal and Informal Problem Priorities

As shown in the first section of this chapter, the order in which problems are investigated is framed by the message priority assigned to the problem and with this, the entire working day of a support employee is aligned to the message priorities. Urgent messages are responded to first, to avoid possible compensation payments or angry users, who potentially call out an escalation. Escalations are for support employees, a dramatic experience as many people, including the company's Board of Directors are involved, observing and evaluating the situation and, with this, the support employee's past and current work. Whilst stressful for the support employee, escalations are also very expensive for the vendor. As the ethnographic account has shown, a complex process is triggered if a customer calls out an escalation which involves additional work force, as well as additional communication and documentation (and is thus expensive).

The priority levels set by the user determine the day-to-day working schedule of the support. However, in some cases the formal framing of the vendor-user relationship at this stage fails practical requirements. It is then, when the support, in search of time, approaches the user to renegotiate priority levels. In doing so, the support, the user and the problem enter a grey zone in which arrangements are made which change the initially set time frame to solve a problem. The example in the chapter shows how priorities, and with this time frames, are re-negotiated for reasons such as the expert being in a different time zone and, therefore, not available or simply if there is a local holiday which interferes with the message solution process. This highlights how the user-vendor relationship is not only based on rules and formal agreements, but also on relationships, which allow both sides to sometimes cross formal boundaries (and adjust priority levels, not according to the urgency of the problem, but according to practical issues).

In other cases, where re-negotiation of message priorities is not a suitable strategy to gain time, the support, if unable to forward the message to other experts, might choose the strategy of suggesting a solution which has not been thought through entirely. Having been sent back to the customer, the message in the inbox of the support employee changes its status to "in progress by user" and hence temporarily leaves the formal responsibility of the support employee. Before the support has to carry out further actions, the user must fulfil his part of the service contract: to implement the solution and inform the vendor of the outcome[44]. The length of time the message is with the user is recorded in the system as "in progress by user" and therefore changes the statistics, showing how many days a message has been with the vendor and how many days with the user. In cases where the user-vendor relationship is tense and users are dissatisfied with the support service, these statistics can be used to prove that the delay in solving a message was caused by the user.

Even though the latter practice creates the exception, it is interesting the way in which support employees create space in the tightly and formally framed relationship between the vendor and the user. In particular it is

---

44 As mentioned earlier, there is a clear boundary between what support employees are allowed to do in the vendor's system and what not to do. Whilst getting remote access and reproducing the problem is common practice, the vendor is not allowed to change any settings, customise or modify the user system. Solutions have to be described in the problem message and are then implemented by the user organisation.

fascinating, how the user agrees at times to change the priority levels to 'help out' the support employees rather than stressing his formal rights. It seems that relationships of trust, of giving and taking, exist which can, at times, overwrite formal procedures.

Whilst 'buying time' is sometimes necessary, on most days, the support employees can handle messages without re-negotiating time limits. It is then that we can witness another type of 'overflow' in the formally regulated user-vendor relationship: Within the boundaries set by the priority levels, the support exercises its own discretion and decides which problem is handled first and with what level of attention.

The Power of Informal Priorities

Whilst, at times, several very high priority messages arrive making the above explained negotiations necessary to gain time, users are generally found to be careful when raising messages to very high priority. Most messages arriving are either of high or middle priority (customers rarely seem to use the priority 'low'). Thus, the support staff regularly encounters the situation of having several messages with the same priority. It is then, when the support employees can exercise discretion and decide for themselves, which message to solve first. As the ethnographic account shows, messages which are, for instance, sent by customers well known for exaggerating the importance of the message or for being unfriendly, are dealt with later, whilst messages from friendly users are dealt with earlier. In some cases, the support employee might simply not be in the mood to think about a certain problem and thus works on another message. Whilst we find space for the support's own discretion in respect of the order in which problems of the same importance are in investigated, similarly 'un-regulated' is the way problems are addressed and reported to the user. It is for the support to decide on which type and extent of help is given. Certain users might get more help than necessary to fulfil the service contract, whilst others will only get the quality and detail as defined in the Service Level Agreement.

To summarise, the order of investigating problems is determined, firstly, by formal and secondly, by informal prioritisation. Within the formal boundaries we find an unexpectedly un-regulated relationship which is surprising in two ways: First, it seems that the user and support at times, leave the official ways of interacting and re-negotiate priorities based on a relationship of trust, and second, other than the formal message priorities, there were no rules in place organising the order in which messages are to be solved. Whilst a formal mechanism of prioritising messages internally has been introduced after the completion of the fieldwork, the support employee providing this insight reported that the way messages are now pre-arranged by the system is only to be seen as a guideline. The final decision upon the order and also the detail with which problems are solved is still with the support employee.

4.11 Conclusion

Software support activities play a major role in securing the success of most organisations, even though in different ways. On the one hand, we have the organisation seeking support services to secure their day-to-day business; on the other hand, we have organisations offering support services as products. For the vendor studied, falling into the latter category, offering support services provides a secure and steady income, mostly unaffected by economic turbulences. Even if companies lack available capital, they cannot cancel their support contracts with their ERP software supplier, since in most cases, the entire business is built upon and reflected in the ERP system. Given the significance of support services for the different types of organisations, it is surprising, that only few researchers, taking on solely a user organisation viewpoint, have tried to investigate this phenomenon (see, for example, Light (2001), Nah et al. (2001)) or as Gable et al. (2001) at least acknowledge the lack of research in this area.

Investigating the support department of a major ERP vendor, this study shows, for the first time, the complex processes and policies in place within such a global organisation's support department. Most intriguingly, this study has shown how fragmented and geographically dispersed expertise is matched with specific user problems through applying a basic classification scheme to each message. Whilst this facilitates the mobilisation and global distribution of problems, the complexity and uniqueness of user problems is also taken care of by leaving 'un-ruled' space for the user to describe the actual problem in his own words. Whilst this mechanism appears to be very effective, as the data shows, in some cases, it is subject to overflows; this is when problems are multifaceted and complex or simply 'unwanted'. In the case of multifaceted and complex problems, concerning not only one component and one support team, but several and responsibilities might be unclear. In other cases, messages are ping-ponged around because the problem looks 'troublesome'. Troublesome problems are problems which appear to be very complicated, long-winded or are simply sent by a user known for being difficult; problems which are better avoided.

Whilst this chapter has shown the complex mechanisms in place when solving a support message, it has also highlighted how one particular category, set by the user during the message creation, the message priority, frames the day-to-day work organisation of each support employee. Whilst the authority of the message priority appears to be crucial at first, mostly because of its connection to the service level agreement and with this, to potential compensation payments, the account provided unique insights on how the formal frame in some cases overflows and informal agreements between users and support take place.

The ethnographic data and following analysis has furthermore highlighted the boundaries of categorising problems. Whilst the categorising of complex problems allows the distribution and matching of problems and expertise, important details about the local context are lost in this process (cf. von Hippel, 1994). It is this user-specific detail which is, however, sometimes crucial in order to understand a problem and hence, to find a solution. Not for the majority of messages arriving at the vendor, but not uncommon for problems dealt with by the third level support teams, a ritual re-embedding of problems in their local context via remote login, by creating a 'virtual local', can be observed.

Overall, the discussion in the chapter provides a narrative, introducing us to the working practices within this vendor's labs and furthers our understanding of how the user-vendor relationship is managed at this moment of the product life cycle. More specifically, the account introduces how ERP system providers deal with the challenge of offering support services for a complex and localised product to a diverse user base – insights as yet unknown in academic literature and unheard of even to the vendor[45].

In the following chapter, I move away from ERP system support towards a phase which is situated almost at the other end of the product life cycle: the software development phase.

---

45 Aware of my efforts to investigate, in particular, the informal practices within the support team, I was interviewed by the vendor in 2008 in the context of an initiative to improve the solution finding processes in the support division.

5 ERP System Development

5.1 Introduction

We are not only throwing away 20 years of development methodology but we are throwing away processes that have been well established for years. The way people work, the comfort zones people had. This is a huge change.
(Tom, Senior Vice President, Interview: February 2006)

The history of software development, and more specifically the management of software developers, reads like an accumulation of problems, which were hoped to be solved by theorising on and implementing new management styles. Pioneering the movement in the 1970s as an answer to the existing software crisis, Royce introduced one of the first software development models which became widely known as the 'Waterfall Process'. The Waterfall Process emerged out of the urgency to manage developments of large scale software systems, which cannot be done by following a two phase approach of analysis and coding. Applying the process, it was hoped to increase control over the development process and the developers respectively, and with this, reduce the amount of failed, late and over budget projects. Furthermore, a more structured approach was hoped to allow organisations to better understand what the developers do in their day-to-day work and with this, not only be able to increase control but also to reduce the organisation's dependency upon the developers. Even though widely criticised, often for not being iterative (which is, however, contrary to what Royce (1970) actually suggested in his work) today, the Waterfall Process is still applied (Sawyer, Presentation, 2008).

Since the 1970s many other 'best practice' development processes were suggested, such as the Spiral Model (Boehm 1986), the Rational Unified Process (Kruchten 1999), and the Agile Software Development approaches (see also Chapter 2). Interestingly, the theorising of what might be the best way to organise the development process is carried out with little knowledge of how people actually work in different settings, for instance, if and how work differs depending on the software industries, national and organisational cultures (Ailon 2006; Barley 1996). Whilst some attempts have been made to highlight the differences between software package development and bespoke system development (cf. Carmel and Saywer 1998), as well as the work practices in software package labs (Dube 1998; Cusumano and Selby 1997; Carmel and Sawyer 1998; Sawyer 2001a; Sawyer 2000; Sawyer 1996; Sawyer and Guinan 1998; Zachary 1994, 1998), existing studies are limited in that (1) they are carried out by the same researchers (2) from an often 'external perspective' (rather than from a participant observation viewpoint, from inside the labs), and (3) fall short in distinguishing between different types of software packages, such as ERP systems versus other types of software packages. As mentioned earlier, ERP system development distinguishes itself from other types of software packages, in that it is highly complex, built to represent the unique processes of an organisation across departments and furthermore, has to provide a very different level of flexibility and adaptability than other types of software packages (such as office products). Furthermore, the market conditions for ERP package providers are different than for other software (package) providers (Sawyer and Guinan 1998). Therefore, development practices in such settings are most likely to be different from other industries and need to be looked at more closely. In order to do so, what is needed are ethnographical accounts investigating software development from the inside and to show how work is organised in different settings. Such accounts would helps us to further our overall understanding of ERP system production, which is currently limited by an uneven focus on the user organisation and therein, on peripheral activities of ERP system production (such as the implementation phase) as well as allow us to contribute to other disciplines in that such accounts can build the basis for the theorising on management methods.

With this book, I advance our understanding of ERP system production with the main contribution of this chapter being of ethnographical nature. The chapter highlights how a vendor struggles in attempting to re-balance its relationship with the market. In the light of stagnating and even falling sales numbers, the vendor decides against closing the unprofitable division and instead, to re-organise its software production process and with this, the way the experts and expertise in the labs are managed.

This chapter includes data collected in the vendor's labs from October 2005 - February 2006 and is divided into two sections. The first section highlights what was understood as being the new strategic direction and associated changes in the development process. In the second part of this chapter, I change the perspective and, rather than focusing on the strategy and associated discussions, I highlight, in chronological order, how the changes over time affected the working practices in the labs, starting with the moment in which the first detailed announcements were made. Throughout, a developer's viewpoint will be adopted. Thus, the account reflects the way the developers perceived, reacted to but also named certain practices, with in particular the latter, not always being in accord with existing academic notions[46].

Within this chapter, I present data mostly collected by observing the events in the labs (cf. chapter three). Therefore, unlike in the previous chapter which drew on data mostly collected by directly participating and carrying out related work, this chapter is written from an observer's, rather than from a participant point of view. Most of the time I talk about 'the developers' or particular individuals[47] and address them with a name to avoid the often- used, and from my point of view 'degenerating' expression of 'my informants'. In telling the story, I pay special attention to the Change Manager, Tom, who plays a major role in this context. By concentrating on Tom, I present not only the company's new strategy, but also convey the general focus on Tom in the labs. Even though Tom's actions were in compliance with the ideas from the Board of Directors, for the developers the changes and their effects seemed to be something Tom, as an individual, was made responsible for.

5.2 Tom's Strategy

> *You have to have a chaos to make change. Therefore sometimes you have to hire people from the outside to do that. Cause it's not easy to do. It's not easy to throw away established processes and start over again. We have changed a lot of significant things.*
> *(Tom, Senior Vice President, Interview: February 2006)*

> *The week before I was in some meeting (...) they always stress the point that from now on they will go first for the easy things [functionality], put it on the market as soon as possible, even if it*

46 This was particularly the case for the notion of Scrum and daily scrums. Whist daily meetings (in the labs also called 'daily scrums') are common practice when following Scrum principles it is only one of many techniques from which one can choose. Daily meetings are thus not an obligatory element of Scrum. However, for the developers, there appeared to be a close connection between daily meetings and Scrum.

47 For an introduction to the most important actors, see Chapter 3.

> *is not perfect. Second then comes quality and the intervals for new patches / service packages will be higher, like in the case of Microsoft. This will be necessary since the software will be not as perfect as it is now. Corrections while it is already on the market will become more common. In one meeting they said that till now [vendor] wanted to deliver 100% solutions but that will change. "Time to market" rules. (Fieldwork Notes, Week 5)*

The day I started working in the labs was also the first time the newly hired Senior Vice President, Tom, visited the vendor's labs to communicate his ideas to the developers. Tom was said to be hired from a major competitor in order to 'turn around' the CRM division. I was told that the reason for this move was, that the vendor, having entered the CRM market only recently, suffered from stagnant sales numbers and customer base. Tom with his experience in the market was hoped to bring the CRM division back on track. To the employees of the company, he was introduced as some sort of hero, which is also reflected in the following Intranet announcement:

> At [competitor], [Tom] had overall responsibility for the 21 vertical product lines (...). [Tom] played a key role in taking verticals from a $10 million- to an $800 million-a-year business in four years. (Intranet: October 2005)

I was introduced to Tom and the current situation within the CRM division by my supervisor, Jordi, who was leading the CRM development support team. On my first day in the labs, my supervisor asked me if I wanted to go along to a meeting, which would mainly address the developers, but would also be of relevance to "us", the support team. He explained that the company had hired a new Senior Vice President for the CRM division worldwide, and as rumours had it, from a managerial viewpoint, was hired to turn around the rather unsuccessful CRM division. To explain his ideas, the manager had organised a "question and answer session", which was supposed to take place just after lunch on the Friday at the end of October, my first day in the labs.

For the meeting, the entire lab gathered in the lunch area in the open-planned office next door. Curiously, I asked Jordi who the new manager was, what he looks like and how I could best recognise him. Jordi answered with a smile and said: "Don't worry, you can't miss him". At first, I did not understand what he meant by this, but when Tom walked in, I understood. A man, about two metres high and 150kg in weight, was standing in front of us, introducing himself with a southern US accent as Tom, the new Senior Vice President for CRM.

In his speech, he explained the new strategy, the resulting consequences and referred to everything as 'my ideas' (rather than the 'the management's ideas' or 'our ideas'). The session was organised in a question and answer style and it seemed that people and the manager were communicating, (to me surprisingly) openly. In my fieldwork notes, I tried to capture the situation:

> Everybody seemed very interested and jokes were accepted too. People laughed. His way of explaining things was very colourful - lots of examples. To me it seems that his strategy was to get questions and by answering them he went for wide explanations to say everything he wanted to say but wrapped it up in an answer to a question. He stressed all the time that he will say everything he knows and not lie. Seemed like people did believe him - might be a corporate culture thing. (Fieldwork Notes, Week 1)

The same day, I summarised his explanations about why he wanted things to change:

> The initial problem was that [vendor's] CRM is not successful and for 3 years there is no growth in the customer base. Tom explained that this is mainly due to three factors: First, the CRM module is tightly coupled with the ERP backend. Consequently only customers, who run an ERP system, best the vendor's ERP system, can buy the CRM module. Tom argues that in order to reach a broader market the system has to be re-designed in a way that it can run stand-alone (without an ERP backend). Secondly, Tom explains that the current user interface is tailored for ERP users but not for CRM users, who are a completely different clientele. Consequently, it will be necessary to completely renew the CRM user interface, to increase user satisfaction and acceptance. Thirdly, Tom says, the CRM division is currently lacking important customers which are running the CRM system successfully, and which can be used by marketing and sales as 'reference clients'. In particular, once the system is re-designed, the reference clients would be a necessity to prove to potentially new clients that the vendor is living up to what he promised. That the

> system can run stand alone and that the new user interface is indeed better and more intuitive. (Reworked fieldwork note to facilitate reading, Week 1)

As it becomes clear from the above fieldwork note, Tom planned on implementing several major changes, to (1) run the system stand alone, (2) change the user interface and, (3) acquire new reference clients.

The ERP market is dominated by a few big players selling a wide selection of different modules, which are potentially suitable for an organisation in search of an ERP based IT solution. For example, Oracle and SAP offer modules for almost any department within an organisation and across industries, including Human Resources, Material Management, Production, Procurement, Sales etc[48]. If a company needs to buy new software and already has an ERP system, decision makers usually decide in favour of the same vendor, not necessarily because the software is the best possible option on the market, but to avoid integration problems. Historically, ERP systems are known for being very 'proprietary' and were designed to interface better (and, in some cases, only) with applications provided by the same or partner organisations This changed during the last few years, due to a growing demand for new functionalities crossing organisational boundaries, such as Supply Chain Management and CRM tools. This, together with technological development such as Service Oriented Architecture, put pressure on ERP vendors to open up. Whilst this is a threat for the vendor in that competition would increase, there was also a chance for products such as the vendor's CRM module. If the vendor managed to offer it as a *'stand alone' product* and facilitate the integration with the third party (also ERP) systems, the potential customer base could be increased.

The second point Tom made during his talk was that, in order to succeed in the market, it would not be enough just to re-design the application in a way that it can run stand alone, but *reference clients* are needed. Tom argued that if well-known companies implemented the system standalone, and are convinced about the applications' features in general, other companies would be more likely to buy. The concept of reference clients is common practice in industry, in particular in areas where complex products are sold. Because of their wide functionality it is often difficult for the potential customer to assess system features (Finkelstein et al. 1996; Pol-

48 See also Solution Map examples in the Appendix.

lock and Williams 2008; Salzman and Rosenthal 1994). Buying decisions are therefore often made on the basis of recommendations or reports from other clients, running their system in a similar environment.

The third thing addressed by Tom, was the *CRM user interface*. As Tom explains, until now the management made the mistake of ignoring the particularities of the fast changing CRM market by building the CRM user interface with the existing, well known ERP user in mind. In a one-to-one interview Tom explains further:

> Let's face it. [vendor] is very successful in the ERP business. No one is more successful than [vendor] in ERP. But if you look at all the peripheral products like CRM, they are not very successful. And why? Cause they do what they know really good. Which is ERP. But these other products they are in a different row. They are all very user based products. Whereas ERP is not. ERP is a back office product with different users. And to meet the requirements is different and that's hard to understand if all you have ever done is ERP. (...) What we try to do is change the whole mentality about the user. The software you build has to be usable. You have so many users.. you have to get them buying. That's a whole different philosophy. Different from how you used to do it at [vendor],. It is hard. It has really taken a lot out of their comfort zone. (Tom, Senior Vice President, Interview: February 2006)

Tom emphasised that ERP users are different to CRM users and therefore a different type of software has to be offered, software which is "usable". Tom explains further:

> The average user at a call centre is 18 years old, right out of high school. If they have a high school degree, you have to have a much more intuitive UI [User Interface]. Most people using the ERP application are business analysts. They are specialists. In the front office it's not that way. Sales, call centres - it's very different. User adaptation is very important and also task completion. Task completion in the front office has to be very very fast. Whereas in the back office it's not a big deal. (Tom, Senior Vice President, Interview: February 2006)

As Tom explains, the difference between an ERP and a CRM user is that ERP users are typically well trained. In sales centres, which are targeted by the vendor, the average user is young and inexperienced. Hence, the User Interface needs to be more intuitive and easy to understand. Furthermore, whilst users in general profit from an easy to comprehend user interface, in the case of call centres, task completion needs to be very fast; best if the task can be completed whilst being on the phone with the customer.

In order to re-design the system to comply with these requirements, Tom emphasises the importance of the user-vendor link which could be supported by the new software development approach Tom was planning to introduce. My diary entry for the day Tom visited the labs continues with:

> To realise the changes, Tom decided on a different software development method than the vendor's CRM division used to apply: Scrum. Applying Scrum, the new user interface should be finished by April [Tom's speech took place at the end of October] and delivered to the market in August. During the development process the user should be included. He asked for getting people from the street into the labs to test the product.
>
> The developers commented that this is a challenging schedule. People are insecure and afraid that they will have to work more than 8h/day. After the new Senior VP mentioned that he hasn't seen his family in the last 20 years, that he is now working 16h per day and that everyone who can't deal with the new approach had better go, my colleague mentioned (she is with [vendor] since the labs were created in [city]) and that she hopes that he doesn't expect her to do the same. Family is very important to her. I got similar comments from other people I spent lunch time with. People seem to be scared. It was said that Tom has the unconditional support of the Board of Directors and the allowance to change everything (he did the same with [competitor] earlier). (Fieldwork Notes, Week 1)

The new software development approach named as 'Scrum', was not yet known to most developers. This, together with Tom's references to work life balance seemed to create insecurity in the labs, which, as I will show later, persisted for several months.

Before highlighting in chronological order the events taking place after Tom's visit to the labs, in the following, for the reader's better understanding of what was happening in the labs, I discuss the issues surrounding Tom's new software development approach. Instead of explaining in my own words the situation and plans, I let Tom answer the questions of why and how he wanted to change established practices. In the context of this discussion, I outline briefly the way the developers described to me how 'things used to be', as well as complement Tom's comments on Scrum with a summary on the principles of Scrum in theory (according to literature). Followed by this overview on Scrum theory, I furthermore highlight how the (wanted) difference between Scrum theory and Tom's actual practices shaped the developers' behaviour and opinion about the changes.

5.3 A New Software Development Approach Is Needed

The existing software development approach at the vendor's CRM division was described to me by Tom and the developers as linear, similar to what is known as the waterfall process[49]. Thorsten, a Solution Manager working in the labs, explained to me in an interview that, usually at the beginning of an 18 month development cycle, he, in the role of the user representative, would write down the initial requirements he collected by interacting with the user in a short, non-technical specification. This specification is then synchronised with other Solution Managers working on related modules and finally handed over to the development group. The developers than discuss the specification in terms of its feasibility and feed the information back to the Solution Manager. Once the Development and the Solution Managers agree upon a final specification, the project managers break down the tasks and distribute working packages,

49 The 'Waterfall model' is mostly associated with a paper published by Royce (1970) and follows the idea that the software development cycle can be structured into subsequential phases and be implemented in a linear manner. Each development phase (system requirements, software requirements, analysis, program design, coding, testing, operations) has a defined starting and end point. In its original design of 1970 the model supports the idea of revisiting certain phases during the project duration (iterative development), however only to a certain degree: Rather than moving freely between phases, Royce suggests to allow only the revisit of the directly preceding / proceeding phase (except when testing fails and the requirement phase has to be revisited, in which case, all phases are said to have to be re-visit). The model has been and is still widely criticised for being not flexible enough. However, it has to be noted, that many critics overlook that, indeed, Royce did suggest iterations, only he did so with the above described restrictions.

(with a deadline of approximately three months) to the developers. How the developers realised their tasks was left to the individual preferences of the developer. Thierry, a developer, explained for instance, that usually, he would start off with doing research, take it easy and think about the best way to code it. Once he found his way, (and with the deadline approaching) he would start “serious programming”.

The existing process was well documented and sequential - one step at a time, iterations exceptional and long term planning the rule. Whilst the developer liked the approach for providing a certain type of planning security, Tom considered it “dangerous” to develop software according to a long-term planning schedule. He explains in an interview:

> If you are building software, planning far in advance is dangerous. Because then, you can’t react to trends, market changes, competitor changes. ‘Cause once you put that plan in motion and you have planned so far out, what happens is you can’t react. This is the way things were done at [vendor]. Planning was done two years in advance of the release. And then when the release came out, people started up building things they won’t need anymore. But because the planning was done, no one was willing to go back and undo that. (...) You just can’t do that. You have to be able to react to the changing strength of the market place worldwide. (Tom, Senior Vice President, Interview: February 2006)

Tom explains the weaknesses of the current process. The long-term planning, up to two years he considers as “dangerous” as market conditions change and the product should be continuously adapted. Otherwise, he comments, that if the developers work on the basis of an out-of-date specification, this would consequently lead to a situation in which a product is delivered to the market, which might not match the current market expectations. Not seeing the advantage of investing in such a product, customers would then decide in favour of other providers, who are able to fulfil current demands. Tom summarises: “If you cannot do it, someone else will do it” (Tom, Senior Vice President, Interview: February 2006).

By contrast, the process Tom had in mind was based on short development cycles, after which each requirement would be reassessed. With this, Tom hoped to bring the CRM division into a position in which the product can be aligned closer to the ever-changing market conditions. The ideas behind the new approach Tom borrowed from different project management approaches ('Scrum' as well as 'Sync and Stabilise'), which he combined with his own experiences. Why he did not decide on a straightforward implementation of for example 'Scrum', he explained in the interview:

> In the book of Schwaber [which was also handed out to the project managers under the authority of Thorsten, the Vice President for CRM working in the labs], the first 50 pages he talks only about how great he is. He didn't really develop Scrum, he was only the first one who put it down on paper. But the principles of Scrum have been around for a long time. The problem with Scrum is: it works good for certain types of projects. But for some it doesn't. Also, everything is done in black and white in this methodology. Once you are on the task you can't change, you can't do this and that. In reality it's just not realistic. For example, in Scrum they talk about a 15-30 days project. Well, there aren't many 15-30 days projects, especially if you do releases. It's great if you do small functionality, fixes, but if you have to do a whole release, and you have to do it in a Scrum way, the methodology is just not realistic. It's almost impossible to do a full release on Scrum. You have to have more flexibility. (...) If you take a release: 40 projects that are all large in nature. You can use pieces of Scrum but you can't use all 'cause it wasn't designed for it. Too many interdependencies, too many moving parts, too many groups. (Tom, Senior Vice President, Interview: February 2006)

From Tom's perspective, Scrum executed as described in theory, is not suitable for every kind of project. Programming a new release makes it, from Tom's viewpoint, necessary that multiple projects run simultaneously. This results in a high amount of dependencies and hundreds of people having to work together, which from Tom's point of view, requires extensive project planning and control, mechanisms which are not supported (to the desired degree) in Scrum. The 'textbook' Scrum approach, instead of trying to emphasise control through project plans, asks for short lists with requirements, which are subject to change, depending on the market requirements. The idea of agile software development is to embrace uncertainty; Tom, by contrast, prefers to control through firm planning and control mechanisms. Tom explains further:

> Project planning becomes really important. (...) sometimes in Scrum they have a tendency to avoid to do a proper project plan. And that's not always a good thing. Sometimes you need a project plan to rationalise, organise tasks and when they should be done and in what order. It's also good to track where you really are. The sooner you catch that you fall behind you can correct those things. The earlier you can catch slips, problem areas, you can course correct quickly. (Tom, Senior Vice President, Interview: February 2006)

Important in this context is that even though Tom explained in February the reasons for introducing a methodological mix rather than 'pure' Scrum to me, the developers (and until February myself, in the role as researcher) were not aware of this. In particular, as the developers were asked to exercise daily meetings, which is a feature typically associated with Scrum, they concluded, based on Tom's initial announcements, that it was Scrum that they were supposed to do. The project managers, wanting to be prepared for the change, started to search the web, downloaded and shared PDF files dealing with the Scrum methodology. Only underlining this assumption, after a couple of weeks the management handed over a copy of the book "Agile Software Development with Scrum" (Schwaber and Beedle 2001) to each project manager.

Below is a compressed outline of Scrum, as described in theory, to provide an impression of what, in particular, the project managers and also some of the developers, might have read and understood under the notion of Scrum. It is this understanding, on which they not only acted upon, but also based their judgement of the management's efforts on.

Excursion: What Is Scrum?
'Scrum', first mentioned as a development method in a paper by Takeuchi and Nonaka in 1986, belongs today to the family of agile software development methods.

Agile Software Development
Summarised under the umbrella of agile software development methods are methods supporting the values stated in the "Agile Manifesto":

> **Individuals and interactions** over processes and tools
> **Working software** over comprehensive documentation
> **Customer collaboration** over contract negotiation
> **Responding to change** over following a plan
>
> That is, while there is value in the items on the right, we value the items on the left more. (Agile Alliance 2008a)

The agile manifesto summarises the main characteristics of agile software development: it is based on particular values rather than a framed methodology. The comparative demonstration of the values show the difference between the values attached to process driven methodologies (on the right side) and agile software development Methodologies (on the left side). Whilst the values on the right site are deeply-seated in methodologies such as the Waterfall model, these are not neglected by the agile movement. Instead, whilst emphasising values stated on the left side, Agilists ask: In which way and why are the processes, documentation, negotiations and plans used? Are they really necessary? If the answer within a particular project is 'yes, they are necessary', also Agilist will support such values.

Scrum Methodology
Even though the original ideas surrounding the Scrum methodology were already around in the 1980s (Takeuchi and Nonaka 1986), its use for the software industry was restricted by the limitations of a programming environment, which would support a quick turnaround, fast build, fast change and rapid testing (Schwaber 2008). It was in 1993, when one of today's Scrum supporters, Sutherland, picked up on the ideas of Takeuchi and Nonaka. Self-empowered, multi-skilled teams where everyone followed the same vision and is up-to-date with the project's progress at any

time appeared to be key factors for the success of Honda, Canon and Fujitsu, the organisations Takeuchi and Nonaka (1986) were writing about. Incorporating these thoughts into their lightweight, iterative, incremental development approach, supported by a flexible Small Talk environment and inspired by the success of Borland, who managed to produce 1000 lines of deliverable code per person per week using a similar approach, Sutherland and Schwaber organised the first 'Scrum meeting'. Exchanging their ideas with others, Scrum as a development method became over the years, more and more popular and is, today, defined as a lightweight management process, which does not require any particular engineering practice but a focus on people (Highsmith 2005).

A development cycle with Scrum is commonly divided into three stages (Bach 1995b):

- Pre-game Phase (Planning and Architecture)
- Game (Development Phase)
- Post-game Phase (Closure)

In each phase a particular set of activities is suggested to be carried out, which have, however, to be considered as 'typical' rather than as 'dogma' (for a detailed discussion see Kruchten (2007)). In the following is highlighted, what can be described as a typical summary of what is Scrum practice, mainly based on Schwaber and Beedle (2002):

The 'Pre-Game Phase' in a Scrum Project

During the pre-game phase, the product backlog is developed. The product backlog consists of a comprehensive list of requirements and features which can come from anyone, including sales or marketing staff. The product owner, the person representing the people investing in the project (such as the user) is responsible for maintaining this list and also the only one allowed to prioritise the requirements. During the pre-game phase, the team is chosen, decisions about additional tools and resources are made and risk assessment, controlling activities as well as the identification of possible training needs evaluated.

Furthermore, the high level design of the system is planned. Any planning is carried out according to the current requirements on the backlog list but is never to be considered as unchangeable and definite. Throughout the development cycle, changes are expected to happen.

The 'Development Phase' in a Scrum Project

The pre-game phase is followed by the **development phase**, which is divided into several sprints. Sprints are iterative cycles with a duration of up to four weeks. Sprints start with an initial one day meeting. The first four hours of the meeting are dedicated to the product owner explaining to the team which parts of the product backlog are most important to him, and the team deciding on how many requirements from the list they think they can realise within the next sprint. Following the idea of empowering the team, it is the team and not the management who decides upon how much they can do during a sprint (Schwaber and Beedle 2001). It is also the team, which, during the remaining four hours of the first day takes the product backlog items they committed to, breaks them down into small tasks and assigns the task to individual developers. The task list from this meeting becomes the sprint backlog (in comparison with the product backlog, the sprint backlog remains fixed during the whole sprint). During the sprints environmental variables such as resource control, requirements and quality are constantly monitored; variables are expected to change.

Change is taken into account after each iteration – during the sprint phase, usually up to 30 days, the team is not to be disturbed. The sprint phase, together with the closure phase, are the only time frames in which changes are monitored, but not immediately taken into account. The time when changes are discussed are in each sprint review / sprint planning meeting.

During the sprints, teams have daily meetings, the daily scrums. The daily scrums are for the team and are meant to ease communication between team members and to create some kind of daily commitment to certain tasks. Usually, the daily meetings are only attended by the Scrum team members. Whilst other stakeholders are welcome, they are asked to remain silent, again following the principle of not disturbing developers during the 30 day sprint. Stakeholders are only allowed to express their opinion during the sprint planning and review meetings, at the beginning and end of each sprint.

Daily meetings should be held at the same time at the same location every day. The same set of questions is discussed at each of these meetings:

1. What did you do yesterday?
2. What will you do today?
3. Anything in your way?

The emphasis during the meeting is on the exchange of information between team members, and not to report to the ScrumMaster (former project manager), also participating in these meetings. There are three questions to be answered on the lowest level of granularity, so that progress can be seen. High level granularity would only result in repetitive comments such as "Yesterday I worked on program A and today I will do the same" (Cohn 2003). With the information from the daily meetings, the team updates the sprint backlogs whilst the ScrumMaster updates 'the list of unmade decisions and obstacles', he is asked to take care of. In Scrum jargon, this list is called a 'block list'.

After the sprint during which an increment is developed, the informal, four hour sprint review meeting takes place. The review meeting is hosted by the ScrumMaster with the whole team as well as, customer representatives and the management being present. During the meeting, the team demonstrates the increment, changes of variables are discussed and finally, the next sprint planning meeting announced.

The 'Post-Game Phase' in a Scrum Project

Once all items are off the backlog list and everyone agrees that all environmental variables have been taken into consideration, the product enters the closure phase. Further testing activities are carried out and documentation and other administrative tasks necessary to ship the product are finished off. Similar to the sprint phase, as mentioned earlier, also during this closure phase, no changes or additional developments are allowed.

Changing Jobs: Assigning New Roles

Following a Scrum methodology means for the organisation, not only renaming and re-organising the different phases within a development cycle, but also changing job roles and profiles. The roles taken up in a Scrum team might incorporate different activities from what the employees were used to. For example, the product owner, whose role is often taken up by the user representative, has to allocate a significant amount of time for frequent meetings with the developers and other stakeholders at the end of each sprint – time which might have been used differently before.

The traditional project manager role does not exist in a Scrum project. The role closest to this is the ScrumMaster. The ScrumMaster is responsible for managing the process. However, instead of controlling the team, he plays the role of a 'sheepdog', a facilitator, removing obstacles for the team, so that the team can concentrate on their work (Schwaber and Beedle 2001). At the beginning, the ScrumMaster is also responsible for teaching and coaching the team, as well as enforcing the rules Scrum is based on.

The Scrum team is the main force for development and consists of up to 10 people. The numbers vary depending on which author is writing about Scrum, however, the general idea is to have a small team with less than 10 people, to allow easy communication. A Scrum team is, in contrast to more traditional teams, cross-functional. The team consists not only of developers but also architects, designers, testers and quality assurance people, to allow cross functional development in comparison to linear development. What Takeuchi and Nonaka (1986) described in their article about overlapping development phases can be already realised by setting up cross functional teams. The Scrum team is empowered and makes their own estimations and task assignments. The challenge for the team members is, however, to learn how to make accurate estimations, handle the 'freedom' and with this, also the increasing responsibility for their own work. In a Scrum team, excuses such as "I followed the process" are not valid. Everyone is encouraged to think, exchange information and if there are doubts, discuss them with the team.

For the management, the job title does not change, however their role does. The management is asked to adopt a particular management style which complies with the idea of Scrum of empowering the team. The management is, for example, not allowed to interfere during a sprint, or to dictate in the sprint meeting what the team has to do. The team decides. The management task is to participate and give general guidelines, take into account industry standards and make final high level decisions. Furthermore, and this is reported as being hard for the managers (Schwaber and Beedle 2001), managers are asked to accept the rules of agile software development, which include reducing documentation and emphasising face-to-face communication. A management, which is used to receiving ten page reports weekly, and multiple chart analysis about the project's progress, might get the feeling of losing control.

5.4 "What Is It That We Are Doing?"

The only time Tom communicated with the developers directly, was to explain his ideas during his initial speech in the labs in October, 2006, after which he immediately left the labs. With Tom's departure, the developers were more or less left alone with what might be thought of as a 'partial picture' of the new management approach. That is, it was a programme of change that was only partially communicated and understood, thus leaving room for alternative readings. As a result, the developers, rather than being passive actors, took things into their own hands and based upon the most recognisable, Scrum theory, started to gather information to complete the picture. Unsurprisingly perhaps, this meant that there were many different interpretations of what was going on, being circulated in the labs, which led to a situation in that there was ambiguity between management's intention and the developer's readings, resulting in some kind of 'temporary arrangement'. In this temporary arrangement the different groups were working towards alternative programmes of action, which on the surface, seemed to match but underneath, they were based on different realities.

In the following paragraphs, I show how the developers try to find ways to fulfil what the management is looking for, to comply with the new rules. In this regard, it is interesting that the developers decided to take matters into their own hands to fill the interpretative gaps left after Tom's fast departure and further absence. The developers demonstrated and acted upon how they saw themselves: as 'experts', capable and willing to think for themselves.

5.4.1 Conforming Interpretations?

One of the first practices introduced in the labs, was the common Scrum feature of having daily 15 minutes meetings. These meetings, at which only three questions are discussed and during which one is not allowed to sit or talk for longer than 2 minutes, were considered by the developers as typically characteristic of the Scrum approach. As a result of the similarity, the dropping of the word Scrum within Tom's presentation and the handed out book to the project managers about Scrum, led almost immediately to a renaming of the practice from 'daily meetings' to 'daily scrums'. Known by all under this notion, the daily meetings become for the developers, a 'clear' indicator, for commencing Scrum implementation.

Dominating the daily life in the labs, the daily scrums became some sort of a 'ritual vehicle', setting a 'common ground' for the management and the people in the labs. The daily scrum became the one variable everyone agreed upon – although with different interpretations attached.

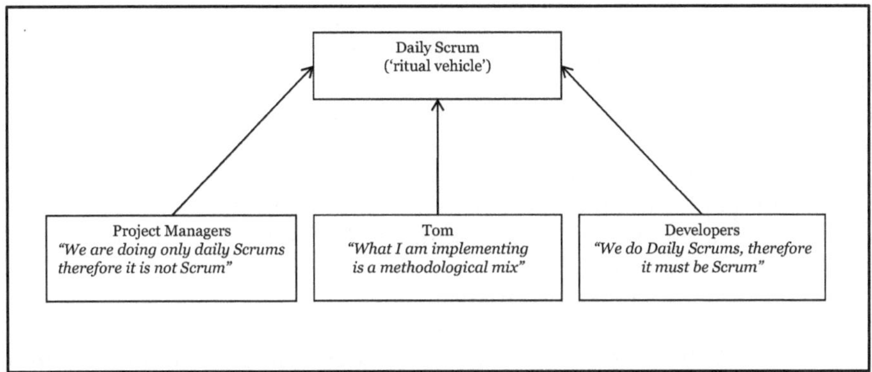

Figure 10: Attachment to the Ritual Vehicle

It was the daily scrum, which became the vehicle uniting – however only on the surface - both forms of interpretation to a degree that everyone assumed to move in the same direction. It was only after approximately three months (calculated from Tom's visit), when inconsistencies between what the developers thought to be Scrum and what the management ask them to do, became more obvious. Interestingly, however, the people in the labs did not change how they thought of and discussed the new development approach, but kept latching on to the notion of Scrum and instead searched for justifications, explaining the inconsistencies. Arguments such as 'it's Scrum with some modification to fit into the vendor's organisation' or 'this is just the start' were commonly expressed. The situation based on this mutual kind of misunderstanding remained stable for several months until eventually, the 'silent arrangement' stared to falter.

I do not know how the project managers experienced the time in which inconsistencies became more and more obvious, and what caused them to have doubts. It was a gradual change which is difficult to show, because I believed in a Scrum implementation myself and mostly interacted with the developers, who believed through the time of observation in a Scrum implementation. Nevertheless this unfolding of the situation is interesting and to picture what happened, within this section, I draw on my own experiences as a researcher, being involved and part of the labs. I show how my perception gradually changed and how other people from outside the labs saw the situation.

5.4.2 The Participating Researcher Discovers Inconsistencies

One of the first things which made me reconsider was a conference paper I was working on for the International Conference on Software Engineering (ICSE). During my time in the labs at the weekends, I wrote a paper called 'The implementation of Scrum at one of the biggest ERP vendors worldwide". Within this paper, I tried to describe the processes and the practices in the labs, and connect them to Scrum methodology. Whilst I wrote this paper, doubts about whether this really was a Scrum implementation started to cross my mind. First disregarding the doubts, in January, I handed in the paper, but found myself doubting even more some weeks later and decided to dig deeper.

Knowing that the developers in the labs believed in a Scrum implementation and therefore would provide no source for clarification, I searched for a contact from outside the labs, someone within the vendor's organisation and who had a familiarity with Scrum theory. I found Fritz, a trained 'ScrumMaster', working in Silicon Valley, California[50]. I contacted him and asked him for his opinion on the current developments in the North American labs. He had already heard about my efforts and asked me detailed questions of what we are actually doing there. Having described to him the managerial approach from my perspective, he manifested my doubts (something I did not actually want to happen, as once more, it would destroy my idea for a good research topic) by commenting:

> Our teams [teams using Scrum outside the CRM division within the vendors organisation] are self responsible but not totally. However, if the project managers tell you what to do then this is definitely not Scrum. (..) You don't have to do Scrum. (..) [But] to plan five month ahead [like CRM does] and the Line Manager dictates tasks - well, I don't know. It's neither good nor bad but it's definitely not Scrum. (Fritz, Scrum Trainer, Interview: February 2006)

From Fritz's point of view, it seems that the criteria for evaluating whether a team is doing Scrum or not, are dependent upon whether they plan

---

50 Being German, Fritz insisted on carrying out the interview in German. The quotes are an author's translation.

ahead and, if it is the manager who decides upon the scope and the planning. If this is the case, he concludes that it is not Scrum. Applying a higher level of categories, he continues:

> The things you don't do [if you do agile software development] are that you write first a specification, then design and then start coding. That's not agile. There are some Scrum projects which did a specification but then that's incremental. (..) Sometimes you also have to make sure intellectual property is protected. With a thin specification this is possible. (Fritz, Scrum Trainer, Interview: February 2006)

Having concluded that it would not be Scrum, Fritz appears to search for a higher definition and discusses whether one could call it 'agile'. Again, he applies categories which are, from his point of view, the main characteristics of agile development and summarises that CRM is not doing agile software development. Drawing from this, Fritz concludes that what Tom is implementing is traditional management. Not Scrum, nor agile.

> The thing Tom is doing in CRM is not Scrum. From what I have seen this is totally traditional project management. My impression is that this has nothing to do with agility, cause with agile software development you don't plan ahead. What I saw was exactly the contrary. (Fritz, Scrum Trainer, Interview: February 2006)

A few weeks after this one-to-one interview, mumbling from the project managers' side could be heard. I overheard that some of them addressed the Vice President with their doubts about whether this is going to be a Scrum implementation. Antoine, one of the managers having spoken to the Vice President, recalls in an interview:

> When I spoke to [Vice President] he made it clear that we are not implementing Scrum. We are implementing some aspects of Scrum but what we are doing is not Scrum. (Antoine, Project Manager, Interview: January 2006)

Interestingly, Antoine, at this point in time is moving away from the initial arrangement of 'we do daily scrums and therefore implement Scrum' (of which also he was part of) and is using the theoretical concept of Scrum to justify that, similarly to Fritz, it was *not* Scrum that they were doing. Whereas, before the daily meetings dominated any discussion, the situation seemed to have changed. Different characteristics of Scrum methodology became more important, such as iterative design and development:

> Yes, we didn't sit with them [Solution Managers] at the beginning of every month to see what they need and what they would sacrifice if we don't have time. It's the waterfall I would say, the approach we are following with the Solution Managers, the waterfall approach. They just sit, define their needs, write them down and we work with that. There are no real iterations. (...) When I look at the reports we have, the project reports, everybody says: ok specification review complete. You know? So they say it's complete. No one says, ok we have completed but we will come back later (...) They are still in the same way. Specs, review, design, review, code. On this aspect nothing changed. (...) Especially, look, how we are using the Indian colleagues: We send them the mock-ups and the Indian guys just implement. There is no way for them to do iterations. They ask people in [Headquarters] to finalise the UI [User Interface] specifications before sending them to India. In this aspect it's far from real Scrum. It's the traditional waterfall approach. (Antoine, Project Manager, Interview: January 2006)

Antoine underlines in his statement that it was not Scrum what they were doing in two ways: First he explains the idea described in Scrum theory, of the team sitting down with the product owner (in the case of the vendor the Solution Manager) to decide together which features are going to be realised within the next sprint which was not implemented. This initial meeting is commonly referred to as 'Sprint Planning Meeting', if we were to apply Scrum terminology like Antoine did. Second, Antoine commented on the lack of iterative development, which was also identified by Michael as a point counting against calling it Scrum or even agile software development t. For Antoine, it appears to be a traditional waterfall approach - with "specs, review, design, review, code" - but with some special features, like checkpoint meetings to see if the development is conforming to the Solution Manager's idea.

> For all of us - I will not call it iterations - there will be checkpoints. So, Solution Managers will come at specified times and say "Yes what you have currently is what we agreed upon". (..) Now, will there be anytime when we say: Ok, we have no time.

> Choose what we have to deliver. Do you see? To ask them to prioritise. I don't know if there will be that kind of discussion. This is corporate action. And for having participated in several meetings I know how hard it is to reduce the scope. So, once again no conferment with Scrum. (Antoine, Project Manager, Interview: January 2006)

Michael, another project manager comments similarly:

> I read a book about Scrum and some articles. We definitely don't do Scrum. I think it's not possible in such big companies such as [vendor]. (Michael, Project Manager, Interview: December 2005)

Over time, Remy also expressed similar doubts to Armand and Michael. Also leaving out the 'daily meetings', he commented in an interview in February, that the amount of documentation changed as well as the time scale on which they were now working, and concluded that this is a sign of the vendor moving toward what is, for him, 'agile development'.

> What changed from working in the past is that we used [name for past development method] and everything was documents. Now, it's closer to agile development. We don't need a lot of documentation. In the past it was 3 month specifications, 2 month design and then development. Now it's 1 month or 20 days for specification and then development and design is done in parallel. If something is changing we can change it. (Remy, Project Manager, Interview: January 2006)

The project managers were the first to question the authority of the daily scrums. Over time, it seems that other features of Scrum theory became more important and questions were asked why they were not implemented. Slowly, the project managers stepped back and whilst still exercising daily scrums, their statement seemed to change towards, 'we are doing *only* daily scrums and therefore, it is *not* Scrum'. The figure below illustrates this change.

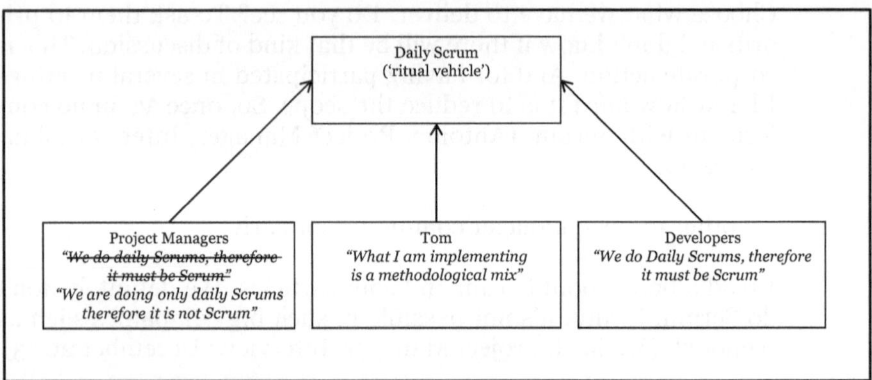

Figure 11: Detachment from the Ritual Vehicle

Antoine expressed this, most assuredly, many months later in an email:

> The only things what people kept from the readings they did is daily Scrum. (..) That means [for them], we are doing Scrum. But no, we are not. (Antoine, Project Manager, Email: November 2006)

It is interesting to see how the different positions emerged over time and how the practice of the daily meeting held the network together for several months. The employees as resourceful experts took things into their own hands in an attempt to fulfil the management's expectations. Skilled, and used to solving problems, the developers latched on to the pieces of information they had to complete the picture. Only after several months did the project managers realise that, by concentrating on the notion of Scrum mentioned by Tom during his first speech, they came to the wrong conclusions. Realising this, the project managers were the first to move closer to Tom's idea of implementing a methodological mix[51].

---

[51] With regards to the conference paper, it was declined, with reviewers comments being similar to my doubts during this time: "What you describe as the introduction of Scrum is really not an introduction of Scrum. It sounds much more like an introduction of a "work more and harder" than an introduction of a people-centric agile methods. In real Scrum, developers estimate effort -i.e. they are in control of what can be done in an iteration. What you describe is quite the opposite "you give work on an engineer" instead of "engineers choose task and accept responsibility for them". Your description sounds like a company that messes up a Scrum introduction. If that is the case, the mess-up will probably overshadow any impact of culture on the results." (Reviewer one).

Interestingly, the project managers as well as the management did not share this, probably not intentional or conscious move of perception, with their teams. When I left the labs about six weeks after these interviews took place, the developers, as well as the support team, who witnessed the changes in the development teams, were still talking about "daily scrums" and expressed their dislike by commenting "It's this Scrum thing.." or "I hate Scrum".

5.5 Summary

In the first part of this chapter, I highlighted how an ERP vendor reorganised his strategy in the light of a product which was not accepted by the market. An imbalance between the competing exigencies of the market and the vendor, respectively, reflected in the sales numbers and analyst reports made it necessary for the vendor to drastically change the strategy and, with this, also the way work was organised. In doing so, the vendor hired a Change Agent from a software provider who specialised in CRM products where he had proven his abilities to develop a successful strategy and introduce change, which is said to have made the competitor what it is today: a CRM system provider able to challenge the vendor in the CRM market, even though the vendor controls significantly more resources and overall, a bigger user base (ERP customers). In a way, Tom entered the company as a hero, pre-announced on the Intranet by quoting the competitor's growth under Tom's regime.

The new strategy introduced to bring the CRM division back on to the route of profitability, appears to be based on three main pillars: (1) developing CRM as a standalone application, (2) paying extra attention to new reference clients and (3) produce a 'usable' system for a CRM user not a ERP user, and do so as fast as possible.

To introduce the changes, Tom asked the developers to follow him and apply a new software development approach, a methodological mix, which would allow the company to develop more closely to the user and deliver faster. As I have shown above, it was this mix which stimulated

"Your description of "GS"'s [the name I used for the vendor within the paper] introduction of Scrum seems to me more of an abuse or mis-understanding of Scrum on the part of "GS" American management. This in itself may be an interesting case study for the agile alliance. You may want to consider a "spin-off" paper as your research progresses." (Reviewer two).

much discussion and also confusion amongst the developers who relied on their own interpretations of the situation, due to Tom's absence and the only partial explanation of his vision. The developers, showing themselves as highly resourceful and motivated employees took things in their own hands and filled the 'interpretative gap' the manager left. The software developers, gathering information from other sources, such as books and the internet, latched onto certain, familiar aspects of Tom's strategy, to complete and fulfil his vision. Unsurprisingly, rather than this being a smooth story, different versions of what might be Tom's interest, developed and co-existed for several months.

These different realities were also reflected in the way the changes were translated into day-to-day life. Following a chronological time line (October 2005 - March 2006) within the following section of this chapter, I show, how the new practices imposed were enacted, how the developers agreed and disagreed at times, and how the new strategic direction, over time, drastically influenced the working climate and day-to-day working practices within this North American software development lab.

5.6 Enactment of the Managerial Changes

Introducing organisational change is not just a question of explaining a proven theory to employees assuming that it will be understood and translated in exactly the same way as the organisational context. Organisations are built out of a network of people who, by having different understandings, values and principles, shape, neglect or accept practices differently. This is particularly true for organisational change taking place in companies with highly educated employees, who are used to thinking for themselves and who are pro-active in searching for suitable patterns and solutions. In the vendor's particular case, change was also difficult to implement as the people working in the organisation had usually worked there for many years. The vendor, especially in Europe, is well known for people entering the company at a young age and leaving the company when they retire. Hence, people are often settled in their way of thinking. Comparing the vendor with companies such as Microsoft and Yahoo, Tom explains:

> Microsoft lives of the laws of Windows per se. But Microsoft develops lot of new products that become successful. And the reason is the way they do it. Their philosophy. Companies like Ya-

> hoo, a company who continues to reinvent, continues to invigorate its workforce by bringing in new college graduates every year. [Competitor where Tom worked before] was the same way. My development group at [competitor] was 80% college grads and the rest senior people. The college grads were refreshed on a regular basis. I know it sounds pretty cold to say that but unfortunately if you want to stay competitive and you want to be able to keep getting new ideas you need to bring in new people. (...) They are excited and they don't think so much about taking risk. (Tom, Senior Vice President, Interview: February 2006)

As it becomes clear from this quote, Tom wanted not only to change the practices in the labs, *but the entire organisation*. He continues:

> It's not just about changing the way people work. It's about changing the culture, the culture in the entire company (Tom, Senior Vice President, Interview: February 2006)

With this goal in mind and the powers given by the Board of Directors , Tom reached beyond the CRM department, and influenced working practices across all labs. In one of the European labs, for example, he did not approve the country's typical hierarchical structure and made attempts to change this:

> First thing I did was I made all my VP's unlock their office doors. I made them take the signs of the door saying if you want an appointment you have to see my administrator. I made them all answer their own phones. And when you introduce yourself to your people, do so by your first and last name. It's ok if they call you by your first name. They don't have to say 'Doctor.'. It was really hard for them. (Tom, Senior Vice President, Interview: February 2006)

In the particular country Tom referred to, titles and a hierarchical working structure, was not only part of the organisational culture, but also of the national culture (Hofstede 1997) - and so, was the family orientation which Tom challenged by asking people to work on Saturdays. Not a problem in the US, a culture in which Tom spent most of his life, he did not approve of the people's resistance and the strength of the workers' union, which he saw as undermining his plans and with this, jeopardising the success of the company.

> In [European country] the legal working time is 8 hours a day. And that's it. You don't see that in [North America]. Cause the labour laws are different. Cause software engineering is considered a profession. The laws for hours that people work are different. But in [European country] it's treated like a factory worker. 8 hours a day. That does have its problems. Don't get me wrong there are people working long hours in [European country] too but it's not the norm. But you can't tell someone they have to do so. I can say that in [North America]. This cultural difference causes problems. (Tom, Senior Vice President, Interview: February 2006)

Tom appears to consider the work of software developers as a 'profession' and his developers as experts, rather than factory workers. In this regard, we might even speculate that the above-described confusion and the self-initiative of the developers in search of guidance was expected by Tom. This, however, seems to be unlikely, since, as I describe later on, the developers in the North American labs perceived Tom as a controlling manager, someone always wanting to know exactly what each of them did.

The changes introduced in the European labs caused major interruptions and gave Tom the title of "the most hated American in the labs" (Email from European Developer, 2007). In comparison to their European counterparts, this kind of change introduced in Europe was not an issue for the Canadians. Even though, used to a more 'European Leadership', which was understood by the developers as a leadership based on consensus, hierarchical boundaries were already minimal and academic titles were never used. Consequently, this part of Tom's ideas remained widely unrecognised in the North American labs. However, in comparison with their colleagues in Europe, who were, except a few, not part of the CRM team, the people in North America had to deal with the introduction of new development practices, which influenced most significantly the way they were used to communicate, interact and organise their daily working life. As we have already seen in the first part of this chapter, of particular importance to the developers was the announcement of new practices, the 'daily scrums', but also there was the 'daily confirmation' and the 'overlapping development cycles'. In the following section, I focus on these three practices. I show the way they are enacted over time, as well as give voice to the developers, letting them express their opinions.

5.6.1 Enactment: The Daily Confirmation

The first change reaching my ears following Tom's visit, was something the developers called 'the daily confirmations', a new way of progress reporting. Whilst the developers were used to working packages on which they could work at their own speed for several weeks or even months, by stating their progress at weekly meetings, they were now asked to work on small packages and state their progress daily, via the daily confirmation, on an Excel sheet. The Excel sheet consisted of several columns labelled with the names of the developers per team, their daily or weekly tasks and a field in which the developers had to enter a percentage showing the progress on a particular task. The Excel sheet was linked to the program MS Project, which translated the percentage entered into statistics and graphs, allowing the project managers, and the upper management, to monitor the progress of each team on a daily basis. Remy explains:

> It's new in our organisation this daily confirmation. Before it was the project manager confirming, one time a week. At the beginning there was some resistance but now everything is accepted. They [the developers] understand now that the organisation needs to see the progress of the work. (Remy, Project Manager, Interview: January 2006)

Even though, as Remy expressed, there was some sort of resistance, the daily confirmation did not seem to be much of an issue to the developers, at least almost no-one spoke about it. As I found out, the project managers did not really enforce the daily confirmation. In Remy's case, the developers working in his team explained, Remy would 'ask' his team to fill it out, but if they forgot or simply objected to doing it, it did not seem to matter much to him. I saw one of the developers, Thierry, working in Remy's team filling out the sheet regularly, whilst other developers, such as Gloria, from the same team, never did it. When I asked her about the daily confirmation, she commented:

> I remember also an Excel sheet that I've never completed. Remy did it for me. (Gloria, Developer, Email: July 2007)

Similarly, for Antoine's team, the daily confirmation was not really an issue. Antoine explained to me that he is not convinced about the way the tool was implemented and decided to complete it himself, instead of giving it to the developers. He comments:

> A: Yes, I do this [the daily confirmation] for them. Because it was difficult, it was not yet very well set up until now, but in the coming days, yes, they will go and individually confirm the work they have done. Everyone will have to confirm by themselves. (Antoine, Project Manager, Interview: January 2006)

Even though Antoine was planning on having each developer confirming their daily progress in the future, in the end, his developers never had to do it either. Before Antoine decided that, finally, it was set up well enough, the purpose of the daily confirmation changed. Whilst the initial idea was to have each developer confirm their progress, with the introduction of the daily scrum, it became the project manager's task, who was supposed to provide data based on the daily scrums.

With this, the daily confirmation disappeared quickly out of the lives of the developers; however, only indirectly. Even though it was not the developers' task to complete the Excel sheet, the upper management still received daily reports about each project's progress, based on the daily confirmation for which the project managers and the developers, respectively, were held responsible. Even though it was not a big issue at first, the practice of the daily confirmation made, as we will see later, the developers accountable - not only to their manager and colleagues within the labs, but also the Change Manager Tom, who was sitting in an office thousands of miles away.

5.6.2 *Enactment: The Daily Scrums*

In Scrum theory (cf. Schwaber and Beedle 2001), the daily meetings are described as an optional tool for the team to update each other and to commit to a task for the next 24 hours. In theory, these meetings are only attended by the Scrum team members. However, 'externals' such as stakeholders are welcome as long as they stay 'outside' the circle of people and do not disturb the meeting. Daily meetings should be held at the same location every day in a meeting room or an area where the team is undisturbed and where blackboards and pin walls can be used. During the meetings only three questions are to be answered:

1. What did you do yesterday?
2. What will you do today?
3. Anything in your way?

With the information given at the daily meeting, the team is supposed to update the current 'backlog' (a list of task for the particular 'sprint' they are carrying out) whilst the project manager updates a list of 'decisions to make and obstacles'. This is the basic idea which is associated with daily meetings in a Scrum context, or any other type of agile project management methods (cf. first part of this chapter).

Whilst the theoretical description of the daily meetings appears to be straight forward, leaving very limited room for individual variances, the way the meetings were carried out and perceived was surprisingly different. The length and detail of the description below highlights these differences and represents the importance of the daily scrums for the developers. It was *the* topic, which was discussed daily. Being most visible and affecting every developer in the labs, it became the symbol, the ritual vehicle for Tom's often 'controversial' changes.

The daily scrums started for most teams just after Christmas and were organised via MS Outlook software, which was used to organise email exchange and meetings within the company. Accepting the invitation to the 'daily scrum meeting' which was sent around by each manager created a daily re-occurring event in the Outlook calendar. Within the electronic invitation, the managers briefly outlined what the meeting would be about. All invitations contained more or less the same information: that there will be a daily 15 minute meeting at which three questions will be discussed. Below is an example:

From: [Manager]
Sent: None
To: [Team]
Cc:[Vice President]
Subject: Daily Scrum Meeting
When: Occurs every weekday effective 1/17/2006 from 9:00 AM to 9:20 AM.
Where: [meeting room]
Hi Colleagues,

I would like to invite you to our daily team meeting to allow everyone on the project team to see the status of all aspects of the project. We will keep this meeting short (about 15 - 20 min). The discussion will be restricted to the following 3 questions:

- What have you done since the last meeting (or what have you done today - for the first meeting)
- What will you do until the next meeting
- What obstacles got in your way

Best regards,
[Manager] (Project Manager, Email: January 2006)

The invitation was sent to the team and, in copy, to the Vice President. From the 17th January onwards, on every working day, this team came together to answer the three questions outlined in the email. Whilst the invitations did not differ much, with regards to the enactment a surprising variance developed. Even though answering three pre-defined questions in teams within the same organisation, in the same labs seems to leave little space for diversity, I was struck by how much the teams differed from each other in the way they exercised and perceived the meetings. Below are some quotes from my fieldwork diary in which I commented on my first impressions after the first few meetings:

> Antoine as usual started on time. He allows discussions of general things which are interesting for the whole team cause he says it makes sense for him. Seems productive their Scrum. So far it's the only team where I can see it makes sense. Also maybe because he is a good team leader and he wants to try Scrum. It's the opinion of the ScrumMaster which reflects on the team. (Fieldwork Notes, Week 12)
>
> Anne-Sophie was lots of chatting at the beginning also jokes about Scrum. Apparently Anne-Sophie doesn't like it. She reminded everyone to do their daily confirmation since she has to report the progress to the higher management. The atmosphere was very different from any other Scrum meeting. Laughing a lot but sort of more hysterical. 3 questions weren't asked explicitly but still answered. (Fieldwork Notes, Week 14)

> Remy's meeting is less dynamic. Also there are jokes and he is funny, however with Antoine there is a completely different atmosphere. He seems more constructive and he takes notes. I guess the difference is that Antoine likes Scrum whereas Remy dislikes it. (...) Bernhard [from Remy's team] is always talking most, commenting on other people's comments. Also, Remy accepts it if people say that they have nothing to say. Well, it feels like that everybody hates it and that they do it cause they have to do it. Including Remy. He doesn't ask the 3 questions either, whereas Antoine does it explicitly. (Fieldwork Notes, Week 13)

The commitment of the managers to the new practice seemed to significantly influence the atmosphere during the meetings. Whereas Antoine, for example, was convinced by the usefulness of the meetings, Anne-Sophie re-assured the team that she did not really like but had to enforce it since the management expected her to do so. With this she sympathised with the developers who criticised the changes that made her popular at this particular moment – a bonding against the forced changes by the management. The problem, however, was that by doing so, she justified actions which disturbed the meeting and the work, such as a lack of motivation to contribute and listen during the meeting. Why should anyone listen, if the meeting is declared by the organiser as enforced and pointless?

Michael, not really excited about the daily meetings either, often started very late and had problems stopping people if they were going too far in explaining and discussing individual problems. Some meetings took over 30 minutes. In my diary I commented:

> Michael started 20min late without any excuse. The arrangement even is different. Everybody stands in front of him – it's not really a circle. People report to him not to the team and they talk for far too long. The atmosphere seems like "we have to do this therefore we do it but we don't expect anything out of it". I guess so far it's the worst Scrum meeting since also Michael doesn't seem to be committed at all. People come with lists reading out all their problems. Today the guy with the list didn't read out loud but was still talking for 5min or so. (Fieldwork Notes, Week 15)

In my role as observer, it seemed to me that, apart from Antoine's team, none of the teams enjoyed the daily meetings even remotely as much as Antoine's team did.

> I went to Remy's meeting. I am not sure if it is any good to do the daily meetings in all cases, apart from Antoine's. People are not enjoying it and complaining how useless it is. Also, especially in Remy's meeting people don't listen to each other anymore. Three questions are no longer asked but everybody says what he is doing and if they are any problems. (...) Maybe it's also the location in Remy case – the circle with 14 people is too big (QA [Quality Assurance] people included) and it's impossible to hear what people say. (Fieldwork Notes, Week 13)

The disenchantment of Remy's developers was amplified by the location Remy chose. The particular corner of the labs had very bad acoustics and because Remy's invited people were from the quality assurance and documentation teams, the circle of people was rather big. As a consequence it was difficult to hear what each developer had to say. The fact that English was not the mother tongue of most developers, but the language chosen for the daily scrums did not help either. Interestingly, none of the developers interrupted the meetings to say that they could not hear anything or the like – for me this was a sign of how little attention the developers paid to what the others had to say during the meeting. The problem with the acoustics was only dealt with because, at some point, the VP and I commented on it after the meeting. From then on people were asked to stand closer to each other.

The Location

Like Remy, three of the five teams I observed chose a place in the lab, where most of the developers of that particular team were sitting anyway. The arrangement of people by teams, was, however, not the way the office was designed. The vendor's office was an open-plan office (see Chapter 3). Because of the open-plan characteristics, in some cases the daily meetings disturbed developers in other teams, who then complained that they could not concentrate. Even though people grumbled during lunch time in front of me, they generally kept quiet and accepted the meetings held next to their desk. Very often, as I explained in chapter three, I found myself in the role of a messenger between the different hierarchy levels. Complaining to me, the people might have hoped that, despite my insistence that I was not reporting to anyone, through me they might get access to the higher management[52].

The exceptions in terms of choice of locations were Antoine and Matthew. Antoine's team held their daily scrums in a nearby meeting room. He took the idea of daily scrum stand up meetings seriously and did not allow anyone to sit down. This led to the rather strange situation, where the developers gathered in a fully furnished meeting room around a table and chairs. Instead of using the office equipment, however, the developers were standing pressed against the walls, in this (see picture below) rather small room. To be able to lean against the wall, the developers had to move the chairs in the room towards the table.

Figure 12: Meeting Room

[52] On one occasion during the early morning hours, several developers independently came to me, asking if I could have a word with the vice president, who put his phone on speaker in the open-plan office. The developers, coming early to work felt disturbed and upset about the ignorance of the Vice President and commented "You know him. Can't you just tell him to pick up the receiver?" Whilst it was not a very hierarchical organisation and everyone 'knew' the vice president, who occasionally even joined after work drinks, the developers did not feel comfortable to criticise his behaviour, rather asking me to do so.

Scrum theory comments on the format of the daily meeting only in a way that people should be arranged in a circle and that it would be best held in a room in which notes can be left on whiteboards. The stand-up practice is very well known in circles applying Extreme Programming (XP), another form of agile software development. In the case of the labs, it was the Vice President's suggestion that the daily meetings should be held as stand up meetings.

Matthew, with a history of Extreme Programming, differed from all other project managers in that he decided to change locations every now and then without pre-announcement. Some of his meetings were held in the corridor outside the labs, next to the emergency exit, some in our kitchen area, and some in the office next door. Depending on the location, people were allowed to sit if there was a table or chairs available. The idea, as he explained, was to push people to be on time and make them think more creatively. After the first couple of weeks, however, Matthew also started to have the meeting where most of his team was sitting, and, even though rigid about starting on time at the beginning, as time went by, his meetings started more and more often with a five minute delay or were cancelled. Even though caused by the developers or the manager being late, the late start was used as an argument against the daily meetings by different developers. The line of reasoning was, that the time they lose each day is not only the 15 minutes during which the meeting should take place, but also the time before and after the meeting. If for example a task comes up just 10 minutes before the meeting, it was explained to me, that people would not start anything new, knowing that the meeting is going to disturb their work in a couple of minutes anyway. Then, with the meeting often starting late and people talking for more than 2-3minutes, some argued that, in total, it could cost them up to 45 minutes each day even though the developers, under time pressure, returned to their desks right after the meeting.

Who Attends the Meetings?

As I described above, the way the meetings were carried out varied between teams. Interestingly, also the question of who attended the meetings cannot be answered in a single way. The project managers in the labs, decided upon whom they included in the daily meetings individually. Again, people in the labs seemed to take matters into their own hands.

As I explained earlier, the labs were organised in teams along the more traditional software development cycle. There were teams of developers, teams from quality assurance, teams from documentation and from testing. This organisation was not changed by Tom. According to Scrum theory, however, these teams should be merged, so that each team became cross-functional. The cross functional teams would then make it possible to develop increments, and to address problems early and in a holistic way. Some of the project managers seemed to be convinced about this idea, and, even though not being asked to do so, they decided autonomously to bridge team boundaries and invite people from different teams, such as quality management and documentation, to their daily scrums. In comparison to Remy and Matthew, who did invite others, Antoine, Anne-Sophie and Michael did not. I asked Antoine after one of the meetings for his reasoning and he told me that, first, he never really thought about it and second, that he could not see any advantage in people outside his team having to listen to the microscopic descriptions of the daily issues the developers are dealing with.

In particular, the first comment surprised me. Antoine always seemed to be very excited about the implementation of Scrum, but appears to have 'overseen' this particular part of the theory. His answer implies also, that his approach has never been challenged since, when asked, he commented that he never really thought about it – and this, even though the Vice President attended many of the meetings as an observer (and thus, I expected him to realise that other teams did it differently and mention this to Antoine). This somehow indicates that even for the Vice President not all aspects of the new practices were entirely clear.

Briefly wondering what the people from the other teams thought about being invited only by certain team leaders, I asked a colleague, Ashleigh, who was working in the documentation team. For her, it did not seem to be an issue and she said she never really thought about it either. But overall, she said that she is happy that she is not invited to all meetings. She commented, smiling, that attending five "of these meetings" every day, would be just very time consuming.

I did not further investigate this issue, being absorbed by other things happening in the field. Who participated in the meetings, was also never part of any discussion I overheard or took part in. It seemed to be accepted as the way it was and even to me, it did not seem to be very important, whilst I was still in the labs. Only by looking back, I started to wonder. Whilst nobody seemed to care much about the mixture of the people attending the meeting, was the question of the usefulness of the meetings in general was heavily discussed.

Perceptions of the Daily Scrums
In terms of what can be learned from participating in daily scrums, the individual developers had different opinions. Antoine's team, for instance, which appeared to me as the team profiting most from the daily meetings, seemed to really enjoy it. One of the reasons for this might be, that this team had a unique advantage which made their daily scrums different from those of the other teams: the team members were almost all working on the same project, the design of the user interface. Antoine had only one team member who did not work on this project. His approach to make sure that the daily meetings were not de-motivating for this team member (as things discussed might not be of interest) was to give him the choice of whether he wanted to attend or not. Interestingly, perhaps because he was given a choice, he came to almost all of the meetings.

As a manager, Antoine was really excited about the idea of the daily scrums. In an interview, he explained why:

> Well, I would say, it's a big advantage for the team in general and for me as development manager, ScrumMaster or whatever you want [laughing], it helps me to know what is going on, what are the opinions and what is the progress of the team. This is a big advantage. For the team itself, it's the same: They share information, they are not stuck in their corner, they get new information and if we implement it thc right way it would help as well to tell the Solution Manager, ok here we have an issue. Can we either reduce the scope or can we do additional iterations because we are not doing what you are expecting. (Antoine, Project Manager, Interview: January 2006)

What became clear during the interview was that Antoine considered the meetings, first of all, as actual information sharing events and only, second, as a progress report. Whilst it cannot be seen in this quote, Antoine described himself as "Secretary of the team", something he referred to in the interview as 'ScrumMaster'. The difference between the traditional role of a project manager and a ScrumMaster is, as Schwaber's book describes, that the ScrumMaster has to give up on trying to control the day-to-day progress of the team but to make sure that the developers can concentrate on their work, rather than being distracted by administrative or political issues (Schwaber and Beedle 2001). Antoine was the first manager who seemed to follow this concept and changed his role accordingly. Maybe because of Antoine's positive attitude, his team was also more convinced of the usefulness of the daily meetings. During my time in the labs, I did not hear any of his team members complain about the daily scrum; on the contrary. Six months after I left the labs, a period where the labs did bug fixing and suspended the daily meetings, Antoine sent me an email, saying that his developers actually *asked* again for daily scrums. Even though he knew that his team accepted it, this also came as surprise to him:

> Well, on our side it's business as usual with some false start of the next release :-(Recently, I was really surprised when in a meeting, the team suggested that we resume the daily scrums... I was amazed... Well, my team didn't really hate the experience but they were not crazy about it either... So, when they suggested this, I couldn't believe it :-)) (Antoine, Project Manager, Email: November 2006)

The degree of acceptance of the daily scrum within Antoine's team was not the rule. The other teams' criticisms were expressed frequently. For example, just after a meeting I was chatting with Thierry, a developer who was part of Remy's team, in the messenger:

> CG says:
> so how was the Scrum?
> Thierry says:
> tremendous
> CG says:
> What does that mean?
> Thierry says:
> it means that I learnt nothing in this meeting, as usual
>
> In another conversation, Thierry comments:
>
> Thierry says:
> the fact is that in our team, half of the people don't even hear what the others say because they speak to low
> Thierry says:
> at the end I'm sure everybody is just thinking about what they will be cooking tonight.

(Communicator conversation, Week 16)

As I explained earlier, acoustics were a particular problem for Remy's team. However, even when the acoustic problem was addressed and changed, Thierry's opinion remained the same. Thierry explained that he knew what his colleagues do anyway and if he needed help or wanted to know, in more detail, what they are working at, then he could just go there and ask.

Like many others Jack and Ramsay also agreed with Thierry. In my fieldwork notes I wrote:

> Yesterday, Ramsay said after the meeting "you don't give anything and you don't take out anything out of those meetings. (Fieldwork Notes, Week 12)

> [Jack comments]: The whole point is that we think about our work and see what we want to do and realise where the problems are, right? Ok, but I hate it. It takes far too long. They don't stick to the questions and they are not even asked. One of the guys even brings a list with all the points he wanted to raise. (Fieldwork Notes, Week 12)

Jack, not liking the meetings either, acknowledged that they might be useful in terms of information exchange. However, he complained about the duration of the meetings – being part of Michael's team, his scrum meetings, at times, went on for 40 minutes.

Whenever developers commented on the way the daily meetings were organised, it seemed to be of major importance that the meetings did not exceed the planned 15-20 minutes. On one occasion, I asked Thierry after the meeting if he liked it today. He answered straight away "Yes, because it was short" (Fieldwork Notes, Week 12). A team member of Matthew's team commented similarly, however, her point of view was a little different:

> Asking the Asian girl [who is Canadian], if she liked it, she said yes, cause it was only 10min. That's how it should be she says. To say quickly what you did. Also she liked the location [which was outside in the corridor next to the emergency exit]. (Fieldwork Notes, Week 12)

A day later I happened to bump into her again. Even though still acknowledging the importance of the meetings being short, she appeared annoyed. In my fieldwork notes I wrote:

> She was very pissed off at lunch saying that she doesn't like it cause it's too long and there are discussions which are not interesting and that they should not be part of the meeting. Also, she said the concept doesn't work, since at the beginning when she wanted to say something, she got told off, having her comments declared as being not important to everyone and therefore to be taken offline. However, now she says everybody is discussing. She was very aggressive and when I just asked her to clarify some things she said aggressively "I have the feeling I am explaining myself to you". Whatever that meant. (Fieldwork Notes, Week 12)

Apart from leaving me rather disturbed because of her aggressive behaviour, during lunch time and in front of other colleagues (she might have seen me as a kind of management mole), the points she made regarding the daily meetings were interesting. At the beginning, she had the feeling that her manager, Matthew, was very strict in what was to be discussed at the meeting and what was not to be discussed. Even though acknowledging the importance that the meetings are kept short, she behaved aggressively because she felt that the meetings were taking too long. Making the meetings shorter would mean that the manager decided more often that some discussions are taken 'offline' and that some elements of the daily report are too detailed. Which parts are important or not, however, are decided by the moderator, who is the project manager. It seems that on one occasion, she was stopped because the project manager considered her explanations as too detailed and not relevant for the whole team. Even though wanting the meetings to be short, she did not appreciate being interrupted. For her, the point she wanted to make was of importance to the rest of the team. However, whilst other people, from her point of view, were allowed to speak for 'too long', she was told off.

The 'speaking time' per person differed significantly in all teams, apart from Antoine's team. Whilst in Michael's team, one of the developers explained himself in every single detail, reading his points from a piece of paper (and not being stopped by Michael) in Anne-Sophie's team one person, who was generally very nervous and loud, always commented on what the others said and explained at full length what he did and what he was going to do – generally in a very negative tone. Because of his status as 'architect', he was, however, a very important person 'to please', and therefore rarely stopped. Anne-Sophie explains:

> I think it's very difficult with him in the team. I invest much more in him than in the rest of the team. He is very very controlling. Also since we have a lot of new people we rely a lot on him. He is the architect, he worked for 6 months in [headquarter] and brought some information back that we have to implement. (...) Now I tell him do this [the daily meetings]. He says no. But then he comes anyway cause he doesn't want to miss it. (...) He is a workaholic and he knows it. But he is doing excellent work and very productive. He is very expressive and that doesn't help me to introduce a new concept to my team. Many rely on him cause he is the architect. So they don't want to take too much position. I make the decision but he sort of decides about the acceptance. (Anne-Sopie, Project Manager, Interview: February 2006)

In Anne-Sophie's case, the power of this particular team member was based on his knowledge from Headquarters and also on his distinguishing role as being the software architect, a position which made him formally the expert amongst experts. In this particular case, due to team dynamics, he was so powerful that he could lead the direction of the team. Anne-Sophie introduced the changes, but it was his judgment which decided on the acceptance. Even though not very popular in the team the other developers were dependent upon him and reluctant to challenge his point of view. I witnessed a similar, but less grave situation in Matthew's and Remy's teams. In both teams there appeared to be some key people, on both occasions it was again 'architects' who were allowed to talk for longer and to comment on the work of others. It seemed that there was a clear hierarchy in place which was not determined by the hierarchy developer – project manager but by team dynamics and technical expertise, also represented in the formal title of 'software architect'.

Next to the daily confirmation and the daily meetings, the third major change determining the discussions in the labs, was the idea of unit tests and overlapping development phases. The latter recommended in various literature as a successful software development approach for fast changing markets was introduced by Tom to do exactly this: allow him to respond in time to fast changing market requirements.

5.6.3 Enactment: Development Phases and Unit Tests

Tom's decision to cut the total time per development cycle from 18 months to 6 months was accompanied by the idea of overlapping development phases. Whilst in the 18 month cycle each phase of the development cycle, for instance, development, testing and quality assurance, had an assigned time frame, Tom's idea was now to let the different phases of the development cycle overlap. This meant, for example, that development (build) would start before the specification (analyse) is complete, and testing would be done in parallel to development (build). Whilst overlaps in some areas were welcome by the developers, others raised questions regarding the quality standards of the product.

Michael, refereeing to an overlap in the design and development phases, expressed his concerns in an interview by using the analogy of building a skyscraper:

> With [the old development process] everything was very well tracked. (...) The design was better thought through before development started. (...) But with Scrum, design and development is done at the same time, thanks also to the time deadline. For some things there is simply less time. Especially for basic functionality. You simply forget something in the design. To fix something in the bottom when already the top is designed is extremely difficult. For example, if you build a skyscraper. You maybe forgot electricity in the basement. That means you have to dig around the skyscraper. So of course it is shaking and almost falling. Things like that. With [the old development process] things were stable. First basis, than the floor on top of it. Now someone is still working on the electricity, in the basement. But someone else is already building the 22nd floor based on the original design for electricity. (...) I think it's still working but from what we will suffer is that hidden quality. (...). Sometimes you need to think some days about something but there is no time for it. But, I think the quantity is definitely higher. We work quicker now. (Michael, Project Manager, Interview: December 2005)

The problems addressed by Michael are the possible negative side-effects on quality through overlapping development phases. In comparison with the existing style of development, the design and development phase was now partially carried out at the same time, so that development could start before the design was finished. His concern was that if the design, particularly the design of the basic functionality, was not thought through carefully to begin with, the vendor might suffer from quality issues later on in the development cycle. An ERP system, like most software systems, constantly evolves and is never 'finished'. Quality flaps therefore might not be visible in the beginning, but became an issue during the next stage, the next iteration or returns to the labs in the form of a message to the support.

Michael applied the idea of the traditional project management triangle, indicating the dependency of time, resources and quality, to underline his argument of potential quality problems also in the light of a shorter development cycle. He explained:

> If you keep the scope and you decrease the time, there is no way you can keep the other parameters the same. Something has to move. If we have the same resources it has to be the quality. I am really curious. We define the UI [User Interface] but the framework is not finished. The framework of course will change and then we have to review the UI. (Michael, Project Manager, Interview: December 2005)

Traditional project management theory assumes that quality, time and resources are inter-dependent, like the corners of a triangle. If one corner is moved up or down, the other parameters have to adapt. The shape of the triangle changes. In this context, Michael's fear was that by decreasing development time and having different phases overlap, without increasing the resources, the product quality would suffer.

Like Michael, I heard various developers commenting similarly. I recall a discussion with one of the chief architects during lunch time. He was concerned that, by using Microsoft as example, only having six months to complete a development cycle, the vendor would have to adopt a 'Microsoft approach' in which software is shipped quickly, but having such poor quality, that weekly updates are necessary to keep the software running.

Whilst the overlap in the design and development phase was described by Michael, and others, as possibly harmful in terms of quality, the overlap in the development and testing phase was, by all project managers, very welcome. Remy for instance explains:

> In the past, the development is given to QA [Quality Assurance] to test. Now they are working with us from the beginning. We don't have to wait until the end to find problems. Solution management, quality assurance and developers work together. QA is writing test cases and testing in parallel with development. Not wait until the end to see that we have a lot of correction to do. (Remy, Project Manager, Interview: January 2006)

Organising the product production process in a way that development and testing overlaps, was positively acknowledged as decreasing the boundaries between different teams. Not having to wait until the product was almost completed and then testing the entire programme at once, the overlap was considered as potentially saving time and increasing quality. For this kind of early testing of individual parts of the program, 'unit tests' as a corner stone of Extreme Programming (XP) engineering practices, were introduced to the labs. The idea of unit tests is to test the smallest testable part of an application to locate bugs earlier, and quicker. Tom explained:

> It [Unit tests] forces you to look at the lowest element if you are testing. This way you can isolate the problem easily. The problem with [last release] - and that's a perfect example - you put [last release] together and you don't do any lower level testing. The problem is it takes forever to debug. No one understands what level, where... It becomes very very difficult. We fix a lot of symptoms but we don't find the root cause a lot of times. And you don't know who is responsible either. (Tom, Senior Vice President, Interview: February 2006)

In addition to making testing quicker and producing higher quality, Tom also saw unit tests as a way to make developers more responsible for their actions. Whilst it is difficult to find a problem in a million lines coded by different developers, unit tests allow testing on a smaller scale and, with this, to identify the developer who programmed the faulty program.

Despite the potential increase in control which, however, was not acknowledged as such by the developers, the unit tests were widely accepted, after a few complaints about the additional work to program the tests in the first place. Even Anne-Sophie, who was most critical regarding the changes, commented:

> When something is finished, it's 'cause it had unit test and code review. The quality increases and doing it by small pieces is much better. (Anne-Sopie, Project Manager, Interview: February 2006)

Remy explained further, and related unit test practice to documentation. Documentation, generally, was not the most favourable task of the developers and was supposed to decrease according to Tom's plans. Remy saw unit tests as a way of doing so:

> Unit Test can be used as documentation cause with agile we have less documentation. We can look into the unit test how for example to call a function. The benefit is that we gain a lot of time for functions that are changing. In general people change the coding and we always lost lots of time to manually test our code. Now we create a unit test and it's tested. Unit Test coding is also transported to quality system and tested automatically. Lots of advantage of this form of documentation. You see the error from the beginning. QA will not waste their time to find minor errors. Unit Test can find bugs. This will for sure enhance quality. (Remy, Project Manager, Interview: January 2006)

Overall, the introduction of practices to have development phases overlap, was seen as controversial. Whilst an overlap in regards to the design and development phase was discussed critically, an overlap of development and testing phase and the parallel practice of unit tests appeared to be welcomed by all managers.

As highlighted in this section, the three most visible and dominant changes from a developer's viewpoint, accompanying Tom's assignment as Senior Vice President in the labs, were the daily scrums, the daily confirmation and the overlapping development cycles. Highlighting these practices, I gave voice to the developers, the project managers as well as to Tom. As it becomes clear, even though welcoming some of the changes, overall the new practices were looked at critically, and a general perception of increased pressure dominated the atmosphere during this time. This feeling of pressure seemed to be mainly caused by a perceived increase of 'visibility', in particular, in relation to the practices of the daily scrums and the daily confirmation. Whereas in the past developers' work might have been slightly 'obscure' to those outside the team and even to immediate colleagues, with the new practices the developers started to feel more exposed to various types of monitoring.

5.7 The Feeling of Becoming 'Visible'

If you commit to things, you better make sure you have done it. It's measurable and if actually somebody comes and checks...
(Tom, Senior Vice President, Interview: February 2006)

When the daily meetings started, I observed one of the teams getting an introduction by their manager about why and how the meetings would take place. What the manager, Remy, explained, was that the daily meetings were a tool for the exchange of information and self control – ideas which originated in both, the Scrum theory and reasoning given by the upper management. By explaining to the team members what one is going to do within the next 24 hours, a commitment is said to be established, which gives each developer a daily goal. Remy comments, that apart from making yourself aware of what you are going to do during the day, the meeting is also a place for information exchange, at which problems can be raised. Other team members might be able to help or, if they encounter similar problems in the future, they might remember that this problem was discussed before.

However, even though the developers seemed to listen, the comments made after the meeting did not correspond with what was communicated as the reason for the meetings. When I spoke with different team members after the first few meetings, many described them as "useless" and understood the daily meetings as being a tool to increase control by asking for a daily progress report. Gloria, working in Remy's team, wrote to me in January, right after the first couple of daily scrums:

> Scrum... I prefer to ask you instead of Remy.... Which is the goal or goals of the meetings.... Because I remember Remy say something about share information but at the end I feel like he was worried about that someone is stuck with something. (Gloria, Developer, Email: January 2006; English corrected slightly to facilitate reading)

Gloria expressed in this email what I had heard from various developers, particularly at the beginning: Yes, they say it was for information sharing, but it was as if they were worried about us not progressing fast enough, and that is why they ask every day. It is it because they do not trust us.

The project managers' position regarding the daily meetings varied. Michael, for instance, did not understand how this would give him more control. He also highlighted that, for him, the meetings made more sense if people worked on the same project. That was however not the case in his team. Michael explained:

> Daily meetings are very efficient if people work on the same topic; for example 'CRM On Demand' has different releases, different deadlines so it doesn't interest them very much what the others have to say. Personally, I think the meeting doesn't do that much. Because the team is small enough that I still have the overview. I can tell you at any time who is working on what. I talk to them on daily basis. It's rarely the case that I would not talk to a single person during the day. For me, I have the overview also without the daily meetings. So, what I read from the theory, the meetings should be more for the commitment in front of the team. Ok, this is what I am going to do today and how I accomplish it. And the next day to say, how you did it and if you succeeded or not. Because if it were just for me, I think it wouldn't make any difference cause I have the overview anyway. But from that perspective maybe it makes sense. The other advantage is, there might be a potentially common problem on which someone else is working and that they see that's similar to what I do and then they can profit from the solution of someone else. (..) These are the two advantages I see. That people know what the others do. The question is if it is really necessary to do it daily. If everyone wants really hear that someone else moved from one field forward from one day to the other. (Michael, Project Manager, Interview: December 2005)

Whilst Michael felt in control of what everyone is doing every day without the daily meetings, Antoine felt differently. Antoine explained:

> I have the impression that I am more in control because every single day I talk to the developers and see where their problems are and if they need help at all. And every single day I can go into

> the system and confirm in the product plan how their work is going, and if there is progress. The other way we used to do was that we know we are doing something, that we are somewhere in the process and close to the end we always came to the conclusion that we are far behind the schedule. With this as long as people are really honest to themselves, I think you know exactly where you are. So, yeah, first impressions: very very positive. (Antoine, Project Manager, Interview: January 2006)

Unlike Michael, Antoine believed that he was now more in control about the developers' progress. He claimed that, through the daily meetings and the daily confirmation, he could evaluate where they were in the process and how long they were going to take. Interestingly, he interlinked this with an appeal to honesty and self responsibility. He commented that the value of the meeting lies in being honest, not (only) with him, but with 'themselves'.

The question of control was not only discussed with reference to the developer – project manager (ScrumMaster respectively) relationship, but also in terms of the changing relationship between the project managers and the management. A project manager is responsible for the team's progress and, with this, for the success of the project. As such, a project manager relies on the performance of the team. In the case of the vendor, it was the project manager's task to inform the management on an everyday basis, through the daily confirmation, on the progress of the team. If the performance of the team was not in compliance with the management's expectations, it was the project manager who was asked to justify why the developers did not complete their tasks.

Reactions to this intensified day-to-day supervision varied amongst the project managers: Whilst, for instance, Antoine showed understanding, Anne-Sophie did not appreciate that she had to report and justify every day. For her, reporting every day was like questioning her abilities to lead the team and make sure that it was on the right track. In an interview she commented:

> What I don't like is, that if you are 5 percent low you have to justify. And that's easy, 5 percent, to fall behind. I know I catch up but I have to justify. I don't like all this justification. Of course the principle is good cause you know where you are and you can raise issues. But all the admin it requires to see where you are: That's a

> lot of work for a Manager. Its more admin then I had before. Definitely. (Anne-Sopie, Project Manager, Interview: February 2006)

Rather positive, Antoine comments:

> And for me also in the beginning I thought, oh my goodness this is some pressure. They want to check me every day! Of course they want to check me every day! Of course I should check myself everyday! And if I said this will take five days its normal that on a daily basis I do some checkpoints. Ok, today I have done 25 percent and if after three days I have only done 20 percent of the whole task there is a problem. People are feeling pressure because they didn't used to even report to themselves, their purpose of their own work. As I said to you we always know we are working on something, we are somewhere in the process but no idea of how much we have done and how much is left. So, this feeling of pressure, yes, it's justified but it's a wrong feeling. It's normal that you want to see where you are. (Antoine, Project Manager, Interview: January 2006)

Whilst first nervous, Antoine started to feel more in control and also considered it as 'normal' that 'you want to see where you are', and whilst understanding his colleagues' feeling of pressure, he found that more detailed control was necessary.

Whilst for the project managers the daily confirmations played a major role, for the developers the issue of control through the daily confirmation was slightly different, more indirect. The status report the developers gave during the daily meetings was noted by the project managers who then used this information to create the daily confirmation for the management (in most cases, except where developers filled the Excel sheet out themselves). If the progress was not as expected it was, first, the project manager and, only second, the developers, who were called to account by the management. The figure below demonstrates the reporting chain.

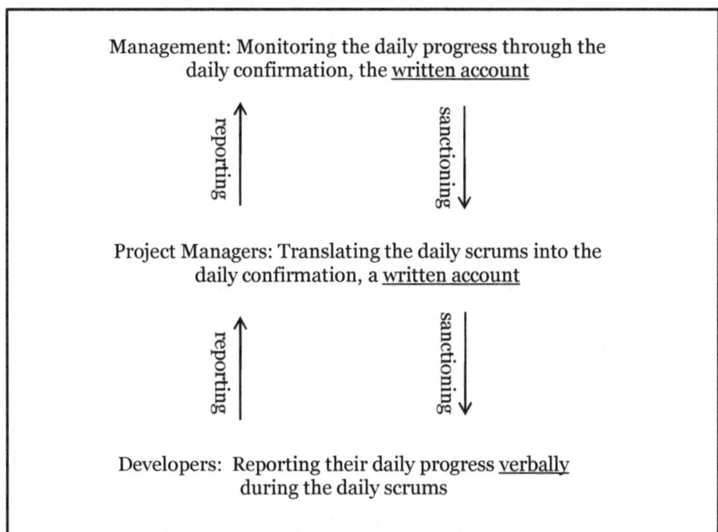

Figure 13: Pyramid of Reporting

The figure shows the perceived reporting hierarchy. The developers made their statements verbally at the daily meetings. In most cases (especially later on in the timeline) it would then be the project manager's turn, who would fill out the daily confirmation, on the basis of what the developers reported in the daily scrums and reflecting on each developer's performance and the team's performance as a whole. As cumulative numbers, these numbers were fed back into another system which then provided the management with an overview of the day-to-day performance of each team. If the numbers were not satisfactory it would be, first, the project managers who would be addressed. It was then up to the project manager to further communicate (or not) and sanction the individuals or the team (or not).

Whilst it is interesting to see the developers' viewpoint as well as that of the project managers, it is important to also look at the management's position. Did the management actually seek more visibility and control or was this some type of side-effect of the new practices which were introduced?

The Management's Position

Whilst some of the developers and project managers agreed, or disagreed, upon the necessity of the new practices and, as a separate issue, on the increased day-to-day control, it seemed to have been in the management's interest to increase control. Either way, through the daily meetings as well as the daily confirmation, Tom explained that he hoped to make people accountable to themselves and to him, as the manager. In an interview he explained his position:

> Tom: What happens quickly in a Scrum type approach: You learn very quickly who produces and who doesn't because it becomes very obvious in small teams, who is doing the work and who is falling behind. And so there is a lot of team pressure. (...) Teams that aren't performing very well - it becomes really obvious.
>
> CG: The same with the daily confirmation.
>
> Tom: Yeah, if you commit to things you better make sure you have done it. Its measurable and if actually somebody comes and checks... (Tom, Senior Vice President, Interview: February 2006)

There are two interesting arguments in this quote. First, the idea of control through team pressure, and second, that commitment makes for accountability. The question of pressure through the team was also discussed between Thorsten, the Vice President and Michael, a project manager. From what Michael told me at the interview, similar to Tom, the Vice President also advised that one 'advantage' of the daily confirmations and the daily scrums was the evolving team dynamics. Michael explained:

> I talked to [Vice President]. He said it should push the potential low performer of the team. I am not convinced about that. Cause as [other Manager] said yesterday you can be easily fooled by someone saying that they are working on the design document and tomorrow too. I try to avoid that by asking when it will be finished. Of course they can say it takes 5 days but then it's my task to judge how much time it's going to cost. The rest of the team they don't know. So they don't push him. Because they work on different projects. (..) The topics should be assigned to the locations but it's not the case today. (Michael, Project Manager, Interview: December 2005)

This situation was more or less the same in all teams except Antoine's. In Antoine's case, all developers apart from one worked on the same project. In this case, Antoine could monitor the projects' progress more easily and compare the developers' performance. Additionally, the team members could potentially control each other as, by working on the same project, difficult and easy tasks are easier to identify and if a team member is slow or lazy, the team will most likely notice this. In these cases, it is more difficult to find workarounds, to decrease the pressure by giving for instance very generous estimations for task completion as feared by Michael.

The second part of Tom's comment in the first quote within this section on the management's position is related to accountability. In his statement, he emphasises that, if the developers commit to something, then they had better ensure that they have carried it out, in case someone actually comes and checks. Tom underlines that there is always a chance that someone comes and checks. Within the same interview Tom explained in more detail this need for tight control:

> There are so many moving pieces to this thing, it's easy to fail. Which is why you need a lot of tight control, a lot of small projects to finish them quickly get them done and move on to the next. (Tom, Senior Vice President, Interview: February 2006)

Exercised on a day to day basis and communicated directly already during the first initial meeting, the tight control was not welcome. In order to avoid it, 'escape strategies' evolved amongst the developers and project managers. One of the most popular instances was the 'hiding strategy'. A developer explains:

> If I don't have anything to tell I could still lie and say I have done this and that (...) and if I have to I put code I just say I tried and it didn't work. (Fieldwork Notes, Week 11)

Another, more drastic step was to leave the team / vendor organisation. As this was the most radical measurement, as it will be discussed in Chapter 6, most developers adapted to the situation by becoming more introverted, solely interested in activities which were directly related to the task at hand and with this, only relationships and communication channels which led closer to this goal, were kept alive.

5.8 Conclusion

The market in which an organisation acts, determines its strategy and vision and, as a result, also the production practices and working climate (Carmel and Sawyer 1998; Dube 1998). This is also the case for ERP system providers which act in a market which appears to be much more dynamic, fluid and complex than what we know from the bespoke system market (cf. Sawyer 2000a). Only by considering one factor, the number and heterogeneity of stakeholders, we find expectations and complexity in the case of ERP system multiplied. Instead of serving, for instance, one or a few user organisations, ERP vendors, such as the organisation observed, serve over 40,000 user organisations, are noted at several stock exchanges and are one of the biggest employers in some countries. Each day for instance, we find the vendor in the news and there are industry analysts whose jobs are to exclusively monitor and analyse the vendor.

Such market conditions, combined with close competition, create a dynamic market in which strategies and, with this production methods, have to be constantly adapted (see also Dube 1998). However, to change an organisation with thousands of employees is not an easy choice. Changing the strategy, even if only for a particular market segment, means changing the way the product is developed in this area and, with this move of people out of their comfort zone, expose them to change and lead them into a direction which corresponds with the (new) organisational goals – all whilst being watched closely by other stakeholders, such as industry analysts.

The above account has introduced, from a social, rather than a development process method view, the importance and also the type of strategy initiated at this vendor's site in the light of an unpopular product, as well as the impacts of this strategic change on working practices. It has shown how the vendor, facing a choice of either closing the division or changing the way things were done, decided upon the latter by hiring a new manager. This new manager was known as a successful Change Agent, who was hoped to bring in the missing knowledge of how to develop a CRM system, which was used by a different type of user than the vendor's core ERP system.

Surprisingly unclear, he introduced his new strategy to the developers and left them (unknowingly?) with a rather ambiguous idea about how the resulting changes in development practices should be translated into the day to day work. Tom's unclearly communicated strategy and his absence left the developers to their own destiny which provides us, not only with an interesting account of change management, but with an intriguing insight into how the developers, rather than being a passive workforce, took things into their own hands and filled the information gap.

If we look at this case, it is necessary to understand, that these people, working in the labs, are experts in their field. The vendor's screening process is known for being very selective. For keeping the developers in the company, the vendor claims to pay top salaries (top 10% of the industry average). These developers were not insecure, shy people needing constant attention and guidance, but people, who were used to make their own decisions and, as this case demonstrates, even in the absence of guidance, search for solutions. The developers lashed onto the word 'Scrum', the most acquainted word used by Tom, and rumours were soon established stating that Tom wanted to implement Scrum methodology. The introduction of daily meetings only supported the rumours leading to the strong belief that, in order to please Tom (and not lose one's job), it was necessary to implement Scrum methodology, with minor adaptations, as best as possible.

This 'taking things into their own hands', however, has, as we have seen, not been a smooth process, but a contingency in which competing accounts existed. Whilst Tom was aiming for a methodological mix out of Microsoft's Sync and Stabilise, Scrum and his own experiences, the developers strongly believed in a Scrum implementation and judged new practices introduced by the management accordingly. However, it is not only this kind of confusion which developed and which is interesting; already the various ways in which the daily meetings took place shows how the changes developed their own dynamics.

The changes had a significant impact on daily working life within the labs, as the above chapter indicates. Particularly dominant in this respect, was the transformation of the control structure impacting also the way work is measured. If we apply Saywer's (2004) archetypes of software development teams[53], a shift appears to have developed from a network/group

53 Sawyer (2004) points to three social types of software development teams: (1) sequential (2) group and (3) network. The three types vary in the way software development is seen and evaluated. Whilst sequential software development is based on a linear set of discrete tasks, with people working in very specific functions and in the believe that a good

driven type of software development towards a more sequential type of software development in which day-to-day individual progress rather than group effort is controlled and measured. It was this change of control structure which resulted also in a most visible change of communication patterns across teams (developer and support teams) as shown above and discussed in detail in Chapter 6.

In the next chapter, I investigate the presented ethnographical data from a more analytical viewpoint, addressing in particular the topics of strategic change in the light of shifting market conditions and the associated, unexpected struggles. Bringing the world of the support and developer teams together, the next chapter highlights furthermore, how the informal work organisation and communication patterns changed across departments.

process produces good software, in a group situation, developers are organized into interdependent groups and are evaluated not only for their technical skills but also on how well they work with others. For the network type, Sawyer (2004) writes: "Software development is seen as a process of constant development with a specific focus on the outcome/product. (...) Group members are valued for what they can produce. This implies a complex network of ties between people and a hub-and-spoke management approach." (page 96).

6 Analysing the Labs

6.1 Introduction

Tracy Kidder (1982), in his remarkable book on building a computer introduces us to a world of multiple and complex decisions shaping the creation of the first computers. Telling the story of the management of innovations, Kidder (ibid.) provides us with an intriguing and fascinating account of working practices and culture within an organisation. In the course of telling the story of Data General, Kidder (ibid.) introduces us to one developer who, wanting to find out the competitors' secret to success, enters the rival's labs undercover and opens up the machine. Unfolding the 'black box' and investigating the interior of the machine, the engineer finds not only technical components, but also the work organisation of the rival company reflected. Kidder's engineer comments:

> Looking into the VAX, West had imagined he saw a diagram of DEC's corporate organization. He felt that VAX was too complicated. He did not like, for instance, the system by which various parts of the machine communicated with each other; for his taste, there was too much protocol involved. He decided that VAX embodied flaws in DEC's corporate organization. The machine expressed that phenomenally successful company's cautious, bureaucratic style. (p: 32)

Kidder's book is most interesting in many ways and a 'must read' for anyone concerned with the creation and emergence of technology. What we can learn from this developer's experience in relation to this study, is that if we want to understand technology we cannot disregard the organisation behind it. Whilst focusing primarily on the user site and how, in this context, technology and society undergo a mutual shaping process, STS falls short in acknowledging the role of the organisation in this shaping process (cf. Vaughan 1999). Acknowledging this gap in current research, for this project I focus on the organisation, and more specifically on the way that work is carried out within the software labs. Like Kidder's (1982) engineer unfolding the machine just to find the hierarchical organisation reflected in the product, I unfold the policies and practices influencing and reflected in the technology.

Continuing this attempt of opening up the black box, this chapter first discusses the ethnographic data of Chapter 5, followed by a discussion, bringing the world of the support (Chapter 4) and the world of the developers (Chapter 5) together.

6.2 Introducing Competing Management Practices

Historically, the software production industry has gone through various phases in which different management approaches were suggested to handle the new challenge of managing software developers and their work (cf. Friedman 1989). With hardware costs sinking in the early 1960s and labour becoming a bigger proportion of the total cost of producing software, the question of how to best develop a usable product whilst keeping costs and quality under control became a widely discussed topic. Already in the 1960s, during the influential Garmisch Conference (Friedman 1989), various academics and practitioners pointed to this problem and started to search for solutions, proposing different approaches as to how best manage the software production process. Kraft (1977), Friedman (1989) and Curtis (1988), from different points of view, provide us with detailed accounts of the management problems in bespoke software production during these early years, when labour became more expensive than hardware and projects were commonly over budget, producing at times, questionable results.

The vendor, being part of the software production industry since the 1970s has gone, like the industry, through different phases of finding and experimenting with the 'best practice' software development approaches of any particular time. A developer from the fieldwork site describes, in an informal conversation, three main phases the vendor went through: Until the early 1990s, the vendor was said to have an informal development process in which the developers were acting with extreme discretion (akin to Friedman's (1989) 'responsible autonomy'[54]). With a change in

54 Friedman (1989) categorises as part of his effort of making sense of the present and history of management styles all management into the two categories: 'direct control' and 'responsible autonomy'. Behind the categories are different kinds of viewpoints mainly in relation to whether employees are generally motivated or if they need close supervision to give their best. In a scenario where management methods for direct control are introduced, management tends to handle people like any other production factors. This goes along with close supervision, division of work into small tasks (deskilling). Management styles falling into the category of supporting the idea of responsible autonomy would allow greater freedom to fulfil tasks, greater responsibility for tasks. With Friedman's words, responsible autonomy is an attempt to "harness the adaptability of labour power by giving workers

management, over the years, more and more processes and methods were implemented, which meant that the vendor could increasingly control developers and at the same time, ensure the work process was in compliance with industrial standards and certifications (such as ISO certifications). Recently a third set of changes was introduced, positioned in the middle of the two extremes; attempting to control the day-to-day progress of the developer on the one hand, with on the other, the management aiming to reduce rigid processes and facilitate an environment of creativity. A developer characterised the vendor's approach as a swinging from one extreme to the other, like a 'big pendulum'. On the left site, there would be 'flexibility', on the right site 'processes'. According to this developer, until the 1990s the pendulum was high on the left, and then swung over to the right. The most recent management approach would be placed somewhere in the middle between the two extremes.

As the ethnographic account in the preceding chapter has shown, the settling between the two extremes has not been unproblematic. Whilst the management found that change is necessary to bring the CRM division back on track, the developers, whilst not necessarily disagreeing with the 'need' for change, were unclear and also somewhat sceptical about the new practices introduced. The lack of clarity expressed itself in the developer appearing not to know what exactly they were supposed to introduce. As experts in their own fields, they thus took things into their own hands, filling the interpretative gaps and coming to the conclusion, that it must be a Scrum introduction – disregarding practices and evolving situations which were contrary to the idea of Scrum or agile project management in more general terms. Whilst the daily meetings and daily confirmation were highly disputed and watched with sceptical eyes, other practices, also generally indicating an iterative and potentially agile development process such as overlapping development phases (see, for instance, Takeuchi and Nonaka 1986), got much less attention and were, if at all, discussed only amongst the project managers. Whilst partially sceptical also towards the changing of the development phases in that they were now supposed to overlap, overall, this appeared to have been a much more welcome change than the daily confirmation and meeting practices (and thus was much less discussed).

leeway and encouraging them to adapt the changing situation in a manner beneficial to the firm" (p: 78).

Even though unclear to the developers for many month, the managers' idea was to base the new approach on three different types of managerial practices: Scrum (Schwaber and Beedle 2001; Takeuchi and Nonaka 1986), Sync and Stabilise (Cusumano and Selby 1997) and customised ideas of good project management. Such an approach of mixing competing managerial practices has been found to be not unusual (Adler and Borys 1996; Barrett 2004; Fitzgerald 1997; Kruchten 2007; Turex et al. 2000). Adler and Borys (1996) for instance, summarised various existing management theories putting forward the idea of a mix: to define rules for routine tasks and empower employees for non-routine tasks. A similar vote in favour of a methodological mix can be found in Barrett (2004) (see Chapter 2). Whilst current research introduces us to the possible advantages of such a mix, the vendor's case demonstrates some of the potential pitfalls as well as possible ways to monitor and thus avoid certain problems.

The mix introduced at the site observed included practices aimed at encouraging team work and acted according to the principles of responsible autonomy (akin to Friedman 1989), but at the same time, increased the feeling of being controlled. The dichotomy of the managerial approach expressed itself most dominantly in the form of the two practices: the daily meetings and the daily confirmation.

The theoretical concept of the daily meetings, as outlined in the previous chapter, is to bring people together and increase information exchange within the team. The meeting aims to encourage team responsibility and team spirit. The project manager attends the meeting as facilitator (without aiming for supervision or control) (Schwaber and Beedle 2001). The daily confirmation in turn, not being related to the agile practice Scrum[55], but based on the manager's idea of 'Best Practice Management', has been introduced from a different motivation. The daily confirmation was designed to monitor each developer's, as well as the team's, progress on an everyday basis. With this, the two practices presented an opposing picture. Whilst one supported team work, the other encouraged individual progress and facilitated close managerial control.

---

55 In Scrum theory we find, at first glance, a similar practice: story cards. Each developer makes notes on the story card, on how much work (in %) is still to do in order to complete a task. Following the idea that only reporting forward, rather than backwards, is productive, numbers such as 'percentage completed today' are not directly recorded (they can however be calculated from the numbers given). Whilst following the principle of reporting forward in time, these numbers are not made available to the upper management.

The management's intention appeared to be to combine the strength of both (akin to Adler and Borys 1996; Barrett 2004) but with an overall tendency to use the practices as measures of control (cf. Chapter 5). However, instead of the polar practices completing each other, a situation of mutual shaping between both now localised practices and the environment took place, leading to a 'merged product' of both being designed to control[56]. Like technology, the managerial practices underwent a localisation process. The data presents a detailed description of this process from which reasons for this development can be identified. One of the main reasons appear to have been that the manager (Senior Vice President and Change Agent) communicated, during his on-site visit, that he would control each process and everyone constantly (and therefore people had better 'watch out'). Thus, the developers concluded that the general intention of the management was to increase control, and that the points of control will be the key indicators for their performance assessments. Combined with a lack of supervision of the changes, with the Change Manager being located in another continent leading to a general confusion about what the developers were supposed to do, the practices and perceptions developed their own dynamics.

Whilst we could now conclude this discussion on mixing competing practices and dispute that general recommendations to do so, have to be followed with care and depend upon organisation specific variables, this account, whilst interesting, would become a type of implementation study on managerial practices. If we look, however, behind the causal reasons presented above, a closer analysis of both managerial practices allows the identification of more general reasons on how such dynamics could evolve: It appears that in this case, an 'inherent' characteristic of both practices has been stimulated: the slightly hidden characteristic of accountability.

6.2.1 *Managerial Power and Accountability*

Accountability can be defined as the giving of accounts in various forms, such as reasons, stories or excuses for a particular situation or event, which can be rooted in *verbal* and *written* exchanges of information (Garfinkel 1967; Munro 1999). If we follow the idea of accountability as a source of managerial power as theorised by Munro (1999), we find possi-

56 It has to be noted that one team did not appear to have suffered from this effect. However, the situation for this team (Antoine's team) was different. For a detailed discussion on this topic see Chapter 5.

ble explanations why the practices were, eventually, perceived as tools of managerial control: Even though 'theoretically' following different purposes, both practices introduced in the labs incorporate the inherent characteristic of making people accountable, the daily scrums in verbal, and the daily confirmation in written form.

The power of accountability in the case of verbal statements is based, if we apply Munro (1999), on the immediate emphasis of the account given by the person to be controlled. In the context of the daily meetings, this would mean that the feeling of control would be the result of the project manager calling the developers to account during the meetings. Interestingly, however, no incident was observed, in which the developers were called to account directly during the meetings, but yet people felt as if they were made accountable for their actions and thus controlled very closely. Interestingly, it seems that in the labs, it was already *the fear* of being called to account and being humiliated, which led to an increase in managerial power. Having to confirm in front of the team the progress or delay, was considered by many as potentially humiliating and an offensive practice; the developers were afraid of losing face.

Mostly based on statements made during the daily meetings, the daily confirmation provided the management not only with information about the team's day-to-day progress in a similar way to the 'mutated' daily meetings; the daily confirmation also provided a *durable* account. Whilst the account given at the daily meetings had limited validity in that verbal statements are quickly forgotten and recalling a verbal statement after a period of time is often considered as invalid (Munro 1999), in written form, the day-to-day progress could be made available to anyone, at any time, and was thus detached from time (the actual moment it was reported) and space (the North American labs). This put the actors, to whom the data was sent on a daily basis, in a powerful position: sanctioning did not have to happen immediately, but could follow at any point in time. Thus, the project managers and developers, respectively, did not know if and whether they would be called to account when reporting a fallback. In cases where there was no reaction from the management, the team which did fall behind was never sure if, for instance, an account was tolerated or if the management overlooked set backs or if, indeed, the management did not look at the written report at all. In all cases, however, there was a chance that sanctioning might come later, possibly even months later, at the end of a project. Being detached from time and space, the existence of the written account in form of the daily confirmation, created a type of panoptical supervision (Foucault 1977) with an geographically detached and thus invisible but also unpredictable observer, who might be paying attention to the data (or not), or might do so later.

Overall, what we find in the labs, are competing practices with, however, similar inherent characteristics. It is the characteristic of accountability which has been stimulated in both cases, leading to an emphasis on controlling elements which became particularly visible in the case of the daily meetings. In their theoretical form considered as team building exercise, in the local context they became and were perceived as instruments of control. Similar to the shaping process of the technology at the local site, a shaping process of methods appears to have taken place, with a highly contextual but yet not unpredictable outcome. To understand and monitor the possible modifications of methods and to predict effects of managerial practices on the work organisation in different settings, analysing the variable of 'potential to make people accountable' as outlined above, in reference to Munro (1999), appears to be a potentially useful exercise in understanding and monitoring such a localisation process.

Furthermore, what can be learned from this account is how one contextual variable (contextual in that it is not an inherent part of the practice) significantly stimulated / uninspired the power of accountability: the time available to complete a task. It appears that the perceived pressure and intensity of managerial control has been amplified in this case, by not giving the developers enough time to fulfil their tasks (as to how they perceived sufficient time to complete a task). The perceived lack of time increased chances of falling behind and consequently the possibility of being 'caught out' and humiliated, directly or indirectly, in written or verbal form, in front of the team and the management. As such, the variable of time increased the potential managerial power, rooted in instruments of making people accountable.

As the case has shown, the overall increase in perceived control was not positively perceived by the majority of employees in the labs (see Chapter 5). Various reactions developed over time, which are analysed in the following.

6.2.2 *When Control Mechanisms Are Not Welcome*

Control (or the perception of control) is said to not always provoke negative feelings, but can also be perceived as relief and comfort (Adler and

Borys 1996). Most explicitly, this is also visible in Dube's (1998) description of a software package vendor, which changed the management approach from a more controlling style towards what Friedman (1989) describes as responsible autonomy. In this case, the employees and the management were found to have difficulties not with the presence but with the absence of individual accountability. Dube (1998) explains the situation by referring to Katzenbach and Smith (1993). Katzenbach and Smith (ibid.) argue that it appears to be difficult for people to trust and accept when it is no more their individual progress which is monitored closely, but the progress of one or many teams or the project in general, which is the basis for their evaluation.

Whilst reducing individual accountability led to a situation of discomfort in Dube's (1998) case, in the labs it was the opposite. It was the newly introduced measures to control individual progress (rather than the progress of the team and the organisation), which created a feeling of discomfort. The developers were reluctant to accept the new management approach unchallenged, and thus developed practices to escape the imposed changes and their effects, by either hiding behind generous estimations or unclear high level statements in progress reports. In other cases, the rejection of increased managerial control showed itself also in more drastic ways, such as through the eventual resignation of some developers. Whilst this was discussed as an 'option' already during the time of fieldwork, to my knowledge, no developer left the team during this time. However, this situation seems to have changed. In a recent email (2007) a developer from the support team summarised her impressions, when she walked over to the developers' office, 18 months later (the support was relocated to another office a few months after I left the labs):

> I don't know if Tom considered that his CRM changes were a success but here in North America, almost everyone is leaving. Rasi has joined [support division]. Dimitiry, Benjamin are joining utilities. Tamsin has left. So many others have left or moved to [other departments]. I go to the other office [the developers' office] and I don't recognise anyone anymore, except for Remy and a few others. Apparently Thorsten [Vice President] was always saying that the lazy people are leaving. But it seems that when Dimitry decided to leave, he said: maybe there is really a problem. Too bad! And they only hire people with 3 or less years of experience! (Sara, Third Level Support Employee, Email: September 2006)

One of the main problems of the high staff turnover, as becomes clear in the quote, is that in particular people widely considered as 'experts' were leaving the CRM division (interestingly, most left only the CRM division but not the vendor)[57]. Referring to Dimitry, who has been considered as an exceptionally good developer and software architect[58], the support employee describes how lab gossips had it that now, with this resignation, the Vice President started to (officially) reconsider the strategy of his supervisor Tom, Senior Vice President.

Experts leaving a company can cause various problems for the employer: not only a new employee with required knowledge has to be found, but also, a gap of (acknowledged) expertise, trust and communication has to be closed. Even if the organisation manages to find a new employee with equal experience, this does not mean that the new employee is accepted and considered an expert amongst the developers. It is a status which has to be earned (cf. Sonnentag 1995). The membership to the various communities is not granted automatically. Values have to be accepted, entry barriers overcome and the arrangements within the groups reformed. This process of socialisation takes time and can potentially fail, resulting in problems such as dysfunctional teams and de-motivation which in turn reflect on the product. Large scale software systems such as ERP systems are not the result of one person but the effort of many.

Whilst some developers took the drastic step of leaving the CRM division, most developers appeared to respond to the pressure by complaining and 'turning inwards', in that they started to focus only on the immediate problems associated with fulfilling their daily working package - to avoid any kind of (possible) direct or indirect sanctioning. One of the effects of such internalisation was that existing communities and networks were no longer maintained and new colleagues, replacing the developers, were not initiated into the group and left isolated. A change in informal working practices took place affecting not only the developer teams, but also interfacing teams included in the occupational communities.

---

57 This has been confirmed by a follow-up telephone interview with the Vice President in August, 2007.

58 I remember occasions in which we approached Dimitry for help. Even though he was very easy to talk to, his expertise made us going 'there' only if nobody else was capable of helping us (see also Chapter 5).

In the following section, I discuss both the way working practices and communication patterns changed within the developer department and how, eventually, other interfacing departments were affected. The case reveals an interesting dynamic, connecting the, at first glance, separated teams of developers and support employees.

6.3 Communication Structure and Working Practices

The situation I encountered when entering the labs was that of a socially active lab in which a constant humming indicated multiple discussions around the coffee machine or at the developers' desks (see Chapter 3). However, with the passing of time and despite the daily gathering of the teams for the daily meeting, I noticed how the labs had become suddenly 'quieter'. Fewer people walked around and even though this might just state the obvious, the sound of clicking keyboards appeared to be more dominating than before. Whilst a decrease in chatting was considered as a success by the management (interview with Thorsten, Vice President, December 2004), this expression of 'turning inwards', as a result of the newly introduced practices, had serious effects on communication structures within the developer teams and across the departments. The developers did not feel as if they were having enough time to do anything unrelated to their immediate task. Helping others meant losing valuable time and to fall behind. As a consequence, this increased the risk of being caught out and potentially, directly or indirectly, embarrassed in front of the group during the daily meetings or through the daily confirmation – what in the long run would also reflect negatively on their performance review.

The following email, which was sent to me a year after I left the labs (2007), summarises a development, which had already started during the fieldwork, from a developer's perspective and shows the effects of the developers change of habits:

> We have no time to chat, to read mails, to have 1 hr lunch. (...) I think is better for the upper level to have people working like horses... And not taking a coffee at the machine. I don't go to any meeting that is not related to what I am doing. I don't have time So, no more all hands meeting [meetings for all employees], etc... I think I can do it for another year cause I am learning and I like that.. But later on.. If it continues like that, I will try to change the

> department. A lot of people left. (Gloria, Developer, Email: August 2007)

The quote provides us with two examples of how this process of isolation expressed itself in the day-to-day working practice. First, it shows a certain dissatisfaction with not having enough time to interact with others in informal ways, such as taking a coffee at the coffee machine; and second, how some developers started to focus only on their immediate tasks and stopped attending meetings which were not directly related to what they were doing.

Both points can have significant impacts on the working climate and also the product itself. A software package is a complex product which consists of millions of coded lines, which are assembled in a specific way to build a unit. Such 'co-development' demands the sharing of ideas, visions, goals and strategies, which is done in formal ways for instance, during all-hands meetings, bringing the organisation together. Not attending these meetings can lead to various problems in adjusting the different pieces of code and acting according to a corporate vision and common goals. Furthermore, attending meetings in general, also provides an occasion for social interaction across departments, which in turn, leads to a constant adjustment and re-production of an organisation (Boden 1994; Sawyer and Guinan 1998).

Not 'attending' the informal chats at the coffee machine, equally influences the exchange of important informal information on tasks and the organisation (expertise is shared in such settings, since a single person cannot understand all aspects of complex technologies such as ERP products). Even though programming can, at times, be a very individualistic task, for the developers, interacting with colleagues during the day and outwith working hours seemed to be important (see Chapter 3). Communities were formed, in which values were shared and communication channels built across hierarchical and departmental boundaries, satisfying the social needs of the developers. With the changes, and by taking away the time to socialise, the developers actively complained that they did not have time to have a coffee or that they did not have time to have lunch together. This picture of a social developer, dependent upon others, is interesting as it does not correspond with the widely promoted picture of individual and self focused developers presented in current literature (Carmel and Sawyer 1998; Cusumano and Selby 1997; Dube 1998; Sawyer 2000a). The current picture of software package developers does not acknowledge the social character of programming, and disregards the need for distributed expertise in such settings. The expertise to build complex systems, such as ERP systems, cannot be held by one person only or by all people equally. Expertise in such settings is distributed and needs to be shared. Thus, it appears unrealistic to assume that developers in such settings are 'unsocial' and that the sharing of expertise can be done by formal means only.

In this regard, an interesting relationship between the communication breakdown in the developer department and the performance of other teams revealed itself. In the following paragraph, I show the impact of the changes on the informal network existing between developer and other teams, as well as on the product and the user-vendor relationship. In this context, it has to be noted that only issues are highlighted, which occurred near to where I was situated: between development and support groups. As a well-known pitfall of ethnographic research, other relationships which were outside my scope of observation, such as the developer-tester relationship, cannot be highlighted (these were, for instance, said to have improved (cf. Chapter 5)).

The Support-Developer Link

At the vendor, the third level user support is situated in the same labs as the developers, officially to facilitate communication between both groups. When I entered the labs it was an established practice that the developers and support would work closely together. Regularly the support staff would ask the developers about user problems and the developers would regularly pass by a support employee's desk for a chat about 'how the users are doing' (see Chapter 4). As such, the developers and the support built a community in which expertise was shared and which at times, even included the user (in the form of a user problem). The figure below illustrates this support-developer-user community.

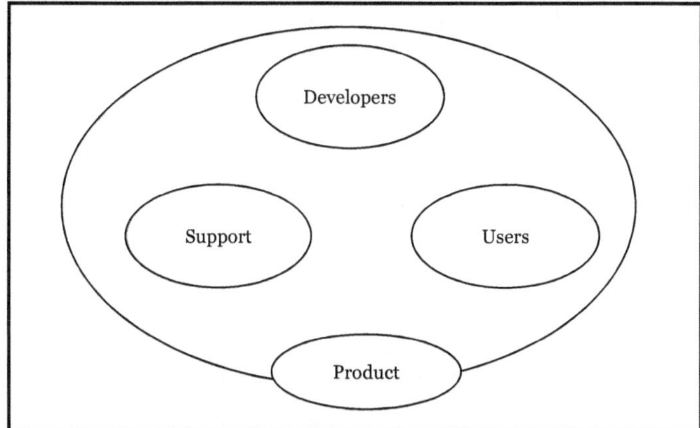

Figure 14: Support-Developer-User Community

Even though not given any formal consideration, this informal socialised working practice was crucial for the support, the developers and the users in three ways. First, the support received fast and informal help with complex user problems from those programming this part of the application, which in turn, allowed the support to respond to the users faster than they could otherwise have done. Second, the developers were constantly up-to-date regarding the problems that the users encountered whilst implementing and using the system. This feedback could then be directly included in the current development. Third, the user could influence the design of the system indirectly (and unknowingly), by having the support discuss their problems and demands, directly, and without any further intermediation, with the developers[59].

As outlined earlier in this chapter, over time, a perceived increase in control and pressure made the developers isolate themselves from any kind of (time consuming) communication. As a result, the inter-departmental co-operation between team members and across different teams, was cut down to a level of 'absolute necessity'. This shifting behaviour became quickly visible. With the start of the daily meetings (the daily confirmations were introduced first, but were not immediately responded upon) the visits of the developers to the support employees' desks became less

59 For a discussion on potential problems when discussing requirements with intermediaries (such as consultants or solution managers) see for instance Curtis at al. (1988), Keil and Carmel (1995) and Saywer (2000a).

frequent and requests for help from the support side were more often answered with "Sorry, I don't have time". The community disintegrated, leaving the support with its user alone, as illustrated in the following figure.

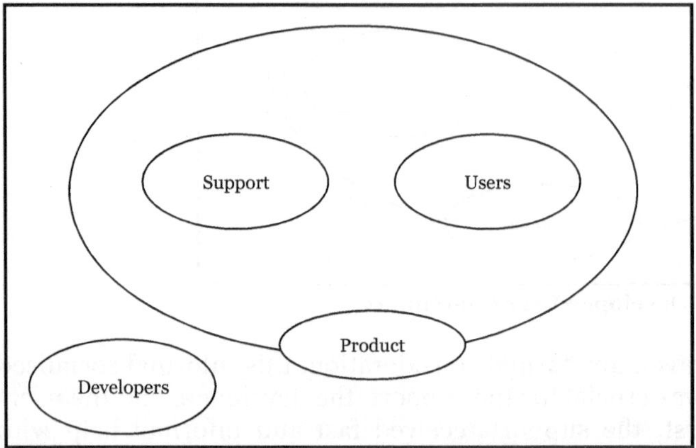

Figure 15: Support-Developer-User Community Dissolving

Within months, the support staff, previously reliant on help from the developers, found themselves confronted by messages which they could not solve on their own. Not being able to count on the expertise of the developers, the support employees found themselves helpless; this helplessness was less a question of the support not being skilled enough to solve problems by themselves, but the result of an unexpected change of working practices for which the support staff was not prepared. It was common practice to share expertise, which was also reflected in the way knowledge was formally transferred between the developer and support. When new features were launched the developers would explain these to the support employees in so-called 'hand-over sessions'. These meetings (I attended several) had a duration of 2-3 hours and provided high level information – enough to give an idea about the new functionality and the way the programs were embedded in the overall system, but not enough to solve complex user problems; this was also not necessary. Both parties were used to sharing and exchanging knowledge on the run, when complex problems arose. In some cases, the support was even entrusted with supporting new features before the formal hand-over session, since one could always ask.

However, with the developers turning inwards, the support was suddenly left alone. The tactical arrangement between the developers and support faltered, with the developers withdrawing from the informal network. The existing community including the support, the developers and the user disintegrated. Formal ways of exchanging expertise were considered by the support teams, but avoided, as seeking help formally was not only a long-winded process, but also an official acknowledgement of a lack of competence in a certain field. Instead, the support used workarounds. As I have outlined in Chapter 4, messages come with a certain priority attached, determining the time given for the vendor to respond to a message. Statistics were constantly checked and the vendor had to stay within the formal guidelines to avoid sanctioning on the basis of the Service Level Agreement. With the lack of support from the developers, the support team found itself in a situation in which deadlines were omnipresent, but answers scarce. To avoid problematic statistics, the support would occasionally send messages back to the users, suggesting a solution which was not entirely thought through, affecting the user-vendor relationship negatively (see Chapter 4).

Additionally, the signing off after the hand-over sessions (that the session took place and that all necessary information was transferred), became a much more important act. Whilst the support would sign off the documents lightly beforehand, now, they would only do so, if they felt that they were now equipped with enough information to solve most of the early problems (it was clear, that a complete transfer of knowledge was not feasible, also, since many errors happen unexpected and possibly in a part of the application which was not even modified within this particular development cycle). Not being able to solve customer problems in time, might lead to a negative customer rating and, as a result, to a potentially uncomfortable situation during the yearly appraisal (see Chapter 4).

With the passage of time, as a result of the newly arranged communities, which now only included the user and the support employee (and the product respectively), new working practices evolved, and with these came new ways of guaranteeing more fully fleshed out answers to support problems. Several months after I left the labs, I received the following email from Sara, showing how the support appeared to have 'recovered' from the lack of co-operation with the developers:

> Yes, I have the feeling that Scrum had a very stressful effect on developers. The turnaround here was very low and that's when

> people started leaving the company. Of course, it was difficult for me at first because I couldn't get help from them. But I think now, I know the application much better than before and I rarely ever ask for their help. (Sara, Third Level Support Employee, Email: September 2006)

This mental and practical detachment was, some months later, reinforced by a physical detachment. The support was moved to another office within the same building. With the support team being, in numbers, large enough to have lunch catered for their own eating area (see Chapter 3), the exchange of information during lunch time also disappeared.

Whilst the emancipation of the support staff assured once more a certain quality of user support, there was no replacement for the informal feedback the developers received by discussing support problems with the support teams. With the informal communication channel eliminated, the developers and ultimately the users, could not profit any more from the earlier fast and non-bureaucratic method of information exchange[60].

6.4 Conclusion

Finding the right management approach to accommodate the different interests of the market, the organisation and the employees during the software development phase is difficult. Investigating the vendors' attempts to find the 'best of breed' management approach, has highlighted the complications, even for one of the biggest independent software providers with many years of experience. Introducing us to the many struggles the vendor was facing, the account demonstrates how we cannot ignore the organisation of work, shaped through management practices,

60 Formal ways of information exchange were in place before and after the changes were introduced. Solution Managers, who had the responsibility for collecting and representing user requirements, at times still consulted the message inbox of the support to see which kind of functionality and problems came up at the user site. However, this was described only as a "last resort" of information: Whilst formal classification schemas are used to distribute support messages (cf. Chapter4), the content of messages is informal and unclassified, often related to several problems at once. The message subjects, which appear in the list if messages are selected according to a particular component or problem, are not-standardised and often cryptic (not all users are native speakers of English) or of such technical nature and uniqueness that without an understanding of the context and the technical particularities, information was difficult to gain by 'browsing' through messages.

if we want to understand the shaping of the technology. Similar to Kidder's (1981) engineer opening the computer and finding organisational patterns reflected, this research aims to open up the black box of this 'mysterious' organisation, show the way work is carried out at such a site, and with this how the technology shapes and is shaped from within the organisation.

More specifically, this chapter discussed the new managerial approach and the challenges associated with expert labour in the light of a fast changing and competitive market. In this context, the analysis of the presented data has shown how, under certain circumstances, the introduction of a methodological mix does not necessarily create a situation in which different practices are complementing each other (akin Barrett 2004). Applying the idea of accountability as a source of managerial power to the case, the data highlights how practices implemented supporting the idea of responsible autonomy (cf. Friedman 1989), can mutate supporting the opposite, direct control (cf. Friedman 1989). With this, this research takes a different stance to conventional analysis of implementations of management methods (such as Dube 1998), by emphasising and analysing the inherit characteristics of managerial practices and their potential to transform into instruments of power in more general terms. In this context, the application of the concept of accountability as a source of managerial power has also shown the important role deadlines can play, if accountability is used as a basis for managerial power. Extending earlier theories on accountability and power by Munro (1999), the case indicates that accountability, as a source of managerial power, can be altered, depending on the time available to fulfil a certain task.

Furthermore, the empirical data shows how the developers - who cannot be considered as 'ordinary' employees who can be easily reconfigured - apply their own discretion (cf. Chapter 5) and find escape strategies to avoid unwanted managerial control. In cases where escaping was not possible, isolation strategies could be witnessed. This, what appears to be a newly developed self-focus of the developers, is interesting in many ways. First, the data indicates that the self-focus is not a 'natural' behaviour for developers. The developers appeared to be upset about the lack of time to have lunch together or meet for a chat at the coffee machine. This shows the developers as 'social beings', who only started to behave in more individualistic and self -focused ways as a reaction to changing circumstances. Interestingly, these observations conflict with existing research in this area. The common cliché of a software developer tends to be a picture of a mostly isolated expert, with little need for social interaction (see, for instance, Carmel and Sawyer (1998)). Whilst this perception could not be confirmed by this research, the picture drawn by the above authors has also been found to be a rather simplistic assumption. In the light of the highly distributed nature of expertise in such settings, it is very unlikely that in the context of software packages, individualistic programmers succeed. The interdependencies between programs suggest the need for close interaction between developers.

The internalisation of the developers has also had a significant impact on the organisation of work and the working climate within the developer teams and beyond. The ethnography indicates an intriguing and unexpected connection between the users, the support and the developers, which appeared to fulfil various important tasks. The co-operation between the support and the developers allowed the support to quickly respond to complex user problems. This, in turn, provided the developers with constant up-to-date feedback from the user's side, which could be included in the current development. As such, it gave the users a chance to influence the design of the product (unknowingly) by simply reporting a problem to the support. We have seen how this fruitful co-operation among these three parties, across the product life-cycle and organisational boundaries, was disturbed by the developers' reaction to the perceived increase of control. As such, the data highlights not only the potential side effects of introducing a different management method into an existing working environment, but also the importance of informal networks (including internal and external parties), as well as their mere existence in the software package industry.

Moreover, from a research methodology viewpoint, the findings underline the importance of designing research in a way in which boundaries between departments and product life phases are not merely accepted or ignored, but investigated and included in the analysis. It is only when we widen our approach and aim to grasp at least part of the complex relationships which can be found in software development labs, that we can aim to understand complex technologies, such as ERP systems.

Within the last chapters, I have outlined the broader research context in which this study has taken place, explained and justified the research design, and presented and analysed the data collected in the North American labs of one of the most successful ERP system providers. In the following, I provide a detailed summary of this research and revisit some of the main findings in the light of my research questions. Also, limitations and the future prospects of this area of research are discussed.

7 Discussion and Conclusion

7.1 Introduction

Numerous and diverse user organisations, dynamic and constantly changing markets, strong competition and rapidly changing technology characterise the market in which Enterprise Resource Planning (ERP) system (enterprise software systems, supporting a wide-ranging variety of organisational functionalities) vendors act. Responding to these challenges is crucial for the organisations' survival and therefore, requires careful management of the product and the product life-cycle respectively. This is a study about a vendor producing ERP systems, carried out in the traditions of Science and Technology Studies and, more specifically the Social Shaping of Technology perspective, highlighting some of the dynamics and complexity which these ERP vendor organisations face, as well as the reaction to the challenges. Putting the organisation and organisational practices at the centre of attention, this research advances our understanding of ERP systems from a work organisation point of view. In other words, it is the organisation that is the point of entry, providing a vendor centred perspective.

This vendor centred viewpoint arguably provides us with a different understanding than typical STS studies, where scholars enter the field focusing on the mutual shaping of the technology and the local site. By changing the perspective from 'outside' (outside the vendor organisation) to 'inside' (within the vendor organisation), this research provides a new understanding of ERP systems as well as highlighting the need for an extension of the current research agenda to move away from a user organisation's to a vendor organisation's view on packaged software. It is only then, when we understand both sites that we can aim to comprehend such global systems.

This research provides such a vendor perspective and highlights the unexpected struggles and complex processes within a global ERP vendor organisation, which is aiming to maintain its status as market leader. In particular, this research shows for the first time, (1) how a ERP system vendor manages to serve a diverse and geographically dispersed user base, using the example of the ERP system support phase, the point in which the system, in customised form, re-enters the vendor organisation and (2) how, from a social perspective, a ERP system vendor organises its product development phase.

Before addressing these topics in the context of the main research questions, a brief excursion into the literature will highlight, in more detail, the current gaps in literature which prevent us from having a better comprehension of the strategies and practices surrounding Enterprise Resource Planning systems (for a full review, see Chapter 2).

If we stand by the life-cycle perspective on current research adopted in Chapter 2, we find the majority of academic studies are carried out in the periphery of software package production, in relation to the moment of implementation of such global systems at the user site. 'Implementation studies' research has characterised the overwhelming majority of literature in this area (for detailed reviews of the implementation literature see Botta-Genoulaz et al. 2005; Klaus et al. 2000; Moon 2007, as well as Chapter 2) and, whilst intriguing and useful, a focus on this part of the product life-cycle has led to shortcomings in other areas. Surprisingly little attention has, for instance, been paid to the phase of software package development, which could help us to understand the way the technology is created. Whilst there are studies on software development, most research addresses bespoke software production, ignoring the rise of packaged solutions. Exceptions include researchers such as, Carmel (1997), Cusumano and Selby (1997), Carmel and Becker (1995), Carmel and Bird (1997), Carmel and Sawyer (1998), Dube (1998), Sawyer (2000a), Sawyer (2000b), Sawyer and Guinan (1998) and Zachary (1994, 1998). Further and new research is needed, addressing the topic from different angles (such as ethnographic work place studies) and carried out by different researchers, as well as within different settings.

Furthermore, a more exclusive focus on the particularities of ERP systems is needed. Current research considers ERP system development only as part of the broader group of software package development. This is surprising if we consider the different markets in which standard software package producers act and, therefore, are shaped by. Whilst Carmel and Sawyer (1998) explicitly highlight how contextual conditions of different markets reflect on working practices and thus, packaged software development differs from bespoke software development, the authors fall short in making such a distinction on a more finely granular level in that ERP markets and ERP vendors differ from, for instance, spread sheet software packages. Similar generalisations can be found in other studies and later work of the authors as well as in Cusumano and Selby's (1997) often cited work on "How Microsoft develops software". The authors imply, that all developers within Microsoft, regardless of which product, follow the same software development approach, "Sync and Stabilise". Such generalisation of development methods and also of the day-to-day working practices already within one settings, seems unhelpful. It is highly unlikely that within one organisation such as Microsoft, providing such a wide range of products varying from word processing software to ERP systems, that the software development phase is organised in the same way across the organisation (and hence all apply the Sync-and Stabilise framework)[61]. Overall, it is questionable, if software developers working on different types of software packages can be considered as similar and hence included in the same research.

Whilst ERP system development, particularly in the social sciences, has been neglected by academic research, other areas of the product life-cycle have been hardly investigated at all, such as the software support phase or the software sales phase. With regards to the sales phase, it is interesting that not even a research agenda has been outlined in this context (see Chapter 2). Even the most recent and most comprehensive work on ERP packages approaching the topic from a life-cycle perspective (Pollock and Williams 2008) falls short in not acknowledging the mere existence of this phase. Whilst there is a need to include the moment of system sales in future research, the existing ignorance towards the sales phase highlights and underlines once more the almost exclusive focus on the user organisation's viewpoint and the technology in our discipline, disregarding almost entirely the vendor's perspective.

In respect of the software package support phase, under-researched, but acknowledged, we find a few accounts provided by Light (2001) and Nah *et al.* (2001), who have introduced us to parts of the problems of ERP system support from an 'outsider', user organisation perspective. Also, we find Gable et al. (2001) supporting the importance of research on software package maintenance activities by outlining a new research agenda, emphasising the particularities of support in such settings. However, even though acknowledging that there is a vendor's perspective on support work, Gable et al. (ibid.) argue that ultimately, all software is used by organisations and thus research adopting an organisation's viewpoint is to be emphasised. As such, also Gable et al. (ibid.) fall short in taking into

[61] As mentioned earlier, a confidential report on a joint effort by the vendor studied and Microsoft to find best practice project management revealed that within Microsoft not only one but many different approaches are used, which depended both on the project and the product in question.

account the importance of the vendor organisations' viewpoint, which, in the context of ERP systems, is always part of the system support activities.

If we look into other fields in search of accounts on technical support, such as the sociology of work organisation, we find intriguing research carried out by Orr (1986, 1996, 1998). Whilst providing a perspective from within technical support departments, the settings in which the study took place are very different. Orr's study was conducted within Xerox, a copy machine vendor. As Chapter 2 and 4 have shown, due to the different type of product and a different time, this account does not translate well into the area of software package support and, more specifically today's ERP system support (see Chapters 2 and 4).

Aiming to address at least some of the many gaps in current literature identified in the context of this book, this research adapts a vendor viewpoint and highlights the working practices within the labs of one of the biggest ERP providers worldwide, by focusing on two phases: the product development and the product support. The research and analysis into these two phases is embedded in contextual, ethnographic descriptions of the strategies, policies and practices in place at such a global ERP vendor in more general terms. With this, this research not only provides insight into two product life-cycle phases from a vendor's viewpoint, but shows a snapshot of how in more general terms, an ERP vendor handles the challenge of responding to the demands of different interest groups, without losing sight of its overall goal: to produce a system which can be applied, and therefore sold to a maximum number of users.

From the gaps identified in the literature and the data collected in the field, the following research questions evolved (see Chapter 1 and 3), highlighting the challenging relationship between the user organisations and the global ERP vendor at two points of the product life cycle, the ERP system support and the ERP system development phase:

1. *How does an ERP system provider manage the challenge of serving a highly diverse and geographically dispersed user base?*

2. *How does an ERP system provider, from a social perspective, organise its product development phase?*

This chapter is divided into two sections. In the first part, the research questions are revisited. To provide a more complete picture of the research, a detailed summary of the analysis made in the previous chapters is presented. For both research questions, this summary is followed by a section, explicitly highlighting the main contributions of this research. The second part of the chapter is dedicated to revisiting the limitations (see also Chapter 3) as well as thoughts for future research.

7.2 The Challenge of Serving a Diverse User Base

How does an ERP system provider manage the challenge of serving a highly diverse and geographically dispersed user base?

Serving a numerous and heterogeneous user base is a challenging task for standard software providers and for ERP system providers even more, since this type of software is developed with the vision in mind (and a corresponding business model behind) of supporting and reflecting the unique processes of an organisation within one system. However, it is not only finding and convincing user organisations to buy a particular ERP system; managing the potentially tense relationship with the many and diverse user organisations remains a challenge throughout the product life cycle. Chapter 4 provides a unique and first-time insight, on how an ERP vendor attempts to manage this relationship - through lenses of the software package support phase.

If we look at the product life-cycle and current research, we know from literature related to ERP implementations, that ERP systems are highly complex products and that it can be difficult to localise these systems in a way that reflects the user organisation's needs. However, what we do not learn from these studies is what happens when problems occur during (or after) the implementation phase, which cannot be solved by the implementation team. We know that the implementation team would contact the vendor's support office and will eventually get an answer back from the vendor (cf. Light 2001). In the meantime, what happens at the ERP vendor's site remains a mystery. This research has revealed part of this mystery by providing an insight into one of the support teams (third level support) at the vendor's site and, furthermore, throws light on the support organisation in more general terms and the way the user-vendor relationship is managed at this stage of the product life-cycle.

In the following, summarising the answer to research question 1 which evolves out of the presented data and analysis in particular in Chapter 4, I highlight some of the main findings in this context, namely: (1) the way problems are made mobile so that they can travel from the user site around the globe to a support expert working at any of the vendor's software labs; (2) how this 'dis-embedding' of messages from their local context, in order to make them mobile, sometimes fails; and (3) how the classification parameters attached to a message by the user, such as the problem priority, influences the user – vendor power relationship.

Making Problems 'Mobile'
Problems reported by the user organisations are numerous and different. To manage the variety and the numbers of messages arriving at the vendor's site each year (up to one million messages) the vendor's support services are based on a process of dis-embedding problems from their sticky and local context to packing them up so that they can be distributed to the support specialists.

When the user organisation encounters a problem, rather than calling the vendor and arranging an appointment for an on-site visit, the user organisation is asked to create an online support ticket. In the course of creating the ticket, various obligatory parameters are offered to the user from which he can chose, for example, which component of the application the problem should be assigned to, and with which priority the problem should be treated. The 'mobilised' problem is formally distributed across the organisation in two ways, as the figure below illustrates:

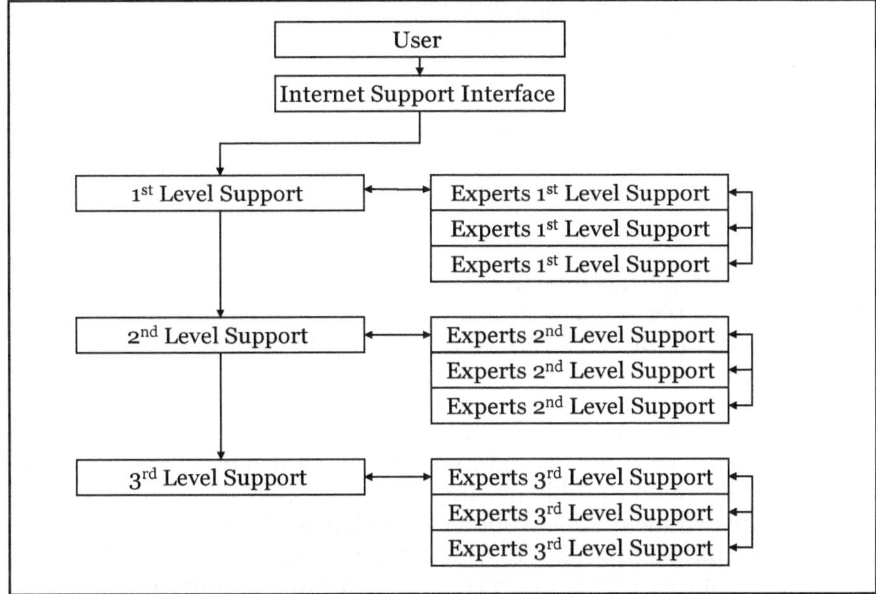

Figure 16: Formal Problem Distribution

The figure shows the different ways of distributing a message, vertically, between the different support levels representing different levels of expertise (first, second and third level support) and horizontally, between support teams, having the same level of expertise but in different parts of the application. As the figure illustrates, whilst horizontal moves between equal levels of expertise but in different areas are reciprocal, vertical moves between the first, second and third support levels, interestingly, appear to be one way only (except emergency situations). Therefore, if the message is not solved by any of the previous levels of support, it is at the third level of support, where the problem ends its journey. With this, for the third level support, assigning oneself to a message is a kind of 'terminal' activity. The exceptions to this rule are cases in which the responsible employee has found that the error is caused by another component and thus lies in the area of expertise of another team. In these cases, the employee is allowed to vertically re-distribute the message (as is the case at all levels of support) and thus, the problem starts travelling again.

Whilst this 'framing' of relationships through dis-embedding messages at the moment of creation, via a classification scheme, and re-distributing problems across the organisation accordingly, appears to be very efficient, the study shows how informal practices developed which, at times, compromised this process. In Chapter 4, we have seen how the framing process fails and becomes subject to 'overflows' when messages are vertically redistributed and assigned to other teams, not because they are in the area of expertise of another team, but to avoid 'troublesome' customers or complex problems (so called "ping-pong games"). I have shown how this informal forwarding of messages, whilst formally outlawed, leads in some cases to a situation in which messages are sent back and forth between teams with both parties denying responsibility for the problem. This process costs valuable time, delays the problem-solving attempts and can sometimes result in 'escalations' raised by the unhappy customer (cf. Chapter 4).

Whilst the classification of messages allows the vendor to lift the user problems out of its local context and by making it mobile, facilitates the re-distribution of the problems, the formal support process also leaves space for the 'wildness' of a problem. Not all aspects of the message creation and handling process are standardised, with certain parts of the problem remaining highly interpretative and 'wild' and therefore, unable to be framed by imposing categories. It is here that the blank text field plays a major role, in that the user can describe the problem in his own words. With this, whilst the vendor needs to set a formal frame to handle the many messages received, space is given to the individuality and complexity of problems[62].

Re-embedding Problems: Creating a 'Virtual Local'

Whilst messages are lifted out of their local context (in the words of von Hippel (1994), the information is made "unsticky") to allow a re-distribution of problems around the globe, at times, this mechanism is unsuitable and unhelpful to the support. If we investigate the message solving process more closely, we can see how differently complex problems are approached and are re-embedded into their (technical) local context. For problems arriving at the third level support, the highest level

62 Surprisingly, on reflecting upon the possible distinctiveness of problems, the support teams also make use of such blank textual fields and formulate each suggested solution from scratch. Per se one might expect pre-phrased templates, particularly, as the vendor sells CRM systems, in which templates and phrasing suggestions are embedded. However, the blank field in which the user organisation can express itself freely, functions as a tool to embrace the variety and complexity of problems which cannot be framed by formal categories only.

of support expertise, a theoretical discussion of the problem is not enough: the problem needs to be inspected in the context of its local settings. The context of problems reported to the user at this stage is unique and system settings at the user site are crucial indicators for finding the solution. As a result, reproduction of the problem in one of the vendor's own test systems is not helpful, with the information being "sticky" (von Hippel 1994) and needs to be embedded in the local context. In such situations the support employees create a 'virtual local'.

The virtual local is created by re-embedding problems into their local context via a remote connection. This allows the support to virtually 'visit' the user site and investigate the problem reported, on site. A common procedure when doing so is to re-produce the problem and explore the error logs of the vendor's system, which run on site, as well as the interfacing systems. Interestingly, in the process of re-embedding problems in the local context, emphasis is given to 'technical' issues, such as parameters set in the system, or the error logs. Disregarding the socio-technical context of the problem, such as, the user's interaction with the machine (as emphasised by Orr 1986, 1996, 1998) in the context of technical support, such investigations take place in a 'silent dialogue' between support and machine, brushing the user aside.

Whilst creating a 'virtual local' is, in most cases used as a mechanism to investigate the problem more closely and, with this as a problem-solving tactic at the vendor, it also serves as a way of clarifying responsibilities. As I have shown in Chapter 4, in some cases the user asks for help relating to problems for which the vendor is no longer liable[63]. In situations where the support employee 'feels' that this might be the case (a judgement often based on prior experiences with the user rather than the type of error reported), remote access to the user's site can be used to quickly clarify and re-establish boundaries.

The Power of Problem Priorities

This research has highlighted the importance of message classification for use in the message solving process. Interestingly, whilst the parameters help the vendor to deal with the many messages which arrive each day, it also provides the user organisation with a tool of power, coming in the

63 For a description on user struggles (on how to not cross the boundaries set by the vendor and hence loose the possibility for support services), see Light (2001).

form of a parameter attached to the message, namely the message priority.

The basis of the formally framed relationship between the user and the vendor is the Service Level Agreement (SLA), in which the legal framework of the support contract is outlined. Within this contract the vendor commits to a certain type of service, also including the response time for problems. Whilst the agreed response time differs, depending on the type of SLA (and on the amount of money the user organisation pays for the support services), in all cases regulations are in place to connect the priority level to a response time frame. As such, it is the message priorities which, set by the user, determine the day-to-day work of the support employee and builds the main pillar of the framed relationship. High priority messages have to be solved first, no matter what other issues or tasks a support employee is working on. More distinctly demonstrating the power given to the users is when the user organisation calls out an 'escalation'. Raising an escalation, the user gets maximum attention not only from one support employee who potentially has to work through the night, but from anyone who could help – all under the observant eyes of the Board of Directors, which usually monitors escalations.

Even though the account shows throughout how priorities can, at times, empower the user, it has to be noted, that priorities also call the user into account. In cases of problems which are classified as high priority problems, the user organisation also has to fulfil certain tasks, such as, for instance, providing a 24h hour contact number. If the user fails to fulfil his responsibilities, the support can educate the user by pointing to 'notes' (pre-phrased information available on the support portal) and lower the priority.

Interestingly, whilst message priority determines support work, we also find here how the formally framed process is subject to overflows. In cases where the support employee finds himself unable to solve a problem within a pre-defined time frame, informal priority re-negotiations take place between the support and the user organisation. It is only with a lower priority and, with this the related extension of the formally agreed response time, that the support worker can gain time to find an appropriate solution. The evolution of this type of relationship between the user and the vendor is very surprising, in that the user in all cases observed did not insist on keeping the message priority, even though he would have had the right to do so, and when asked, lowered the priority to 'help out' the support team.

Re-negotiation of support priorities were not a common habit, but were more of a last resort. In cases where a re-negotiation of priorities was not considered a viable option, but time was desperately needed, other types of informal practices were latched onto, such as providing solutions which might not be entirely thought through. Again, such practices were not common practice, but an act of despair in the light of an empowered user.

Whilst the priorities play a major role in determining which problem is to be solved first within this formally framed relationship, we also find how the support employee exercised power within the formal frame, that is, when all messages had the same priority. It is there, when the support employee judges on the basis of personal preferences (such as type of problem, friendliness of customer) which problem to attend first.

Contributions (1)
As highlighted in the introduction to this concluding chapter, current studies into ERP software production tend to present a user's viewpoint, disregarding the vendor's attempts to manage the product life-cycle. This leads to a situation in which certain phases of the product life cycle, such as ERP system support, are almost entirely disregarded (except Light (2001), Nah *et. al* (2001) who, however, provide a user organisation viewpoint). This research presents the first insider perspective on how ERP system support can be organised, the challenges associated with such a model and overall, how the user-vendor organisation is organised at this stage of the product life cycle. In so doing, it presents, what would be impossible if we were to translate Orr's (1986, 1996, 1998) findings on technical support as well as von Hippel (1994) on 'sticky information' into the context of ERP systems (see also Chapter 2): online support for complex, world-wide distributed systems.

This study has outlined the policies and processes behind the scenes, facilitating the management of globally distributed problems as well as the equally globally distributed expertise. In particular, it showed how, firstly, one key mechanism in organising such support service, appears to be the practice of detaching messages through the means of classification schemes, to lift the problems out and re-distribute them to whoever is awake and at work, having the expertise needed. In this context, I have shown, that whilst for most user problems, this appears to work well, this process is also subject to overflows such as, when the user problem is classified incorrectly, and thus the problem does not meet its expert and needs to be re-distributed or, when the distribution mechanism is used to avoid potentially 'troublesome' users, who are 'unwanted' resulting in the message being sent back and forth between teams. Whilst in these situations the problem remains within the virtual world, for some problems, the detaching mechanism is unhelpful in that it does not provide enough information to solve the problem. It is then, when the support employee remotely connects to the user site, to embed the complex problem in its original context.

Secondly, the data highlights the polar perception of the nature of the problem in that it is either social or technical. Socio-technical problems akin Orr (1986, 1996, 1998) appeared to be non-existent. It is where complex problems appear, that this distinction between technical and social becomes most visible. Most problems are classified as 'technical only', which is reflected in the mechanisms of lifting messages out of their local context and distributing them across the geographically dispersed support labs, in which expertise is shared. Even in cases where the problem is too complex and has to be investigated in its original context, when a 'virtual local' is created to re-embed the problem, it is the *technical context* which is emphasised. Rather than contacting the user, the support employee establishes a remote connection to the user's system, resulting in a silent dialogue between the support employee and the machine (disregarding the user).

Whilst the majority of problems seem to be considered as technical, interestingly, some appear to be seen as 'social only', such as when the users raise their voice and ask for maximum attention by announcing an 'escalation'. Escalations cannot be raised through the portal, but the user has to call the vendor, which points towards considerations of the vendor's site for escalations being potentially connected to social issues. Whilst in the context of an escalation the problem is split once more into two categories, 'customer escalations' and 'message escalations', the vendor seems to be more aware of the importance of the social relationship between vendor and user organisations. In the case of a customer escalation, the general relationship between the vendor and user organisation is considered as 'in danger', which usually results in a vendor's representative visiting the user's organisation on site. Interestingly, in such cases, the representative is *not* a technician sent to solve the problem, which would again underline Orr's claims, but a manager (with limited technical expertise) who is sent to repair the *social relationship.*

Third, this research has shown, that whilst the ERP vendor seems to have managed – not without trade-offs and exceptions - to make complex information 'unsticky' (von Hippel 1994) and mobile, various tensions, in particular related to the power relationship between user and the vendor (represented through the support employee), become visible in the context of this type of online support. The way users express the urgency of their problems is through the classification parameter 'priority'. It is this priority, which appears to put the user organisation into a position of power, leaving a struggling support employee behind. In the labs, informal work practices could be found to escape the power of priorities, such as providing a solution which was not fully fleshed out, in an attempt to gain time. In other cases, where the priorities are set to the upper maximum (very high or escalation), the account shows how even informal renegotiations of message priorities between the support employee and the user take place, revealing the occasional helplessness of the support employee begging the user to change the problem priority.

Equally associated with what appears to be an empowerment of users, or at least, at times, an uneven power relationship, is that the user is always given the advantage of doubt when problem responsibilities are unclear. The account has shown that when in doubt about who is responsible for a software error, the vendor or the user organisation, it is the vendor who has to present proof. Whilst it would be easier for the vendor to do so in a face-to-face support setting in which the support would see how the user interacts with the machine (and with which machine exactly), it can be difficult to spot at first glance whether a problem is the vendor's responsibility.

Overall, what we can learn from this account is, besides a first time understanding of how support work is organised in such settings, that existing accounts on support work in social research cannot be translated unchanged into the context of today's ERP systems support research. Indeed, it can be said, that from this account, it appears that the concept of local and territorial support work, as demonstrated by Orr (1986, 1996, 1998), is inadequate for ERP system support work – even though problems reported to the ERP system support department appear to be much more complex than technical problems of copy machines and thus should make this type of support necessary. At the vendor, what appears to have been established is a process, which allows the 'partial framing' of problems where they are classified and made 'light' in order to be redistributed to the globally dispersed support expertise, but where, at times, if more complex problems occur the support changes to other modes of problem solving. It is then possible, when the problem is re-embedded in its technical context through creating a 'virtual local', to solve what is seen as a technical problem, or where face-to-face/phone contact is established to repair the social relationship.

7.3 The Challenge of Developing Standard Software

How does an ERP system provider, from a social perspective, organise its product development phase?

If developing software is a challenging task, developing standard software which is accepted by the market is an even more complex endeavour. Whilst bespoke system production has its challenges (cf. Kraft 1977), standard software production appears to be much more complex in that it often has to accommodate not only many more competing expectations of different user groups, but is also constantly evaluated by other interest groups, such as analysts, stakeholders and the media (Carmel and Sawyer 1998). Thus, software package organisations are not only under pressure to satisfy existing users but also to fulfil the expectations of the various groups which shape public opinion and with this the user's attitudes, expectations and buying decisions. Whilst it is Carmel and Sawyer (1998) who explicitly point to these 'external' challenges (without using it in their later work), it is Dube (1998) who, unrelated to these authors, argues that it is such complex and fast changing market conditions, which force package vendors to re-assess and re-adapt their strategies at times, and implement solutions which, in some cases, drastically changes how things are done within organisations.

It is such drastic changes from existing strategy (and consequently working practices), which have been witnessed in the vendor's case during the time of the investigation. The vendor who had successfully offered ERP products for more than 30 years, moved into the CRM market in 1999. However, the new market followed different principles and had different characteristics to the ERP market, which, whilst using similar strategies for both markets, resulted in an imbalance between the competing requirements of the market and the product provided (mainly its range of functionalities), and consequently, in a rejection of the CRM system by the users. Being based on a business model which demands a wide distribution of the system into multiple organisations, from an economic point of view, the rejection of the CRM product by the market resulted in a negative return on investment and an urgency to re-adapt to current market conditions. This situation left the vendor with a choice of two options: to either close the unprofitable division, or to find ways of building a more useable product. The first option - closing the division - was considered as a worst case scenario, as this would signal to the market that the vendor failed in overcoming its problems and in competing with financially considerably weaker and less powerful competitors. This damaged reputation would also disturb the carefully built relationship with the market in other areas, such as the ERP market segment (cf. Scott and Walsham 2005)[64]. As closing down the division was not a realistic alternative, the vendor introduced a new strategy with the help of a new manager, hired from one of its main competitors in the CRM market[65]. As discussed in detail in Chapter 5, the new strategy was communicated as being based on three main pillars. First, to develop CRM as a stand-alone application; second, to produce a 'useable' system, not for an ERP but a CRM user, who provides the functionality needed and a quick 'time to the market'; and third, to find respected organisations running the revised application (so called 'reference clients'). Looking at the communicated strategy, interestingly, we find familiar patterns to what has been suggested as possible strategic moves of software package vendors in earlier research.

For instance, considering the standard software market and its characteristics overall, we find a general trend (necessary for the survival of these companies) to constantly enlarge the potential user base, to develop a system which can be used by even more users. The vendor's strategic goal to de-couple its CRM solution from the ERP product family and hence provide a product which can be used by both, ERP and non-ERP users, demonstrates the practical translation of the theoretical business concept. Furthermore, we find accounts such as Carmel and Sawyer (1998), who

64 One reason why customers buy the vendor's ERP system is the likelihood of being able to establish a long term relationship and to protect the investment for years.

65 Currently, we see how the market leader SAP has a similar problem: Having developed their 'Business One' solution for millions of Euros, the lack of market acceptance pushes SAP to decide between trying to correct the market image and improve the product or to declare it a failed product. The later would result in a big loss of reputation as well as a loss of trust from early adopter organisations and invested in the Business One solution.

reported upon a particularly competitive market in which standard software providers are constantly urged to develop and deliver more quickly in order to outrun the competitors. With regard to the third strategic pillar in which the importance of 'reference clients' is reflected, interesting accounts can be found in procurement literature, where the importance of reference sites for the final buying decision are highlighted (cf. Pollock and Williams 2008).

Moving on from this strategic discussion (a more detailed discussion is unfeasible given the focus on the fieldwork having been that of the work organisation and representing a developer's, rather than a managerial viewpoint) and concentrating on the working practices in the labs, we find close connections between the new managerial strategy and the way work was done. The data and related analysis introduces us, not only to the working practices within this lab, but to work organisation during a moment of change - an instance, in which existing working practices were considered as unsuitable by the management for the current market situation. In the following, I re-address the discussions carried out in Chapters 5 and 6, and highlight in particular: (1) the mutual shaping of managerial practices and the local site; and (2) the changing working practices within this ERP system lab.

The Mutual Shaping of Managerial Practices and the Local Site

The Social Shaping of Technology perspective, whilst used in various contexts, draws our attention to the transformation of technologies between their initial conception and laboratory location, to their becoming a widespread commercial commodity (Williams and Edge 1996). In this tradition, a line of research has emerged in the area of software package production and commercialisation, investigating the mutual shaping of the commodity (standard software package) and the local site (the user organisation), demonstrating processes of mutual shaping. If we translate the concept of the Social Shaping of Technology into the context of methods and practices implemented within a particular organisation, similarities become visible. The way managerial practices are defined in theory often differ from what we find in practice (cf. Fitzgerald 1997; Turex et al. 2000). Like technology, management practices also appear to undergo a transformation process when implemented at a local site.

Whilst we could distance ourselves from such analysis in the context of this research reasoning that this is the task of Management and not Social Sciences, and instead, move on to discussing working practices within the

ERP system developer teams, such a approach would result in a misleading conclusion. Most likely and similar to the developers (and the reviewers of the conference paper), we would conclude that the practices and changes in the working environment are rooted in the agile development approach Scrum and the problems are a result of a 'failed' Scrum implementation. However, as we have seen in Chapter 5, this was not the case. A mutual shaping between the management method and the local took place and, as such, it was not the method as defined in theory which led to the particular changes of working practices, but its localised (and mixed) version.

One of the most dramatic transformations within the context of this research was related to the agile practice 'daily meetings' (cf. Schwaber 2001), which provides an interesting insight, particularly for the community interested in agile software development approaches. The daily meetings, as part of the Scrum methodology, were introduced as a managerial practice to stimulate creativity, team work and trust. A mix of different practices implemented at the local site, as well as various contextual factors, however, created an environment which stimulated certain characteristics embedded in the methods, eventually leading to an alteration of the practice and, with this an alteration of its (theoretically defined) purpose. Instead of inspiring creativity and team work, the daily meetings became an instrument of day-to-day control.

Chapter 5 provides a detailed description of the specific local settings, the environment and the process of transformation. This offers an interesting empirical insight into how a transformation process can take place and also, a counterweight to current success stories of companies introducing a managerial mix (cf. Barrett 2004). Furthermore, in the context of analysing this transformation, the account demonstrates how, as a source of managerial power, the concept of accountability (cf. Munro 1999) can be applied to this case. In so doing, this research goes beyond the conventional analysis of localisation processes of management methods (akin Dube 1998), and provides a framework whereby analysing the characteristics of the method, highlights potential directions in which a certain management practice could develop (cf. Chapter 6).

Accountability is the giving of accounts or reasoning to other people, which can either be verbal or in written form. Whilst giving accounts is a day-to-day action of everyone, accountability can be used as a source of managerial power (Munro 1999). If we apply the concept of accountability as a source of managerial power to the case, we find that the new practices of daily confirmation and also daily meetings, the latter supposed to increase team work, inherit elements of making people accountable, both verbally, as well as in written form. By combining the daily confirmation and the daily scrum a mix developed, which partially intended by the management, created an environment of control in which the developers felt as if they were reporting their day-to-day progress, both verbally as well as in written form.

We can argue that this development is part of a failed implementation of Scrum features. However, this would be too easy an explanation from which we could learn little. What is interesting though is how this could have happened, how the transformation could have taken place, and what we can learn from it. This research demonstrates one way of explaining the phenomenon and with this implicitly, how to take care to avoid /stimulate the effect: by searching for and monitoring the potential of a practice to make people accountable.

Whilst making people accountable can lead to a situation in which employees feel as if they constantly have to justify themselves, the idea of accountability as a source of managerial power as demonstrated by Munro (1999), has to be looked at by also including the idea of deadlines: the time given to fulfil a task upon which the employee is asked to provide an account. The case demonstrates (and with this advances Munro's (1999) research) that it is the availability of time to fulfil a task which increased / decreased the power of accountability as a source of managerial control. The constant lack of time made it more difficult for the developers to complete all their daily tasks. With this, being accountable in written and verbal forms became more threatening, as falling behind and being caught out, sanctioned, and directly or indirectly humiliated in front of the group, more likely. Therefore, it can be concluded that loose deadlines would have had an adverse effect and the developers, despite being exposed to the same practices, may have felt less controlled. As such, the practices could have been a weaker source of managerial power in this respect than they were in the actual case. As a consequence, to discuss and analyse the various management practices and situations, it is necessary, not only to investigate the elements of accountability within, but also the associated timelines. It is the availability of time which eventually determines the degree to which accountability as part of a managerial practice can become a source of managerial power.

The above discussion allows us, not only to further our understanding of the transformation of managerial practices in the course of their localisation and how to possibly analyse this development, but also shows that if we try to understand how software packages are developed, we cannot stop when scholarly boundaries would suggest doing so. To understand the happenings in the labs, it was necessary to read up and draw upon theories not only from within Social Sciences, but also from Management and Computer Sciences. It is this that makes interdisciplinary research, like research carried out in the line of Science and Technology Studies, such a complex, but yet insightful task[66].

Creating Communities

Since the beginning of history, people have formed communities such as tribes, occupational guilds and more recently virtual communities of interests. In academic research, different notions of communities developed, like 'occupational communities' (Van Maanen and Barely 1984), or 'communities of practice' (Lave and Wenger 1991; Miller 1995; Wegner 2000; Wegner et al. 2002), as well as more recently, the notion of 'network of practices' (Brown and Duguid 2001). From our own experiences, as well as from academic research, we know that building communities and sharing values, interests and knowledge is not unusual when people come together. Whilst the degree to which people are involved in communities differs from individual to individual it is nevertheless startling to discover that in literature related to software developers, a rather uniform picture of the individualistic, goal-oriented and the financially motivated programmer is presented (cf. Cusumano and Selby (1997); Carmel and Sawyer (1998); Dube (1998) and Sawyer (2000b)). Whilst it is difficult to generalise from the case presented within this book, the developers in the labs showed, contrary to the picture drawn in literature, a strong tendency to act within and as a community. Communitarian behaviour in various forms could be witnessed which often crossed team boundaries and occasionally expanded throughout the labs and into private lives. The different groups building communities, which were partially defined by their occupation (the support community and the developer community), built a community which sometimes even included the users, influencing, incorporating and united by the product. This type of community, seemed

66 Whilst it is often difficult to work and research in a discipline other than the one studied as an undergraduate or for a Masters, for this this research, my interdisciplinary background (MSc and Diploma in Management and work experience as IT consultant) provided an invaluable advantage.

to fulfil three main purposes (see also Chapter 6): (1) responding to the (surprisingly strong) social needs of the developers; (2) allowing the experts to share their expertise within and across teams; and (3) facilitating an informal, direct information flow between the user, the support team and the developers.

Communities as Space to Socialise

If we start with the first aspect, we find that the communities in the labs were not only useful for fulfilling day-to-day work, but provided the developers (both from the support department, as well as the development area) with a space to socialise. The socialising habits in the labs varied from the occasional chat at each other's desk, to taking lunch together, to going out in the evening (see Chapter 3, 4, 5) which, in the light of existing literature, is most unexpected. In particular, software package developers are said to be individualistic, expressing little need for social interactions (Carmel and Sawyer 1998; Cusumano and Selby 1997; Keil and Carmel 1995) - findings which are as yet, undisputed in literature and are not supported within this research. Instead, a surprisingly strong communitarian behaviour was witnessed which bound the staff working in the labs together. The people in the labs acted as a community. Even if we argue that this desire for social interaction is particular to the lab investigated due to its international work force and thus it is this case, which is the exception to the rule, in the light of the complexity of the software system which developed, it nevertheless appears to be a slightly simplistic conclusion from other academics, that developers, developing complex solutions, work detached from each other.

Communities as Space to Share Expertise

The case presented (see Chapter 6) shows how the communities established not only functioned as social space, but as an interaction platform to share expertise. Expertise in such settings cannot be maintained by a single developer, but is shared amongst the team members and across teams in formal and informal ways. The different types of sharing expertise became particularly noticeable in the case of the system support division, where expertise is organised at different levels and with different teams. Furthermore, on a more informal level, the case has demonstrated how on an 'on call' basis, the developers and the support help each other out by sharing their knowledge of: (1) the application, and (2) the users' experience (see Chapter 6).

Communities Extending beyond Organisational Boundaries

Whilst we have seen in both cases, the development team and the support team, how people in the labs worked together on a day-to-day basis, socialised and shared expertise, this research introduces us to an example in which the sharing of expertise happens not only within the organisation (for example, between support staff and developers), but at times included the user. A community established itself, which facilitated an unexpected flow of information between the world outside the labs and the vendor's developers and support employees. Within this network, the information flow commonly showed itself as following (cf. Chapter 6): The user reports a problem to the support; the (third level) support, in some cases unfamiliar with a complex problem, informally consults the developers for assistance. The developers, having programmed the application would usually be able to give the support hints, allowing the support to provide a fast and high quality response to the user. The developers, knowing about the user problem by helping the support can use this feedback and include it in the current development. This research shows, how through this kind of communitarian behaviour, an informal direct user-vendor link was established which, whilst unrecognised by the management, was claimed to be missing (and necessary) in software package development (Keil and Carmel 1995).

Building and maintaining any kind of community involves a certain commitment, which requires time and space in which the communities can grow, develop and expand. Time, however, is a scarce resource in organisations and even more so in the competitive ERP system industry (Carmel and Sawyer 1998).

Transforming Communities

For communities to exist and function, available time to act within and for the community, is necessary. Under the new management, however, as we have seen in Chapters 5 and 6, the developers started to feel under pressure and controlled and, with this, time became a sacred resource. As a result of the new management practices, the developers started to isolate themselves and withdrew their membership from the community. The network disintegrated, leaving the support employees alone with the users and the developers without feedback from the user side or shared expertise through support employees (cf. Chapter 6).

A disturbance of existing communities is not unusual when new management practices are introduced. In some cases, the informal working practices facilitated by these communities are unknown by the change managers and hence, accidently disturbed (Brown and Duguid 1991). In other cases, it is part of the strategy to destroy existing working practices to break up resistance and make room for new habits and working practices (Hofstede 1997). In the case of the vendor, whilst for some areas a change of working practices was actively aimed at, for the community under observation, which appeared to be unknown to the management, no precaution or active interruption was planned. As such, it seems to have been the lack of attention to the social processes in the labs which endangered a community which, interestingly, the vendor tried to create formally. The vendor sought closer user-vendor co-operation, more team work, faster and more efficient development and more direct communication. One of the practices aimed to facilitate the realisation of these goals was the daily meetings. However, as we have seen, the daily meetings failed in most cases to fulfil this purpose whilst, due to an overall increased feeling of control and pressure at the same time, the informal ways of information exchange were weakened.

Whilst the disturbance of the communities appears to have had negative effects on the working climate, working practices and eventually the product, one might argue that in particular the community established informally between the support and the users, resulting in unstructured and uncontrolled exchange of information might not always be desired (therefore, the breakdown of the communication channel is actually an advantage). If we consider, for instance, the line of research occupied with the design of software package systems, we find, over and over again, the discussion on how much and if at all, user requirements should be included in the software (see, for instance, Grint and Woolgar 1997; Keil and Carmel 1995; Salzman and Rosenthal 1994; Wagner and Newell 2004)[67]. If too many requirements are included, the software might become too complex to customise and too specific and so fail to address a wider user base (Salzman and Rosenthal 1994). If we accept this argument, the influence of potentially non-key customer organisation through the support channel is not actually desirable.

Whilst this argument cannot be settled by discussing software development in general, looking only at the particular lab and the teams there, it can be said that when taking a micro view, this communication channel appeared to have had a positive effect on the system design. The infor-

67 For a detailed discussion see Chapter 2.

mation communicated between the users and the developers through the support was of major importance to the specific users and with this contributed to user satisfaction by influencing the product design. As it were generally only practical and for the product's 'necessary' changes, including the feedback from the user site into the product, did not compromise the overall product strategy. In cases where crucial changes were necessary to incorporate the users' requests, the developers consulted their manager. Being with the manager, the request became one of many and was evaluated like any other form of feedback (for instance formal feedback from intermediaries).

Contributions (2)
The investigations into the working practices of this software lab have highlighted the struggles of an ERP software vendor of managing its product development phase, and with this its experts, in the light of having to develop a system which should be described by all stakeholders (for instance, user organisations, analysts, media) as 'usable'. Investigating an ERP vendor during a time of change, this research shows for the first time, how challenging it is for standard software vendors to find the best way to produce a system which reflects the needs of the various groups of interest, and with this, the current market conditions. As the study highlights, unlike what is often implied by implementation studies, producing and providing such a system is not (only) a question of a powerful market leader imposing technology on the user. It is about offering a convincing product and managing relationships successfully.

More particularly, firstly, this research has shown the need to reopen the discussion on software package development and working culture in such settings. Existing research across all product life-cycle phases falls short in acknowledging the particulars of ERP systems in comparison with other types of standard software (a methodological error). Barrett (2004) goes as far as explicitly stating what most others implied, that word-processing packages as well as operating systems development are both the same in that both are the development of software packages (p: 779). Whilst implementation studies seem to be often specific in that they discuss 'ERP implementations' rather than 'standard software package implementation', the vast majority of studies in this area are either unspecific regarding which type of standard software is investigated (for example Keil and Carmel 1995) or generalise from one type of standard software to other types of standard software packages (for example Pollock et al. 2007). If we believe current research, then the development of any type of standard software is essentially the same. However, whilst such generalisation might be feasible for some cases, what appears to be the current 'default' that is to generalise, is, however, unhelpful and potentially misleading. This research has shown, by highlighting the complex structures and policies in place in this lab, how ERP systems are highly complex products, which reflect an organisation's practices and strategies, in some cases across all departments within one system. ERP systems are highly customisable and complex (see Chapter 4, 5) and are not comparable with other types of standard systems such as Microsoft Office products. Whilst reaching an equally wide user base, such systems rarely play a critical role in an organisation and are, in many cases, not even customisable beyond trivial things, such as appearance.

The current generalisation led to a uniform picture of an individualistic developer, who works in an entrepreneurial work setting - characteristics which are said to be rooted in the history of the software package industry (Carmel and Bird 1997; Carmel and Sawyer 1998; Cusumano and Selby 1997; Dube 1998; Sawyer 2000a). There seems to have developed a consensus around this view, which is not further refuted or problematised in academic circles. Thus, it appears accepted that no matter if software developers work in software package organisations such as Microsoft, Oracle, SAP or Apple, the software developers are all the same. This research argues that this discussion has to be reopened. The data presented shows how ERP developers acted within their communities, which served as space to socialise, share expertise and even, in some functions, as a platform to communicate user feedback coming through the support channel. Thus, the presented picture of ERP developers differs significantly from existing research and highlights the urgency to re-open the discussion on ERP and standard software package culture and working practices. The current view, based on generalisations from various software package studies, if undisputed, is misleading in the context of trying to understand how ERP packages are shaped from within the vendor organisation and, even more, in cases where Management and practitioners conclude and draw upon these accounts, using them as a basis for new management theories or the implementation of new managerial practices. Thus, this research calls for a more distinctive approach, that is a Sociology of ERP systems, addressing not only the particularities of ERP system development but also the particularities of ERP systems throughout the product life cycle.

Secondly, this study has also shown the importance of crossing departmental boundaries, when investigating the settings in software labs. Whilst we find studies providing us with different viewpoints on software packages and ERP systems, even though mostly form a user organisation viewpoint (see Chapter 2), existing research in all areas appear to fall short in combining different aspects of software production already during the data collection phase. Apart from books bringing together different phases (and theorising upon it) such as Pollock and Williams (2008), most studies do not even attempt or recognise connections to other phases of the product life cycle. Looking at two phases simultaneously (support and development), unexpected information channels revealed themselves in this study, providing an important and new insight into the discussion of software package design and development. Going beyond departmental boundaries highlighted not only unexpected connections between the different teams, but also, how the user is sometimes included in this community and can (unknowingly) influence the design of the product through the 'backdoor' of the support. What could be found in this lab, was a informal but yet direct user-vendor link, which has been said to be missing in software package development (Keil and Carmel 1995).

Thirdly, the investigations into the software development of ERP systems has not solely demonstrated that we cannot stop where formal boundaries are drawn between product life cycle phases and departments, but that we need to look beyond academic disciplinary boundaries and, for instance, aim to understand managerial practices and their effects on the shape of the technology. Whilst highlighting the importance of such a mixed approach by showing how managerial practices influence the formal and informal work organisation and with this the shaping of the product, in this context, this research has also outlined how the framework of managerial power and accountability, as presented by Munro (1999) can be applied to such a case. Showing how the analysis of the impacts of management practices and change can be taken to higher levels of abstraction than many current studies do and, on the other hand, demonstrate the importance of time in such a context, this study applies but also extends Munro's (1999) framework of accountability as source of managerial power. It has demonstrated how the characteristics of making people accountable inherited in some managerial practices, can be stimulated under certain circumstances and result in a shift of purpose of the practices in question. Furthermore, this research, extending Munro's (1999) ideas, has shown how the variable of time determines the amount and strength of the power which can be gained through making people accountable.

Fourthly, in context with the above, this work has shown how mixing methodologies can have pitfalls. Using the analytical framework of accountability as source of managerial power, the study provides material to dispute current success studies when mixing methods, such as presented by Barrett (2004). Whilst providing a missing insight into how software developers work and are managed, Barrett (2004) presents a picture of a software lab, in which different methods, of what appears a mix of tools supporting responsible autonomy and control (applying Friedman's (1989) categories), were successfully implemented. Not arguing that mixing methods is unsuitable (indeed, it is believed that this is most common and practices tend to be localised and mixed (cf. Adler and Borys 1996; Barrett 2004; Fitzgerald 1997; Kruchten 2007; Turex et al. 2000)) the research carried out within the vendor's labs shows, how it is not without challenges and, in particular, how the mutation of practices in regards to their controlling features can be watched. As the vendor's case demonstrated, applying such analytical framework allows discussions to go beyond method and case specific analysis and draw a broader conclusion on the way method affects or may be affected by the local environment.

To sum up, the insights gained from studying this ERP vendor have demonstrated the general need to adapt a vendor organisation's viewpoint and investigate work organisation in software labs, in order to understand the shaping of the product. Current research, carried out in the traditions of SST tend to focus on the mutual shaping process between the technology and the local, widely disregarding aspects of the mutual shaping within the technology producing organisation, which showed themselves in the study. As in any other setting, it is the way people work together and the hierarchical structures, which are reflected in the product (Kidder 1982). It is thus critical to understand what is happening within software vendors' labs, a viewpoint present in this research, if we aim to comprehend more fully the phenomenon of ERP systems.

Overall, in shedding light on the practices in ERP system labs, this research provides a unique and new insight for the academic community as demonstrated throughout. Furthermore, it is also highly relevant for practitioners. For the vendor itself, it was both the analysis and observations of the support and the developer teams, which were of interest. The latter was discussed with the management, on several occasions during, but also after the fieldwork. Interested in the perceptions of the developers, the management was also most intrigued by the informal information sharing between the developer and the support teams the study revealed, of which they were previously not aware. As a reaction to what was described, team goals were adapted and formal practices introduced in an attempt to improve the situation and re-establish formally, what had previously existed informally.

Outside the vendor's environment, insights gained in particular in relation to the daily meetings, and the reasons for, as well as the effects of the local shaping, will be interesting to the community, in that it provides important 'lessons learned' in regards to a practice, which is highly praised within the agile community. A publication in a practitioners' journal is planned to stimulate the discussion on practices such as daily meetings and the potential problems in the context of their inherent characteristic of making people accountable.

The support case was not discussed with the support employees / management of the labs directly (though one support employee had read through the final draft of the case[68]) but become relevant in the context of a vendor's research project in 2008. A new search functionality was planned to be developed, which aimed at optioning comprehensive and contextualised access to classified but also non classified information (such as information from Blogs and Wiki's) through the use of semantic technologies. The vendor's support department, in which information is stored at multiple points and in different, often not accessible formats (see, for example, Chapter 4 and the discussion on information stored within old messages) was used as use case, from which requirements for the system developers were derived. Taking on the biggest share in the split of revenues at the vendor, support services are considered, in particular during the economic crisis where new buys are less frequent, as crucial for the organisation's success (vendor statement, internal employee conference, January 2009). If we believe Humphrey (2001) and his hypothesis that the amount of errors in 1000 lines coded remains constant

68 The support employee commented (email): "Yes, I think you did a great job giving an accurate picture of the situation. I thought it was very honest (ex. ping pong situation). When you talked about us not liking some customers, I thought about my colleague Max who now takes care of [module] with me. He's very moody and often gets upset with customers or already classifies customers even before reading the message. (...). Really, I think you did a pretty good job with the information you collected and that you gave an accurate picture."

(if the same methodology is used) regardless of the size of the program, the constant increase of functionality and thus volume, will increase the amount of errors, a situation the vendor, with a constantly growing support division, appears to be aware of. In the context of optimising support work in that knowledge can be shared more easily, this research could provide important information to the vendor, who was less interested in the formal working practices but on how work is done and information processed, shared and stored informally.

Outside the vendor's labs, this research has also been requested by a smaller organisation, which was looking for a business model on how to set up a support department in North America. In both cases, this research provided practical information, into how to approach the challenge of supporting a complex product and manage the user-vendor relationship at this stage of the product life cycle.

7.4 Reflections

By three methods we may learn wisdom: First, by reflection, which is noblest; Second, by imitation, which is easiest; and third by experience, which is the bitterest. (Confucius 551 BC - 479 BC)

A research project is a long journey and deserves a moment of reflection. Whilst there were many events and experiences which changed the way I used to think about academic work, research methodology and, of course, ERP system production, it was the research design chosen which heavily influenced these experiences and with this the outcome of this research. It is the way we approach a topic, the philosophy we align ourselves with and the choices we make with regards to the method, which determine in many ways the nature and validity of a study.

Whilst theoretically all methods are available to choose from (as I started this research in a Management School, I was also familiar with quantitative methods), the research design is in many ways already predetermined by the way 'things are done' within a particular discipline, the background of the lead researchers, the settings one wants to study and the researcher's own personality. Discussed in detail in Chapter 2, in the following, I briefly reflect on these choices to highlight, once more, the influences these factors had on this research project. It is only if we critically reflect and understand the research design choices, that we can comprehend, evaluate and validate research findings appropriately.

What finally made me choose a qualitative approach, more specifically, ethnography, were three reasons. First, the main objective of this research was to present a detailed picture of the working practices within one of the most successful software package vendors' labs. This was only possible, if I were to gain access to a research lab. With this goal in mind, ethnography, including tools such as observation and interviews, was the most 'logical' choice. Secondly, it was the choice of carrying out participant observation, which allowed me to gain access to the secretive labs of the vendor in the first place. Having had several years of consulting, experience, implementing and custom programming the vendor's application, I could offer the vendor my discretion as a professional to use the data in an ethical and considerate way, as well as my expertise, to actually contribute to programming work, whilst carrying out research. No other method would have allowed me to profit from my technical experience with the vendor's systems in the way ethnographic research did. Being a 'developer' by training, it was only this situation which allowed me, not only to present abstract working practices, but present a unique picture of how it 'feels' to be a developer in such a lab, as well as participate and become part of the many 'silent dialogs' between the developers and the machines (cf. Czarniawska 2004). Third, this choice was also made on the basis of personal preferences. Being no strong believer in quantitative research, to me, participant observation (or, if impossible, 'only' observing events), appeared to be the most natural way to investigate a topic.

Once a particular methodology has been decided upon, it is the choices we make during our projects which, once more, determine the outcome. In this case, for example, I gained access to two labs in the Americas, and having decided in favour of studying one site in depth, I positioned this research project, from the beginning, within a certain category. Instead of carrying out a comparative study between two labs, the data collected introduces in detail the working practices of a particular vendor within a specific lab, within specific teams and with this, reflects working practices within a particular setting during a particular time. Whilst this facilitated investigating the setting in much detail, it also provides a very 'particular' account from which generalisations are difficult to derive. Also, known as a common pitfall of qualitative research, the reproduction of such a specific, qualitative account, is unfeasible (Hammersley and Atkinson 1995).

To tackle the shortcomings, of qualitative, one-site ethnographical research, the following precautions were taken. Firstly, I chose a triangular approach for the data collection (Blaikie 1993; Blaikie 2000). Carrying out participant observation, I, too, interviewed people (also from other labs in Europe and the USA), and consulted secondary data (such as the vendor's Intranet) to gain a more complete picture of the organisation. Secondly, keeping in touch with the developers after leaving the field and also investigating previous practices, I constantly aimed to extend my viewpoint beyond the five month time frame during which I worked in the labs. Thirdly, I situated this study as much as possible within the broader literature to gain a more complete picture. Fourthly, detailed fieldwork notes were taken and partially presented in this book, allowing the reader to evaluate this research but also, to make space for and allow alternative conclusions (Hammersley 1991; Hammersley and Atkinson 1995).

Interestingly, whilst the above-mentioned trade-offs are well known and discussed in detail in literature, these aspects were not the most challenging aspects of this research. The difficulties I encountered were mostly associated with one of its main advantages: the possibility for ethnographic researchers to enter and participate in people's lives. Whilst this was a inestimable advantage, allowing the coverage of the events in the labs in much detail, being incorporated to such a degree became an ethical challenge: Already an issue during the time in the field, it was particularly during the writing up phase, that I was constantly aware of the amount of trust I received, when the people in the labs allowed me to enter their lives and included me in their group. In writing and publishing what these people entrusted me with, I felt I could potentially challenge their careers and betray their friendship. To overcome this barrier, I started to make the characters, gender and location anonymous and together with careful evaluation of whether things were explained to me in my role as researcher or exclusively as friend (and hence are left out of this research), I found a balance which allowed a description and discussion of this vendor's North America lab to advance knowledge, whilst living up to my ethical commitments as ethnographic researcher.

7.5 Future Research

ERP systems are designed to integrate all elements of an organisation's activities. An ongoing challenge for providers of standard software packages, which has also been highlighted throughout this study, is to accommodate the competing exigencies of the market, its own strategic goals as well as its employees' expectations. This research has shown, from a Social Shaping of Technology point of view, the attempts of one of the biggest ERP vendors worldwide to handle this challenge during the moment of ERP system development and support from a vendor organisation's viewpoint. In so doing, the account demonstrates the importance of putting the organisation and the working practices therein, in the focus of investigation and underpins the need for a new research agenda into the sociology of ERP software packages, which takes into account the vendor's viewpoint and experiences.

Whilst I could throw light, once more, on some of the yet unknown issues surrounding ERP system production in this section on future research, the problems with existing research in this regard have been addressed throughout. Thus, this section is dedicated to the more recent changes in the product itself and the possible related influences on working practices and product usage, which have only been mentioned briefly in this book. What became most visible in the labs was that the vendor, as well as the entire software industry, is currently undergoing product changes: the move towards new software architecture, towards Service Oriented Architecture (SOA) (Allen et al. 2006; Bloomberg and Schmelzer 2006). As it became clear in the many presentations I attended in the labs, as well as when studying the literature surrounding this topic, SOA is changing the way we know about ERP systems in all respects. It is expected to change the way these systems are designed, developed, sold, supported, used and also, recycled; it will change all aspects of the system life-cycle. Having neglected this topic in favour of other issues, and because of its importance for future research, I will discuss this change in architecture in more detail in the next section. In so doing, I aim to create some understanding of the new approach for readers between technology and social research, and with this, particularly for readers from my own discipline, Science and Technology Studies. I will therefore disregard technical particularities such as transfer protocols and, instead, put the SOA movement in an historical context and highlight the possible overall impact of the architectural change on existing and future studies, using the vendors' future product vision.

Service Oriented Architecture

The ERP industry, as well as the entire computer industry, is currently undergoing a major architectural change: the transformation from Client-

Server Architecture towards Service Oriented Architecture, the fourth architectural wave in the history of software development. If we look at the change in its historical context, we can see the significance of this development which is far from what might be described as "hype" or "trend", but will change the way we produce and use software today.

If we look at the early years of standard software packages, we find Material Requirements Planning (MRPI, MRPII) systems, the predecessors of ERP, which were based on 'One Tier Architecture', also known as 'monolith' (see also Chapter 1). Whilst systems based on such architecture are very stable[69], their implementation and adaptation are a very complex endeavour. From an architectural point of view, all programs composing the application (user interface, applications and data base) were closely related. With this, a change in the user interface could perhaps cause a breakdown of the entire system (Woods 2003; Woods and Mattern 2006). Whilst today, such a situation is only accepted in exceptional circumstances, in these early years, the degree of flexibility of a user interface was less of an issue. Users were generally limited and experts in their domain, therefore the usability and adaptability of the user interface played a much smaller role (Grudin 1991; Winograd and Flores 1994). Furthermore, the processes these applications supported, as well as the interfacing systems which had to be connected with the monolith, did not often change (Woods 2003).

Over the years, the systems evolved and the One Tier Architecture in which user interface, application and data base were tightly connected, was followed by a 'Two Tier Architecture'. Whilst the user interface and the applications still built one item, with the emergence of the database management system, the database was disconnected, making the system more flexible. In the 1980s, the Two Tier Architecture became the Three Tier Architecture, more commonly known as Client-Server Architecture, which, until today, is the most commonly used architectural framework (Woods 2003). In contrast with its predecessors, Client-Server Architecture supported the decoupling of the user interface, the application and the database, and made the system also more open to third party software. It was this Client-Server Architecture which made terminal computers possible. With computer terminals becoming more and more common, the user numbers and diversity increased. No longer were users

69 Because of the system's stability once implemented, organisations such as banks, still run some of their applications in such an environment.

technical experts, but often clerks or managers without technical training. A demand for user friendly systems emerged (Winograd and Flores 1994), which has been consistent until today. Whilst the architecture and, in particular, the decoupling of the user interface made it easier from a technical point of view to respond to user requirements, the main challenge today is to capture the user requirements and decide, if, which and how they can be translated into the software (see discussion on ERP system design, Chapter 2).

Since approximately the year 2000, we can see a gradual migration of systems onto new platforms which are based on the fourth generation system architecture: Service Oriented Architecture (SOA) (Woods 2003). The idea behind SOA is to structure applications, in (more or less) independent services with a standardised interface facilitating the communication between the different components (Woods and Mattern 2006).

SOA is not an entirely new idea, but has become more popular in the last years, in particular, in the light of standardisation effort on communication protocols (Lomow and Newcomer 2005). At the same time, new legislations emerged (such as REACH[70] or programs to reduce the carbon footprint), which promote and push technologies facilitating business collaborations further[71]. Different vendors have different visions on how to re-design their systems in the light of the possibilities SOA offers but overall, all major players have already invested in SOA-enabling of their applications (Oracle 2005; Woods 2003).

It is to be expected, that this architectural wave will change the way we know ERP systems significantly. The way systems are localised and the role of the user will change. Users are envisioned to be able to design parts of their interface and instead of parameterisation, orchestrate services, generating new and 'tailored' applications – without programming effort[72]. Overall, we can expect that SOA will change what we know as

---

70 REACH (Registration, Evaluation, Authorisation and Restriction of Chemical substances) is a European Community regulation which was introduced in June 2007. It relates to the safe use of chemicals and requires reports which make advanced system integration necessary (European Commission 2007).

71 Only a brief scan of the current (2009) calls for proposals from the European Union, demonstrate the importance of such topics.

72 We find interesting parallels between Kraft's (1977) forecast of the computer industry and programming work and the move towards graphical programming interfaces, in which code is generated automatically. Kraft (1977) wrote: "The application program-

ERP systems today in all respects, touching upon all phases of the product life cycle, from both viewpoints, vendor and user organisation. Such significant change deserves attention. Science and Technology Studies aims to investigate how social, political and cultural values shape, and are shaped by the technology. All these aspects can be expected to be influenced by the new architecture. Whilst we might find researchers who step back, not understanding the new technology and are therefore reluctant to accept this change, it is this transformation which will open up new and most interesting fields whilst, at the same time, make other studies history.

Given the potential with which SOA changes and is already changing the system landscape, and with this the way systems are produced and used, the question evolves whether we should still invest in research concerned with the client-server generation of software. Whilst different researchers would answer this question in different ways, from what I have learned in the labs, as well as the overall understanding gained through extensive research in the area, investigating the current ways ERP systems are produced and used is still important. This architectural change is a gradual and ongoing long-term development, which started (unnoticed, as it seems, by Social Sciences) in the vendors' case, for example, already in the year 2000. It will be years until the vision demonstrated earlier will be realised[73]. Therefore, if we were to come today to an halt with our investigations, we would miss out, firstly, on investigating, participating and thus understanding this gradual change; secondly, on advancing our overall understanding of ERP packages also in its historical context; and thirdly, if we were to not investigate things which might change, technology related research would never happen, as there is always change.

Instead of standing still, we need to be aware of the current technology vendor moves, so that we can position ourselves and not be surprised, if finally confronted with a system, which appears to be so much different

---

mer's role will depend on the expanding use of packaged software which requires relatively minor but regular changes to meet customer requirement. Like coders, their future will hinge on the ability of hardware and software developers to simplify the use of hardware, as higher level languages are created and are combined with improved hardware, the machines will become directly accessible to untrained users. The "man-machine interface" which managers and engineers look forward to is one unmediated by a human programmer." (p: 104).

[73] In 20111, when this book was edited again, the big ERP organizations are still struggling - but nevertheless still aiming for –SOA enabled applications.

from what we know from existing studies. In the course of observing this changing technology, there is a constant need to be vigilant about which type of research is combined, and from which architectural period it derives. Moreover, in observing and participating in technology change, there is a constant need to reconsider and re-evaluate our methodologies and tools with which we approach topics and question in the light of whether they are still suitable. It is awareness and understanding of architectural evolution and a consequent adaption to the situation on all levels which is needed in our line of research.

To summarise, whilst this research has filled some of the gaps in current literature by shedding light on the vendor organisation's view on the ERP development and ERP support phase, it became clear in the course of the investigation and in the context of a comparison with existing literature, that there is a urgent need to extend our current research agenda, if we aim to better understand the phenomenon of ERP systems. In the light of existing and future research, two points became particularly clear:

First, that there is a necessity for a Sociology of ERP Systems, which takes into account not only all aspects of the system life cycle from a user organisation perspective, but also from a vendor's perspective and does so, specifically for ERP systems. In this respect, for the next steps, it is in particular the ERP sales phase, which needs to be investigated and put into the context of existing research.

Second, the move of the software industry towards service orientation has to be watched closely. Whilst much research related to SOA is carried out in Computer Sciences (it is indeed difficult to find an academic paper or an industrial research project, which is not somehow connected to SOA) with vendor rhetoric's dominating the less technical discussions, Science and Technology Studies should not ignore or turn away from this development but set out to understand and investigate this development. Our discipline needs to map out a new research agenda, reconsider existing methods and concepts, and embrace this change.

References

ABRAHAMSON, E. (1991) Management Fads and Fashions: The Diffusion and Rejection of Innovations. *Academy of Management Review,* 16, 586-612.

ABRAHAMSON, P., WARSTA, J., SIPONEN, M. & RONKAINEN, J. (2003) New Directions on Agile Methods: A Comparative Analysis. *Proceedings of the 25th International Conference on Software Engineering (ICSE '03).* IEEE Computer Society.

ADLER, P. & BORYS, B. (1996) Two Types of Bureaucracy: Enabling and Coercive. *Administrative Science Quarterly,* 41, 61-89.

AGILE ALLIANCE (2008a) *Agile Manifesto,* http://www.agilemanifesto.org/, 05/10/08.

AGILE ALLIANCE (2008b) *Articles about Agile Development Practices,* http://www.agilealliance.org/articles, 15/10/2008.

AILON, G. (2006) What B Would Otherwise Do: A Critique of Conceptualizations of 'Power' in Organizational Theory. *Organization,* 13.

AKKERMANS, H. & VAN HELDEN, K. (2002) Vicious and Virtuous Cycles in ERP Implementation: A Case Study of Interrelations Between Critical Success Factors. *European Journal of Information Systems,* 11, 35-46.

ALLEN, P., HIGGINS, S., MCRAE, P. & SCHLAMANN, H. (2006) *Service Orientation: Winning Strategies and Best Practices,* Cambridge University Press.

ALVES, C. & FINKELSTEIN, A. (2002) Challenges in COTS decision-making: a goal-driven requirements engineering perspective. *Proceedings of the 14th international conference on software engineering and knowledge engineering.* Italy, ACM.

AVISON, D. & FITZGERALD, G. (2003) Where now for development methodologies? *Communication of the ACM,* 46, 79-82.

BACH, J. (1995a) Enough about process: what we need are heroes. *IEEE Software,* 12, 96-98.

BACH, J. (1995b) *SCRUM Software Development Process,* http://www.controlchaos.com/old-site/scrumwp.htm, 12/03/2008.

BANSLER, J. & HAVN, E. (1996) Industrialised Information Systems Development. *CTI Working Paper.*

BARLEY, S. (1996) Technicians in the Workplace: Ethnographic Evidence for Bringing Work into Organizational Studies. *Administrative Science Quarterly,* 41, 404-441.

BARNARD, A. & SPENCER, J. (1996) *Encyclopedia of social and cultural anthropology,* London, Routledge.

BARRETT, R. (2001) Labouring under an illusion? The labour process of software development in the Australian information industry *New Technology, Work and Employment* 16, 18–34.

BARRETT, R. (2004) Working at Webboyz: An Analysis of Control over the Software Development Labour Process. *Sociology,* 38, 777–794.

BATE, S. P. (1997) Whatever Happened to Organizational Anthropology? A Review of the Field of Organizational Ethnography and Anthropological Studies. *Human Relations,* 50, 1147-1175.

BECHHOFER, F. & PATERSON, L. (2000) *Principles of research design in the social sciences,* London, Routledge.

BECHKY, B. A. (2006) Talking about Machines, Thick Description, and Knowledge Work. *Organisation Studies,* 27, 1757-1768.

BECK, K. & ANDERS, C. (2004) *Extreme programming explained: embrace change,* Boston, Addison-Wesley Professional.

BERG, B. (1995) *Qualitative research methods for the Social Sciences,* Boston, Allyn & Bacon.

BERG, M. (1997) *Rationalizing Medical Work: Decision-Support Techniques and Medical Practices,* Cambridge, MIT Press.

BIJKER, W. E. (1995) *Of bicycles, bakelites, and bulbs: toward a theory of sociotechnical change,* Cambridge; London, MIT Press.

BIJKER, W. E., HUGHES, T. P. & PINCH, T. (Eds.) (1987) *The Social Construction of Technological Systems,* London, MIT Press.

BINGI, P., SHARMA, M. K. & GODLA, J. K. (1999) Critical Issues Affecting an ERP Implementation. *Information Systems Management,* 16, 7-14.

BLAIKIE, N. (1993) *Approaches to social enquiry,* Polity Press

BLAIKIE, N. W. H. (2000) *Designing social research: the logic of anticipation,* Malden, Polity Press.

BLOOMBERG, J. & SCHMELZER, R. (2006) *Service Orient or Be Doomed!: How Service Orientation Will Change Your Business,* New Yersey, Wiley.

BLOOR, D. (1976) *Knowledge and Social Imagery,* Chicago, The University of Chicago Press.

BOADEN, R. J. & DALE, B. G. (1986) What is Computer-integrated manufacturing? *International Journal of Operations & Production Management,* 6, 30-37.

BODEN, D. (1994) *The Business of Talk,* Cambridge, Polity Press.

BOEHM, B. (1986) A spiral model of software development and enhancement. *ACM SIGSOFT Software Engineering Notes,* 11, 14-24.

BOEHM, B. (2002) Get Ready for Agile Methods with Care *IEEE Computer Magazine*, 64-69.

BOTTA-GENOULAZ, V., MILLET, P.-A. & GRABOT, B. (2005) A survey on the recent research literature on ERP systems. *Computers in Industry,* 56, 510–522.

BOWKER, G. C. & STAR, L. (1999) *Sorting things out: classification and its consequences,* Cambridge, MIT Press.

BRADY, T., TIERNEY, M. & WILLIAMS, R. (1992) The Commodification of Industry Applications Software. *Oxford University Press,* 1, 489-514.

BRAVERMAN, H. (1975) *Labour and monopoly capital: the degradation of work in the twentieth century,* New York; London, Monthly Review Press.

BROWN, J. S. & DUGUID, P. (1991) Organizational Learning and Communities-of-Practice: Toward a Unified View of Working, Learning, and Innovation. *Organizational Studies,* 2, 40-57.

BROWN, J. S. & DUGUID, P. (2001) Knowledge and Organization: A Social-Practice Perspective *Organisation Science,* 12, 198-213.

CARMEL, E. (1993) A discussion of special characteristics for software package development life cycle models. *ACM SIGSOFT Software Engineering Notes,* 18, 23-24.

CARMEL, E. (1997) American Hegemony in Packaged Software Trade and the "Culture of Software". *The Information Society,* 13, 125-142.

CARMEL, E. & BECKER, S. (1995) A Process Model for Packaged Software Development. *IEEE Transactions on Engineering Management,* 42, 50-61.

CARMEL, E. & BIRD, B. J. (1997) Small is Beautiful: A Study of Packaged Software Development Teams. *The Journal of High Technology Management Research,* 8, 129-148.

CARMEL, E. & SAWYER, S. (1998) Packaged Software Development Teams: What Makes Them Different? *Information Technology and People,* 11, 7-19.

CHUNG, S. H. & SNYDER, C. A. (2000) ERP adoption: a technological evolution approach. *International Journal of Agile Management Systems,* 2, 24-32.

COHN, M. (2003) *Towards a Catalogue of Scrum Smells,* Mountain Goat Software, http://www.mountaingoatsoftware.com/article_view/11-toward-a-catalog-of-scrum-smells, 05/05/2007.

COMPUTERWOCHE (2008) *SAP verhängt drastische Sparmaßnahmen*, http://www.computerwoche.de/knowledge_center/erp/1875365/, 9/10/2008.

CORNFORD, J. & POLLOCK, N. (2003) *Putting the University Online: Information, Technology, and Organisation*, Milton Keynes, Open University Press.

CRONBERG, T. (1992) Technology in Social Sciences: the Seamless Theory. *Mimeo Technical University of Denmark.*

CURTIS, B., KRASNER, H. & ISCOE, N. (1988) A Field Study of the Software Design Process for Large Systems. *Communications of the Association for Computing Machinery,* 31, 1268-1287.

CUSUMANO, M. A. & SELBY, W. (1995) *Microsoft Secrets: How the World's Most Powerful Software Company Creates Technology, Shapes Markets, and Manages People,* New York, The Free Press.

CUSUMANO, M. A. & SELBY, W. (1997) How Microsoft builds software. *Communication of the ACM,* 40, 53-61.

CUSUMANO, M. A. & SMITH, S. (1995) Beyond the Waterfall: Software Development at Microsoft MIT and IBM

CZARNIAWSKA, B. (2004) On Time, Space, and Action Nets. *Organization,* 11, 773-791.

DE LAET, M. & MOL, A. (2000) The Zimbabwe Bush Pump: Mechanics of a Fluid Technology *Social Studies of Science,* 30, 225-263.

DENSCOMBE, M. (1998) *The good research guide: for small-scale social research projects,* Buckingham, Open University Press.

DIERKES, M. & HOFFMANN, U. (1992) *New Technology and the Outset: Social Forces in the Shaping of Technological Innovations* Frankfurt / New York Campus / Westview.

DOWNEY, G. L. (1998) *The machine in me: an anthropologist sits among computer engineers,* New York ; London, Routledge.

DUBE, L. (1998) Teams in Packaged Software Development: The Software Corp. Experience. *Information Technology and People,* 11, 36-61.

EASTERBY-SMITH, M., THORPE, R. & LOWE, A. (1991) *Management research: an introduction,* London, Sage Publications.

EDGE, D. (1988) The social shaping of technology. *University of Edinburgh PICT Working Paper* 1.

ESTEVES, J. & PASTOR-COLLADO, J. (2000) Towards the unification of critical success factors for ERP implementations. *10th Annual*

Business Information Technology (BIT) 2000 Conference. Manchester.

ESTEVES, J. & PASTOR, J. (2001) Enterprise Resource Planning Systems Research: An Annotated Bibliography. *Communications of the Association for Information Systems,* 7, 1-52.

ESTEVES, J. M. & BOHORQUEZ, V. (2007) An Updated ERP Systems Annotated Bibliography: 2001-2005. *Communication of the ACM,* 19, 386-446.

ESTEVES, J. M. & PASTOR, J. A. (1999) An ERP Life-Cycle-Based Research Agenda. IN EDER, J., MAIDEN, N. & MISSIKOFF, M. (Eds.) *Proceedings of the First International Workshop in Enterprise Management and Resource Planning: Methods, Tools and Architectures*. Venice, Centro de Studi San Salvador.

EUROPEAN COMMISSION (2007) *REACH,* European Commission, http://ec.europa.eu/environment/chemicals/reach/reach_intro.htm, 05/10/08.

FINCHAM, R. (2002) Narratives of success and failure in systems development. *British Journal of Management,* 13, 1-14.

FINKELSTEIN, A., SPANOUDAKIS, G. & RYAN, M. (1996) Software Package Requirements and Procurement. *Proceedings of the 8th International Workshop on Software Specification and Design IWSSD '96*. IEEE Computer Society.

FITZGERALD, B. (1997) The use of systems development methodologies in practice: a field study. *Information Systems Journal,* 7, 201-212.

FLECK, J. (1988) Innofusion or diffusion? The nature of technological development in robotics. *Edinburgh PICT Working Paper, University of Edinburgh.*

FLECK, J., WEBSTER, J. & WILLIAMS, R. (1990) The dynamics of IT Implementation: A Reassessment of Paradigms and Trajectories of Development. *Futures,* 22, 618-640.

FOUCAULT, M. (1977) *Discipline and Punish,* London, Penguin.

FRIEDMAN, A. L. (1989) *Computer Systems Development: History, Organization and Implementation,* Chichester, John Wiley and Sons.

GABLE, G., CHAN, T. & TAN, W. G. (2001) Large Packaged Application Software Maintenance: A Research Framework. *Journal of Software Maintenance: Research and Practice,* 13, 351-371.

GARBANI, J.-P. (2009) Future Trends In The Enterprise Software Market. Forrester

GARFINKEL, H. (1967) *Studies in ethnomethodology,* Englewood Cliffs, N.J., Prentice-Hall.

GOSH, S. (2002) *Challenges on a global implementation of ERP software*,IEEE, http://ieeexplore.ieee.org/iel5/8054/22257/01038374.pdf?tp=&arnumber=1038374&isnumber=22257, 20/06/05.

GRAY, D. E. (2004) *Doing research in the real world,* London, Sage.

GRILLS, S. (1998) *Doing ethnographic research: fieldwork settings,* London, Sage Publications.

GRINT, K. & WOOLGAR, S. (1997) *The Machine at Work: Technology, Work and Organization,* Cambridge, Polity Press.

GRIMM, C. (2009) Inside a Secret Software Lab: An Ethnographic Study of a Global Software Package Producer. PhD, University of Edinburgh.

GRUDIN, J. (1991) Interactive systems: Bridging the gaps between developers and users. *IEEE Computer Society,* 24, 59 - 69.

HAMMERSLEY, M. (1991) *Reading ethnographic research: a critical guide,* London, Longman.

HAMMERSLEY, M. & ATKINSON, P. (1995) *Ethnography: principles in practice,* London, Routledge.

HANSETH, O. & BRAA, K. (2001) Hunting for the Treasure at the End of the Rainbow: Standardizing Corporate IT Infrastructure. *Computer Supported Cooperative Work,* 10, 261-292.

HANSETH, O., CIBORRA, C. & BRAA, K. (2001) The Control Devloution: ERP and Side Effects of Globalization. *The Data Base for Advances in Information Systems,* 32, 34-46.

HANSETH, O. & MONTEIRO, E. (1998) *Understanding Information Infrastructure,* http://heim.ifi.uio.no/~oleha/Publications/bok.html, 09/07/05.

HARWOOD, S. (2002) *ERP The implementation cycle*, Butterworth-Heinemann.

HIGHSMITH, J. (2005) *Agile Project Management,* China, Pearson Education Asia Limited and China Machine Press.

HOFSTEDE, G. (1997) *Cultures and organizations: software of the mind,* New York; London, McGraw-Hill.

HOLLAND, C. P. & LIGHT, B. (1999) A Critical Success Factors Model for ERP Implementation. *IEEE Software,* 16, 30-36.

HOLLAND, C. P. & LIGHT, B. (2003) A Framework for Understanding Success and Failure in ERP Implementation. IN SHANKS, G., SEDDON, P. & WILLCOCKS, L. (Eds.) *Second-Wave Enterprise*

Resource Planning Systems: Implementing for Effectiveness. Cambridge, Cambridge University Press.

HONG, K. K. & KIM, Y. G. (2002) The Critical Success Factors for ERP Implementation: An Organizational Fit Perspective. *Information and Management,* 40, 25-40.

HOWCROFT, D. & LIGHT, B. (2002) A Study of User Involvement in Packaged Software Selection. IN APPLEGATE, L., GALLIERS, R. D. & DE GROSS, J. I. (Eds.) *Proceedings of the 23rd International Conference on Information Systems.* Barcelona, Spain, Association for Information Systems.

HOWCROFT, D. & LIGHT, B. (2006) Reflections on Issues of Power in Packaged Software Selection. *Information Systems Journal,* Forthcoming.

HUMPHREY, W. (2001) *The Future of Software Engineering: Part I,* Software Engineering Institute Carnegie Mellon http://www.sei.cmu.edu/news-at-ei/columns/watts_new/watts-new-compiled.pdf, 05/02/09.

HYMAN, R. (1987) Strategy or Structure: Capital, Labour and Control. *Work, Employment and Society,* 1, 25-55.

JACOBSON, S., SHEPHERD, J., D'AQUILA, M. & CARTER, K. (2007) The ERP Market Sizing Report, 2006–2011. *AMR 2007 Market Sizing Series.*

KATZENBACH, J. R. & SMITH, D. K. (1993) The disciplines of teams. *Harvard Business Review,* March / April, 111-120.

KEIL, M. & CARMEL, E. (1995) Customer-Developer Links in Software Development. *Communications of the Association for Computing Machinery,* 38, 33-44.

KIDDER, T. (1982) *The soul of a new machine,* Harmondsworth, Penguin Books.

KLAUS, H., ROSEMANN, M. & GABLE, G. G. (2000) What is ERP? *Information Systems Frontiers,* 2, 141-162.

KLING, R. (1980a) Social Analysis of Computing: Theoretical Perspectives in Recent Empirical Research. *Computing Surveys,* 12, 61-110.

KLING, R. (1980b) Social issues and impacts of computing: from arena to discipline. *2nd Conference on Computers and Human Choice.* Amsterdam, ACM.

KNOX, H. (2005) Imitative participation and the politics of 'joining in': paid work as a methodological issue. *Anthropology Matters Journal,* 7.

KRAEMER, K. L., DUTTON, W. H. & NORTHRUP, A. (1980) *The management of information systems* New York, Columbia University Press.

KRAFT, P. (1977) *Programmers and managers,* New York, Springer-Verlag.

KRUCHTEN, P. (1999) *Der Rational Unified Process. Eine Einführung,* Munic, Addison-Wesley.

KRUCHTEN, P. (2004) Putting the "Engineering" into "Software Engineering". *Proceedings of the 2004 Australian Software Engineering Conference (ASWEC'04).* Australia, IEEE.

KRUCHTEN, P. (2005) Software Design in a Postmodern Era. *IEEE Software* 22, 16-18.

KRUCHTEN, P. (2007) Voyage in the Agile Memeplex. *ACM Queue,* 5, 38-44.

KUNDA, D. (2003) STACE: Social Technical Approach to COTS Software Evaluation *Lecture Notes in Computer Science: Component-Based Software Quality,* 64-84.

LAFOREST, F. (1997) Generic Models: A new approach for information systems design. 189 - 196

LATOUR, B. (1988) *Science in Action: How to Follow Scientists and Engineers Through Society,* Harvard University Press.

LATOUR, B. (2005) *Reassembling the Social: An Introduction to Actor-network-theory,* Oxford, Oxford University Press.

LATOUR, B. & WOOLGAR, S. (1986) *Laboratory life: the construction of scientific facts,* Princeton, N.J., Princeton University Press.

LAVE, J. & WENGER, E. (1991) *Situated Learning: Legitimate Peripheral Participation* Cambridge, Cambridge University Press.

LESSER, E. L. & STORCK, J. (2001) Communities of practice and organisational performance. *IBM Systems Journal,* 40, 831-841.

LIGHT, B. (2001) The Maintenance Implications of the Customization of ERP Software. *The Journal of Software Maintenance: Research and Practice,* 13, 415-430.

LIGHT, B., HOLLAND, C., KELLY, S. & WILLS, K. (2000) Best of Breed IT Strategy: An Alternative to Enterprise Resource Planning Systems. IN ROBERT HANSEN, H., BICHLER, M. & MAHRER, H. (Eds.) *Proceedings of the 8th European Conference on Information Systems.* Vienna, Austria, Vienna University of Economics and Business Administration.

LIGHT, B., HOLLAND, C. & WILLS, K. (2001) ERP and Best of Breed: A Comparative Analysis. *Business Process Management Journal,* 7, 216-224.

LIGHT, B. & SAWYER, S. (2007) Locating packaged software in information systems research. *European Journal of Information Systems*, 527–530.

LOMOW, G. & NEWCOMER, E. (2005) *Introduction to SOA with Web Services*, Addison-Wesley, http://www.informit.com/articles/article.asp?p=357691&rl=1, 03/05/05.

LOW, J. & WOOLGAR, S. (1993) Do users get what they want. *ACM SIGOIS Bulletin*, 14.

MABERT, V. (2007) The early road to material requirements planning. *Journal of Operations Management*, 25, 346-356.

MACKAY, H., CARNE, C., BEYNON-DAVIS, P. & TUDHOPE, D. (2000) Reconfiguring the User. *Social Studies of Science*, 30, 737-57.

MACKENZIE, D. (1991) Notes towards a sociology of supercomputing. IN LA PORTE, T. R. (Ed.) *Social Responses to Large Technical Systems: Control or Anticipation*. London Kluwer.

MACKENZIE, D. & WAJCMAN, J. (1985) *The Social Shaping of Technology: How the Refrigerator Got Its Hum*, Milton Keynes, Open University Press.

MACKENZIE, D. & WAJCMAN, J. (Eds.) (1999) *The Social Shaping of Technology*, Maidenhead, Open University Press.

MACLAUGHLIN, J., ROSEN, P., SKINNER, D. & WEBSTER, A. (1999) *Valuing Technology: Organisations, Culture and Change*, London, Routledge.

MEISSNER, G. (2000) *S.A.P, inside the secret software power = SAP, die heimliche Software-Macht, wie ein mittelständisches Unternehmen den Weltmarkt eroberte*, New York ; London, McGraw-Hill.

MILLER, W. L. (1995) A broader mission for R&D. *Research Technology Management*, 6, 24-36.

MOON, Y. B. (2007) Enterprise Resource Planning (ERP): A review of the literature. *International Journal of Management and Enterprise Development*, 4, 235-264.

MOTWANI, J., SUBRAMANIAN, R. & GOPALAKRISHNA, P. (2005) Critical factors for successful ERP implementation: exploratory findings from four case studies. *Computers in Industry*, 56, 529-544.

MUNRO, R. (1999) Power and Discretion: Membership Work in the Time of Technology. *Organization*, 6, 429.

NAH, F., FAJA, S. & CATA, T. (2001) Characteristics of ERP software maintenance: a multiple case study. *Journal of Software*

Maintenance and Evolution: Research and Practice, 13, 399-414.

NUSEIBEH, B. & EASTERBROOK, S. (2000) Requirements Engineering: A Roadmap. The Future of Software Engineering.

O'REILLY, K. (2005) *Ethnographic methods,* London, Routledge.

ORACLE (2005) *Oracle Delivers First Complete SOA and Integration Platform*, Oracle, www.oracle.com/corperate/press/3233257.html, 23/08/2006.

ORACLE (2008) *Oracle Strategic Acquisitions*, Oracle, http://www.oracle.com/corporate/acquisition.html, 28/12/08.

ORLICKY, J. (1975) *Material requirements planning: the new way of life in production and inventory management,* New York, McGraw-Hill.

ORLIKOWSKI, W. (1992) The Duality of Technology: Rethinking the Concepts of Technology in Organisations. *Organisation Science,* 3, 398-427.

ORR, J. (1986) Narratives at work: story telling as cooperative diagnostic activity. *Proceedings of the 1986 ACM conference on Computer-supported cooperative work* Austin, Texas, ACM.

ORR, J. (1998) Images of Work. *Science, Technology, and Human Values,* 23, 439-55.

ORR, J. (2006) Ten years of talking about machines. *Organisation Studies,* 27, 1804-1820.

ORR, J. E. (1996) *Talking about machines: an ethnography of a modern job,* Ithaca; London, ILR Press.

OXFORD ENGLISH DICTIONARY (2009) *AskOxford.com*, Oxford University Press, http://www.askoxford.com/?view=uk, 10/05/2009.

PARR, A. & SHANKS, G. (2000) A Model of ERP Project Implementation. *Journal of Information Technology*, 289-303.

PENTLAND, B. (1992) Organizing Moves in Software Support Hot Lines. *Administrative Science Quarterly,* 37, 527-48.

PINCH, T. & BIJKER, W. E. (1984) The social construction of facts and artefacts. *Social Studies of Science,* 14, 399-441.

POLLOCK, N. & CORNFORD, D. S. (2004) ERP Systems and the University as an 'Unique' Organisation. *Information Technology and People,* 17, 31-52.

POLLOCK, N. & CORNFORD, J. (2005) Implications of Enterprise Resource Planning Systems for Universities: An analysis of Benefits and Risks. *Observatory on Borderless Higher Education,* 30.

POLLOCK, N., GRIMM, C. & WILLIAMS, R. (2008) Passing the User: Searching for Expertise in Globalised Technical Support. IN POLLOCK, N. & WILLIAMS, R. (Eds.) *Software and Organizations: The Biography of the Enterprise-Wide System Or How SAP Conquered the World.* London, Routledge.

POLLOCK, N. & WILLIAMS, R. (2008) *Software and Organisations. The biography of the enterprise-wide system or how SAP conquered the world,* London, Routledge.

POLLOCK, N., WILLIAMS, R. & D'ADDERIO, L. (2007) Global Software and its Provenance: Generification Work in the Production of Organizational Software Packages. *Social Studies of Science,* 37, 254–280.

POLLOCK, N., WILLIAMS, R., GRIMM, C. & D'ADDERIO, L. (2009) Post local forms of repair: The (extended) situation of virtualised technical support. *Information and Organization,* 19.

PORTER, M. (1980) *Competitive Strategy,* New York, Free Press.

QUINTAS, P. (1994a) A product-process model of innovation in software development. *Journal of Information Technology,* 9, 3-17.

QUINTAS, P. (1994b) Programmed Innovation? Trajectories of Change in Software Development. *Information Technology and People,* 7, 25-47.

RANDALL, D., HUGHES, J. & SHAPIRO, D. (1993) Systems development - the fourth dimension: perspectives on the social organisation of work. IN QUINTAS, P. (Ed.) *Social Dimensions of Systems Engineering: People, Processes, Policies and Software Development.* London Ellis Horwood.

REGNELL, B., HÖST, M., NATT OCH DAG, J., BEREMARK, P. & HJELM, T. (2001) An Industrial Case Study on Distributed Prioritisation in Market-Driven Requirements Engineering for Packaged Software. *Requirements Engineering,* 6, 51-62.

ROYCE, W. (1970) Managing the development of large software systems. *IEEE WESCON.* Wescon, Reprint by Institute of Electrical and Electronics Engineers.

RUSSELL, S. & WILLIAMS, R. (2002) Social Shaping of Technology: Frameworks, Findings and Implications for Policy with Glossary of Social Shaping Concepts. IN SØRENSEN, K. H. & WILLIAMS, R. (Eds.) *Shaping Technology, Guiding Policy: Concepts, Spaces and Tools.* Cheltenham, Edward Elgar.

SALZMAN, H. & ROSENTHAL, S. R. (1994) *Software by Design: Shaping Technology and the Workplace,* Oxford, Oxford University Press.

SAMMET, J. (1991) Some Approaches to, and Illustrations of, Programming Language History. *Annals of the History fo Computing* 13, 33-50.

SAP AG (2009) *SAP - Von Walldorf an die Wall Street*, SAP AG, http://www.sap.com/germany/about/index.epx, 15/01/09.

SAUNDERS, M. N. K., LEWIS, P. & THORNHILL, A. (2000) *Research methods for business students,* Harlow, Financial Times/Prentice Hall.

SAWYER, S. (2000a) Packaged Software: Implications of the Differences from Custom Approaches to Software Development. *European Journal of Information Systems,* 9, 47-58.

SAWYER, S. (2000b) Studying Organizational Computing Infrastructures: Multi-Method Approaches. IN BASKERVILLE, R., STAGE, J. & DEGROSS, J. I. (Eds.) *Organizational and Social Perspectives on Information Technology.* Boston, Kluwer Academic Publishers.

SAWYER, S. (2001) A Market-Based Perspective on Information Systems Development. *Communications of the Association for Computing Machinery,* 44, 97-102.

SAWYER, S. & GUINAN, J. (1998) Software development: Processes and performance. *IBM Systems Journal,* 37, 552-569.

SCHWABER, K. (2008) *History of the Agile Movement*, Conchango, http://scrumforteamsystem.com/processguidance/v2/Flash/01. TheHistoryOfTheAgileMovement.swf, 06/01/09.

SCHWABER, K. & BEEDLE, M. (2001) *Agile Software Development with Scrum,* New York, Prentice Hall

SCOTT, S. V. & WALSHAM, G. (2005) Reconceptualising and managing reputation risk in the knowledge economy: toward reputable action. *Organization Science,* 16, 308-322.

SISMONDO, S. (2004) *An introduction to science and technology studies,* Malden, Blackwell.

SOMERS, T. M. & NELSON, K. (2001) The Impact of Critical Success Factors Across the Stages of Enterprise Resource Planning Implementations. *Proceedings of the 34th Hawaii International Conference on Systems Sciences.*

SONNENTAG, S. (1995) Excellent software professionals: experience, work activities, and perception by peers. *Behaviour and Information Technology,* 14, 289-299.

STAR, L. (1989) The structure of ill-structured solution: boundary objects and heterogeneous distributed problem solving *Distributed Artificial Intelligence,* 2, 37-54.

STENHOUSE, L. (1984) Library access, library use and user education in academic sixth forms: an autobiographical account. IN BURGESS, R. G. (Ed.) *The Research Process in Educational Settings: Ten Case Studies.* Lewes, Falmer Press.

STOREY, J. (1985) The Means of Management Control. *Sociology,* 19, 193-211.

STRODE, D. (2006) Agile methods: a comparative analysis. *19th Annual Conference of the National Advisory Committee on Computing Qualifications (NACCQ 2006).* Wellington, New Zealand.

SUCHMAN, L. (1995) Making work visible. *Communciation of the ACM,* 38, 56-65.

SUMNER, M. (2000) Risk Factors in Enterprise-wide/ERP Projects. *Journal of Information Technology,* 15, 317-327.

TAKEUCHI, H. & NONAKA, I. (1986) The New New Product Development Game. *Harvard Business Review.*

TOLLE, B. (1992) *Ada, the Enchantress of Numbers: A Selection from the Letters of Lord Byron's Daughter and Her Description of the First Computer* Mill Valley, Strawberry Press.

TOLSBY, J. (1998) Effects of Organizational Culture on a Large Scale IT Introduction Effort: A Case Study of the Norwegian Army's EDBLF Project. *European Journal of Information Systems,* 7, 108-114.

TRIXTER98052 (2008) *Life at Google - The Microsoftie Perspective,* Wordpress, (Blog), http://no2google.wordpress.com/2007/06/24/life-at-google-the-microsoftie-perspective/, 23/12/08.

TRUEX, D., BASKERVILLE, R. & TRAVISC, J. (2000) Amethodical systems development: the deferred meaning of systems development methods *Accounting, Management and Information Technologies* 10, 53-79.

VAN MAANEN, J. & BARELY, S. (1984) Occupational Communities: cultures and control in organizations. *Research in Organizational Behaviour,* 6, 287-365.

VAUGHAN, D. (1999) The dark side of organizations: mistake, misconduct, and disaster. *Annual Review of Sociology,* 25, 271-305.

VON HIPPEL, E. (1994) 'Sticky Information' and the Locus of Problem Solving: Implications for Innovation. *Management Science,* 4, 429-39.

WAGNER, E. L. & NEWELL, S. (2004) Best for Whom? The Tension Between 'Best Practice' ERP Packages and the Diverse Epistemic

Cultures in a University Context. *Journal of Strategic Information Systems,* 14, 305-328.

WANG, R. & BARTELS, A. (2008) SAP Will Return To Mostly Organic Growth. *Gartner Inc. series on Software Market Consolidation Trends,* 3.

WATZLAWICK, P., WEAKLAND, J. H. & FISCH, R. (1974) *Change: principles of problem formation and problem resolution,* New York, W. W. Norton.

WEBSTER, J. & WILLIAMS, R. (1993) Mismatch and tension: standard packages and non-standard users. IN QUINTAS, P. (Ed.) *Social Dimensions of Systems Engineering: People, Processes, Policies and Software Development.* Hempstead, Ellis Horwood.

WEGNER, E. (2000) Communities of practice and social learning systems. *Organization,* 7, 225-247.

WEGNER, E., MCDERMOTT, R. & SNYDER, M. (2002) *Cultivating communities of practice: A guide to managing knowledge,* Boston, Harvard Business School Press.

WILLIAMS, L. & COCKBURN, A. (2003) Agile Software Development: It's about Feedback and Change. *IEEE Computer Society.*

WILLIAMS, R. & EDGE, D. (1996) The Social Shaping of Technology. *Research Policy.*

WILLIAMS, R., STEWART, J. & SLACK, R. (2005) *Experimenting with Information and Communication Technologies: Social Learning in Technological Innovation,* Cheltenham, Edward Elgar.

WINOGRAD, T. & FLORES, F. (1994) *Understanding computers and cognition,* New Jersey Ablex Publishing Corporation

WOOD, S. (1983) *The Degradation of work?: Skill, deskilling and the labour process,* London, Hutchinson.

WOODS, D. (2003) *Enterprise Service Architecture,* Sebastopol, O'Reilly.

WOODS, D. & MATTERN, T. (2006) *Enterprise SOA: Designing IT for Business Innovation* Sebastopol, O'Reilly.

WORTHEN, B. (2002) *Nestles ERP Odyssey,* http://www.cio.com/archive/051502/nestle.html, 05/05/05.

WYLIE, L. (1990) A vision of the next-generation MRP II. *Gartner Group,* 300-339.

YIN, R. (1994) *Case Study Research: Design and Methods,* London, Sage Publications.

YURONG, Y. & HOUCUN, H. (2000) Data Warehousing and the Internet's Impact on ERP. *IT Professional,* 2, 37 - 41

ZACHARY, G. P. (1994) *Showstopper: The Breakneck Race to Create Windows-NT and the Next Generation at Microsoft*, New York, The Free Press.

ZACHARY, G. P. (1998) Armed Truce: Software in an Age of Teams. *Information Technology and People*, 11, 62-65.

Appendices

Appendix 1: Fieldwork Notes Week Two

Date	Monday, Nov 07, 2005 07:30-16:30
Keywords	New employee training, [vendor product] installation
Main actors	Thierry
Importance	no

Got my desktop [computer]! Talked to Thierry about his introduction training. He said they got around 10 different courses and that it was mad. The new one I talked to just went to a training period of 3 weeks. 1 week [vendor programming language] 1 week [vendor programming language] and 1 CRM. Retail people get one week more.

[I was] complaining about the long installation time for [vendor product]. The one with the broken knees said that I should be happy as [other software product] is a lot more complicated and that it took him a week to install it!
I got [vendor product] cause I will work in the old version. Yu said too [other software product] is too slow.

Thierry's new team will be 12. Existing people plus 4 new ones. He says so far it's not so much of a change and that they will learn the new approach "in the field". Team stays together for 1 year.

Date	Tuesday, Nov 08, 2005
Keywords	[vendor conference] presentation
Main actors	Research centre [location]
Importance	Middle but presentations high

See presentations!

What I did

Went through the Java tutorial. People started early today, and talked a lot. Might be cause of meeting with new team structure yesterday for the developer team. Nothing happened in the morning.

[vendor conference] presentation

Afternoon: [vendor conference] presentation in this other building which looks like an old factory from 2-3pm. Phone conference with [other labs] Research – they just listened. 30 people attended.

Some points:

- Goal: SW [software] to make life and work for costumers easier
- Business is changing
- Do the light and easy stuff first and leave the difficult one to the end. Otherwise [competitor] will take the easy market
- [Vice President] has asked 3 wishes to 100 sales men. (see slide with Usability)
- Easier UI by integrating [vendor] in common interfaces like outlook (showed an example)
- Then users can have a familiar look and feel.
- 1 percent of the business reports are used 70% of the time. And the rest? We have to know better what the customer wants
- Fast trade approach by [Vice President]
- Create teams, coding millions of lines of codes and applications and get them out immediately (guy with broken knees says at lunch later that he thinks quality and customer service will decrease)
- Ultimate goal: fewer screens! Everything which can be automated should be automated.
- Build one generic interface for everything
- Historically [vendor] wants 100 percent solutions. But we should do it differently now and just get the products out to the market.
- All applications will be built on one business process platform
- Graphical modelling for BP [Business Processes] through [vendor product]

Date	Wednesday, Nov 09, 2005
Keywords	
Main actors	
Importance	

Date	Thursday, Nov 10, 2005
Keywords	
Main actors	
Importance	

Slowly it's getting colder.. and there are less people going for a walk after lunch. Today not so much happened. Basically I followed the whole day the configuration guide to configure [vendor's software I was supposed to support]. Yesterday we finished the installation of all the relevant other products I needed additionally to actually being able to run [vendor software] like Perforce, [vendor's Java Engine] and [vendor product]. Interesting as I have never done anything related to Java.

People are still very friendly and help me if I have a question. I feel quite comfortable also in the flat and at the moment I wonder if North America is not a better place to stay than UK. People seem less violent and less drunk (though everybody smokes grass). Last night I went swimming in the YMCA. Was great! There is a steam room as well ☺. Here it seems to me so much better than [company I worked before joining academia]. In fact, I can't believe it.

Date	Friday, Nov 11, 2005
Keywords	
Main actors	
Importance	

Morning: Started to listen to music as well and finished the specification of the [vendors software]. Lunch: After lunch I went for a walk with [developer] who is going back to Europe today after 18 month in North America. Reason: married to R. [working in the vendor's HR department] and they have a child and want the family environment in [European Country].

He said that when he arrived he had a cultural shock – people are very laid back and family working balance is very important. You can even leave and say my family needs me. Also problems are not addressed directly in meetings. He did so and insulted his cross cultural team members. He thinks cross cultural factors are key in this kind of work and asked me to send him book links. I did so and asked him if we can talk about it more... hope he agrees (see mail Neil)

Appendix 2: Fieldwork Notes Week Fourteen

[Comments About the Daily Meetings, Week Fourteen]

Michael: 10min not everybody there. B. was missing. Asked: he didn't mind since they scrummed for 45min Friday and he is annoyed by that

Matthew: Started late as usual, took far too long. Left after 25min and still 3 people to report. Technical discussions and the German big guy just never stops talking

Antoine: 20min. 6 people. I asked him why he does not have QA [Quality Assurance] and Docu [Documentation] people there but he didn't remember why or if they are invited. He meets with QA twice a week anyway. Still it seems he is the only one asking the three questions. He does so always at the beginning of the meetings and then he nails people down asking when they will be finished and to the facts. It's very much controlling. I like it but then it's not up to me to like it or not. People in the team seem happy.

Michael: Supposed to start at 9. As usual not [it didn't start at nine as usual]. People arrived even after nine. The one which looks Russian came late. And Thomas too. Still they are not scrumming – hm..

Anne-Sophie: Suggested to her yesterday to go to other meetings especially Antoine's. Guess it would help her. She says it changed since now she has to control a lot more than before. She tried to keep them off admin work before and support them so that's the same but she gets high pressure from management since people don't fill out their daily confirmation and her project is on red.

[Another Day]

Today I didn't go to all the meetings. Didn't go to Michael but Thomas told me that people complained that it took too long Friday so he said at the beginning of the meeting: just 2 min for everybody and they made it in 10 min. However they started late as usual (around 10min). To Matthew and Remy I didn't go either. Have seen their way and will take a break since I am very stressed on not spending enough time for [the team I was working for]. (...)

[Another Day]
Anne-Sophie seems very helpful. So, yesterday in the queue [for lunch] she told me that she is very stressed about the Scrum cause she gets emails and emails about that they are not on time [with project]. Today the meeting was shorter. 15 min – maybe cause [developer], the nervous guy was ill the days before and couldn't comment on everything that is going on. People don't like to get nailed down so they don't give proper reports I think. It's more like a therapy group with a very understanding team master. She reminds me a lot of [a friend of mine]. When she is reporting to the management she never says the names but just the developers and justifies why. Tom says that the problem is that even if he adjusts his progress to the actual one (which is less than the plan) it doesn't help cause the end date April 28th will not change. Jeanine, the girl who brought the Christmas desert Ice cream said that she is very stressed cause of that Scrum thing and that she doesn't like it. "I feel like I have to work at the weekends cause I am so stressed that I cannot meet the final deadline (..) I don't care about the daily confirmation but about the deadline that I cannot make it." Well, I think she is afraid of the daily confirmation as she mentions before but then she sees the main problem. The final deadline. "then when the testing starts we will just fix bugs, fix bugs, fix bugs". That's also what Antoine said in the interview that maybe people will end up using the testing period for going on developing...

[Another Day]
Talked to Thomas at lunchtime during the walk about Scrum. He says people don't like to be put on the spot and it puts so much pressure on them. "people will burn out and get de-motivated". (...)

In the Scrum with Anne-Sophie it was difficult 'cause she announced that I recommended that she goes to the different Scrum meetings to see how they are doing. She will do so and in fact I guess I made a mistake. When I asked her for an interview she said that she first wants to visits the others (and also find out if they have so much trouble with the planning) before talking to me. Strange that is.. as if I am the judge.

Also went to Thierry to ask him to sit together with all ScrumMasters – his initial idea. He said he will organize it. The guy from India hasn't responded but Tom's secretary. How embarrassing – I did the calculation to CET wrongly and told her that 4pm is 10pm here ;-)

Anyway, tonight for the first time since Wednesday sports (its Tuesday). Will go swimming and meet Thomas for beer afterwards. Beer is always good.. I could spend hours in the office to find out things.. I guess best to go again on Saturday or Sunday to have quiet time to write up and collect some more info. So many things to discover.. what's about CRM on demand, unit tests and SOA???? (...)

[Another Day, Again, Talking About the Daily Scrums:]
Michael: didn't have it (guess they have their weekly meeting)
Matthew: [like Michael]
Anne-Sophie: 13min but less people and still [loud developer] cannot say much since he was ill. He said he has no news and didn't say what he is doing tomorrow [when he got asked the three Scrum questions of what he was doing yesterday, what he will do tomorrow and if he has any problems]. Anne-Sophie [as project manager] didn't follow up.
At the end of the meeting she [Anne-Sophie] asked them if they have any special wishes for tomorrow for their weekly meeting. Some commented. (...) So, [these daily meetings] it's a therapy group but in terms of project management I am not sure.

Matthew sent this:

> Hi,
>
> I thought it would be useful to meet for 15 - 20 minutes to discuss the daily Scrum meetings.
>
> Christine has been watching our meetings and I was curious to get her feedback.
>
> Regards,
> Matthew

To all Scrum Managers. I am confused.. I thought they will sit together and include me. I haven't prepared to give feedback. Great.Some more work. But then it's nice too, since they are asking me. Puh.. but what to say? Guess I will have to cancel Thorsten invitation for food [tonight] once again so that I have time to prepare.

[Another Day]
Antoine: 20min
[Antoine started the daily scrum with] Thanks for your good work last week
When people started discussing he said that the Scrum meeting is there to share information. That is the purpose rather than reporting to him. So, he raised the question how to best share information? They didn't find a solution but one guy recommended that it would be helpful if their office spaces could be closer to each other.

People [in this team] really talk to each other [during the Scrum meeting] but then, he is lucky cause he has only 6 people. We went to the small meeting room around the corner today again. Think it's a good idea. Nobody was sitting. 2 came late, one was excused being in a phone conference with another lab.

Appendix 3: Oracle and SAP's Solution Maps

Oracle distinguishes between two areas: Industry solutions and Horizontal Business Solutions. Screen shots from the Oracle homepage (2008) are displayed below. SAP can be displayed with one figure.

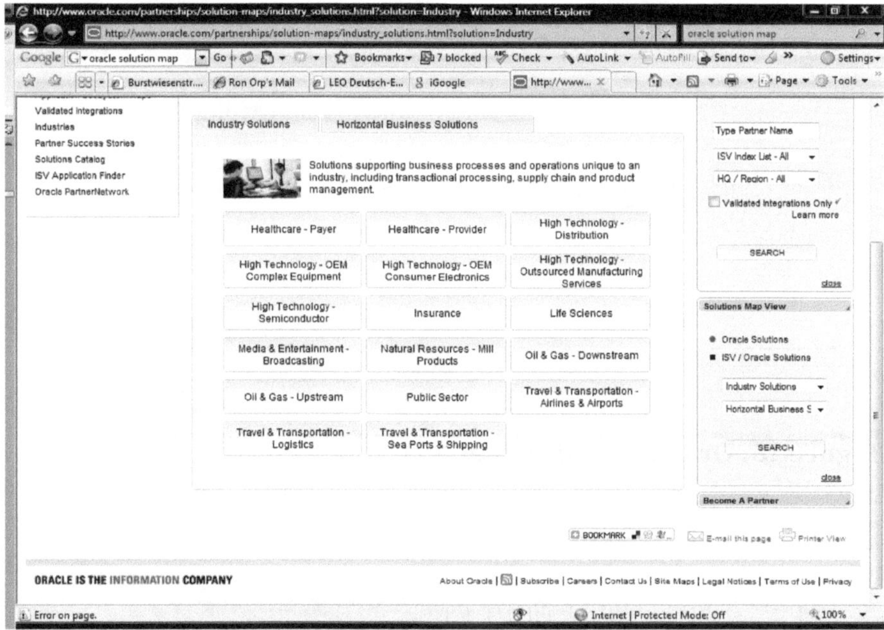

Figure 17: Oracle Solution Map (1)

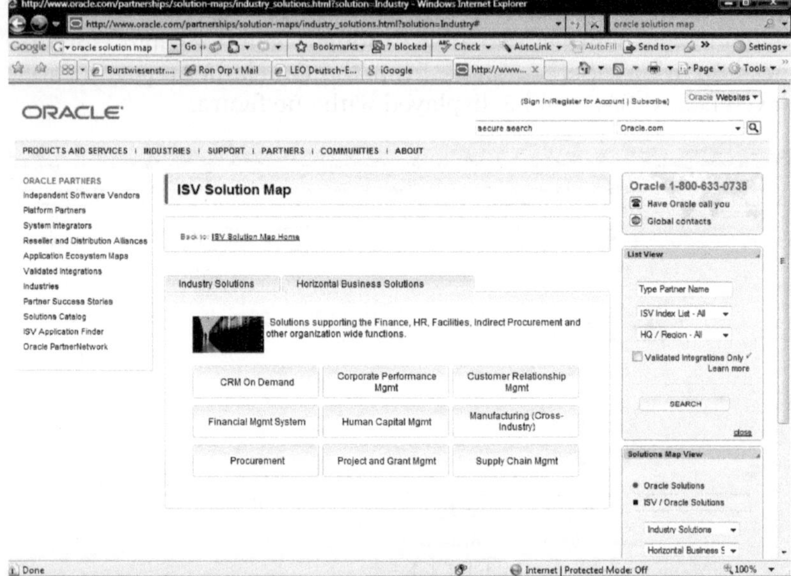

Figure 18: Oracle Solution Map (2)

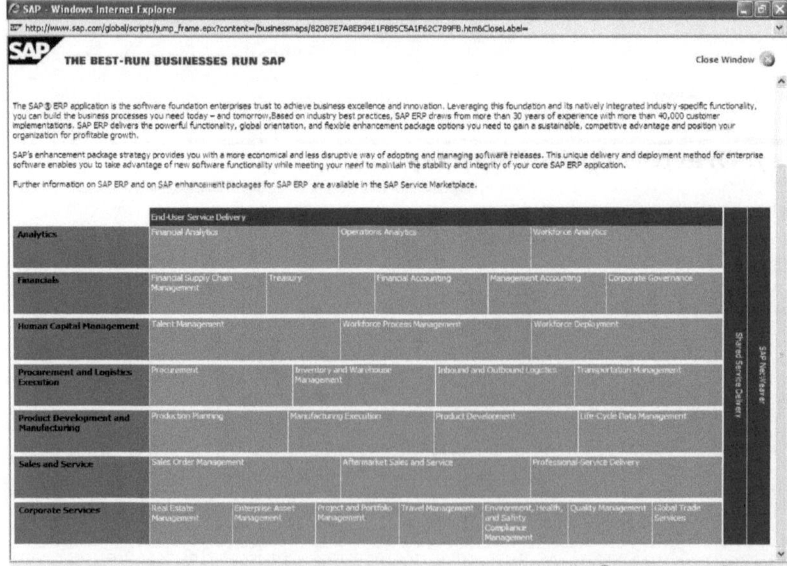

Figure 19: SAP Solution Map

Appendix 4: Published Work

Part of the ethnographical data on ERP systems support described in this book has been included in:

POLLOCK, N., GRIMM, C. & WILLIAMS, R. (2008) Passing the User: Searching for Expertise in Globalised Technical Support. IN POLLOCK, N. & WILLIAMS, R. *Software and Organisations: The Biography of the Enterprise-Wide System Or How SAP Conquered the World.* London, Routledge.

POLLOCK, N., WILLIAMS, R., GRIMM, C. & D'ADDERIO, L. (2009) Post local forms of repair: The (extended) situation of virtualised technical support. *Information and Organization,* 19.